C. Este

A Journey in the Year 1793

Through Flanders, Brabant, and Germany, to Switzerland

C. Este

A Journey in the Year 1793

Through Flanders, Brabant, and Germany, to Switzerland

ISBN/EAN: 9783744797146

Printed in Europe, USA, Canada, Australia, Japan

Cover: Foto ©Andreas Hilbeck / pixelio.de

More available books at **www.hansebooks.com**

A JOURNEY
IN THE YEAR
1793,
THROUGH
FLANDERS, BRABANT,
AND
GERMANY,
TO
SWITZERLAND.

―――

BY C. ESTE.

―――

Nunc retrorsum
Vela dare, atque Iterare curſus
Cogor, reli&os.   Hor.

―――

LONDON:

PRINTED FOR J. DEBRETT, OPPOSITE BURLINGTON-
HOUSE, PICCADILLY.

1795.

ADVERTISEMENT

*T*HE Reader is not troubled with a recapitulation of any literal Errors there may be, which he will at once be able to correct, without any suggestion but his own.

But there are a few verbal inaccuracies on which the Reader's indulgence must be desired, to observe the alterations which follow.

The book went to press at the end of the winter. Soon after, the writer went abroad. In his absence the sheets were all worked off. And so, like two of our most memorable predecessors, his works, for precision, failed. For in the first book, printed with a name and date, there is an error even in the title!—And Lord Lyttleton, after unexampled toil about commas and points, lapsed so egregiously, as to fill with errata no less than nineteen quarto pages!—Sic Apicem Rapax Fortuna sustulit.

ERRORS OF THE PRESS.

READ,

Page
5 The House of *Taylor*, and the Tomb of Hooker.
6 The hill is between *Samer* and Montreuil.
36 The better state of *things* in England.
37 In first instances, and *initiatory* processes.
39 The Chef d'Œuvres of Reubens in the *Churches* at Antwerp.
40 *Incendia Belli.*
47 The woods *growing* to the very walls of Bruxelles.
78 *Doyens* de Cretienté.
110 *Gros* Gibier.
113 *List* of the Game.
130 They formed the *Jus Tractus.*
141 The town *connives not* at such a dubious being:
154 Vos patriam *fugitis*—Vos dulcia *linquitis* arva.
171 With equality, moral, civil, and political.
181 Metamorphose *men* into hired heroes.
190 There *are* at Liege, two small wards.
192 J. Koelholf de *Proprietatibus Rerum*, and St. Augustine.
193 De *aptitudine* ingenii muliebris.
199 14 or 1500 acres, with horses, cows, and all stock in proportion.
220 I am sure *we* must!
224 *Underwald, Uri,* and Schweitz—*cultivating* aids.
228 That, he *does* not pay if he builds.
251 *Omit* the second use of the impressing passage from the Psalmist.
258 *Brutis—Merces—Magis.*
279 The *Bible*, is referred to a date, between 1452 and 1455.
281 Canna neque aurea. Sed arte, &c.

A JOURNEY, &c.

EUROPE, at least the better parts of it, being, by the malignity, of something worse than fortune, plunged into the bitterness of war, produced, among other evils, the following journey:

For those evils, HISTORY must be eager to account—with opinions and emotions, well becoming the offended minister of policy and virtue; but with equivocal continence she refrains herself. It has been her custom, unhappily, to sacrifice use to delicacy. Over each crazy generation of the offending Adam, while they have been present, she has been fain to content herself, solely with expressive silence: and it is not till the requiem shall have been heard over the welcome tomb, that there has been a signal for the sound of unmolested TRUTH!

From those evils, hard to suffer, but harder to atone, what myriads of men, and of the best blessings man is heir to, were doomed, why we know not, to droop and to decay! My family, at first, felt them, except from sympathy, in a very mitigated degree; but still they felt them.—For, of a fortune so small, (Propitii an Irati Dii!) that nothing but caution and self-denial could make it the independence of a very private gentleman, no small part was in France. And finally, I had a son, at that time, there, on a plan of study;

in search of science, no where else, perhaps, so strenuously, so frugally, so extensively to be pursued.

My son, thank God, had done his duty, to himself, and to his condition. He had turned time to good account. He had already forced forward into the foremost classes of that learning, of all others the most indispensible to the *fearful and wonderful make* of man; and on more than one occasion, at once an adept in knowledge and in language, he had shewn himself able to teach at an age when others are, in general, but beginning to learn.

As FRANCE, alas! by accidents never to be enough lamented, seemed daily less and less likely to be allowed to retain for foreigners that free reception and repose, hitherto so amiably imparted to all, I determined to cast about, with due care, for some other region, where there might be, like Monf. DESSAULT, some fit representative of our late countryman Mr. POTT, that is, some great mind; original and just, applying the powers of philosophy and art to the relief and consolation of mankind!—Where there might be, besides, something like that constellation of useful learning from VICQ D'AZIR, from JUSSIEU, from LAVOISIER and FOURCROI—some establishments, if possible, equivalent to the learned societies, and to the public libraries of Paris—and where, altogether, these advantages might be as systematic; as well applied to public instruction, with the same perfection of combined preferences, ample, laborious, incessant, frugal, and free.

Accordingly, the clever and experienced friends I consulted, referred me to an ITALIAN UNIVERSITY.

For EDINBURGH, though it may be rationally proud of first-rate men, and there is still such good arrangement in the place, that it is in vogue to study, and to be distinguished by a wish for skill—yet Edinburgh, for what we wanted, offered only partial aid. Of science, philosophical, contemplative, there might be enough. But art was wanting.

ing. There is no mechanical supply.——The superstitious prejudices of the place forbid it.

As for LONDON, from the nature of the market, with talents in such demand, and at such prices for them, there must be ever many accomplished men in it; but where is there any thing like a sage provision for the collective application of their skill? Where is there any systematic establishment for popular instruction? Where are their public libraries, generously open to all? Where are there any MEDICAL SCHOOLS?—As far as it offers to be a school, it seems challengeable on the various objections as being loose and disjointed; therefore probably impracticable; certainly very dear!

The ITALIAN UNIVERSITY before recommended to me, was PAVIA.—For PADUA, since the time of FABRICIUS, when it had celebrity from him and HARVEY, has been gradually fading away.—BOLOGNA has no academic fame, but for the imitative arts—The POPE's State, heaven help him, has nothing; but for the unassisted study of the antique!—And FLORENCE, though upheld by FONTANA, who is in the first rank of fame, is, through him indeed, pre-eminent as a museum!—It is not his object to form a school.

The idea of PAVIA was thus forcibly impressed, and willingly received upon my mind; yet I did not dare to let it take at once, an entire hold of me. I could not but be scared by the powers of distance and of doubt; for I could not find ways and means, like FRANCIS the First, (though one of the least of his race thus inventive) when he went into the *Milanese;* " to raise new taxes, to sell the administration
" of justice in twenty places at once, to *convey,*

" Convey the wise call it."   SHAKSPERE.

" I know not how many thousand livres, in the shape of a
" silver tomb, from our departed tutelary friend, Saint
" Martin, at Tours." Each of these is a grace, by the grace of God, peculiar but to a few.

However, by degrees I did what might be expected, and suffering my thoughts to ferment into wishes, I determined at once to make an effort rather above my power than below it; to see for myself, and to ascertain for my son, whether the object, obviously of such prime moment to him, really was as it was said to be, and had merit equal to its praises.

Accordingly, taking leave of my ecclesiastical superiors, from whom I never found any thing but elegant consideration and useful kindness—confiding each small charge I hold to men better than myself, and having sold my notes before I had written a word of them (a peculiarity I rather mention to explain the title page, and that there may be no doubt as to my bookseller's taste or my own), I left London in July, and took the strait road to Dover—with my son.

There is hardly any part of KENT that is not interesting—for even the Hundred of Hoo, as the vile amphibious marshy object, is called, between the Medway and the Thames, I once heard much lauded by a neighbouring physician! who said, rather dexterously for his art, "that as " for situation, *de aere et locis*, speaking after the manner of " physicians, bad was the best."

In the DOVER ROAD, among many scenes that are pleasing, perhaps these parts please the most. From the fifth mile-stone to the ninth, both the plain and the hill are with difficulty any where to be much exceeded.—The ground at DANSON HILL, where Sir R. TAYLOR gave the façade, and BROWNE formed the water for Sir R. BOYD.—The hill above Dartford, where the houses of Lord EARDLEY and Mr. WHEATLEY are in the view.—The grounds and woods so well undulated by Lord BESBOROUGH at Ingres.—The bridge at ROCHESTER, with sweet scenery in such strong contrasts above and below it.—CHATHAM Hill, where those varying objects have an effect more captivating still!—From the winding course of the Medway, the bold uplands, the variegated agriculture on its banks, the shipping, the arsenals, with the distances of Essex, Sheerness, and the Nore.— After these, there is BOUGHTON Hill, the plain, with the fine water and woods on the top of the hill.—The four miles of Burham wood, and the four last miles through the valley of Dover.

In all these, there is many a potent, delightful charm, and where the *mind* can work upon it as well as the eye.

On BLACKHEATH, there is the beautiful bubble of PAGE's house, blown up by one man, and broken by another, each within the year! At GAD's HILL, (about the 26th stone) the spirits may revel at the recollection of FALSTAFFE—and they who had the happiness to know the late Mr. HENDERSON, will, with fond regret, also think upon them—for his genius in comedy had no rival, in the last half century at least; and what is now of so much greater moment, he was not more gay than he was good!—The bridge at Rochester, a fine example of the arts in the fourteenth century, may contrast the modesty and skill of the eighteenth, when, but for Lord PEMBROKE, a minister and his workmen had made the bridge at Westminster of their congenial wood!—At Dartford, now of such gunpowder fame, the first paper was made, and the first iron was slit. At Boughton, in the delicious plain and wood on the top of the hill, the view ranges over Canterbury and Harbledown in the bottom, where BECKET's shrine at one place, and his slipper in the other, may virtuously and usefully excite us, like ERASMUS, against the wretched impostors of Rome—though now, indeed, as we all know, talents are never prostituted!— No man, otherwise illustrious, can now be mentioned, with such trash as a wafer in his mouth!

The house of JEREMY TAYLOR, and the tomb of HOOKER, are also in the scene! And at Barham Down, visited even so lately as the Duke of Marlborough's, with the barren and deleterious laurel, you may see, with STUKELEY, the remains of the old Watling Street, where past barbarities

have

have happily yielded to prefent elegance; and where, inftead of Celtic barrows, and the intrenchments of the Romans, there is the ufeful rapture from fo many villas and ornamental farms.

" Well ordered home—Man's beft delight to make."

Stukeley was not a mere, dry, hufky antiquarian, without pith, without tafte. He had both. His ideas and expreffions were vigorous; and he had the power of pleafing, where it was, obvioufly, difficult to pleafe. He paints the valley of Dover, like a landfcape amidft theatric charms; with artificial diminutions as juft, as perfpective herfelf could figure it; converging to their point at Dover; where, the fea, between the pharos, is fo beautifully made to clofe the fcene.

Such is a little of the praife which belongs to Stukeley. Thefe were the relaxations of his more ufeful hours, confecrated by the ftudies of a phyfician, and the efforts of a parifh prieft!—He gave his life to learning, and, as we truft, his foul to God.

As for Dover, if the winds, and they who live by them permit, which, if you happen to have a number of horfes and fervants they feldom do permit, Dover need not keep a traveller long, unlefs he afpires at novelty, and is ambitious to falute, with due emotions, the juft and neceffary office of the Cinque Ports—or unlefs he has the better luck to be drawn up the hill to the fine convivial talents, which, now and then, are to be found at the top of it.

Dover makes a figure, not only in the *Doomfday Book*, but even fo high up as the Itinerary of Antoninus. But the more potent topics of the people feem to be, " that " they have a market—that they have two members—and " that the average returns of their trade, I mean every fix " or feven years, are very curious and *interefting* indeed."

Dover, like fo many other places, has been fomewhat overfhadowed by the ftupendous laurels of the war! Every quarter of a year the port clearances ufed to be about 600

veffels.

veffels—In the quarter prior to my being there in November 1793, the Cuftom-Houfe books happened to report, alas! no more than 59 veffels!

When the firft pier was forming at Dover, "the good Lord Cobham," as he was called, kept a daily table for the workmen; and a Prince, with the heart of a gentleman, made a prefent of feveral thoufand pounds!

The workmen have juft finifhed a new fluice on the North fide, and a new pier head on the South, and they talk with becoming feeling on the liberality of modern manners. On the table and the prefent, they alfo have had in—Hope.

Of the new pier head, Sir H. OXENDEN was the engineer. The object of it is to keep off the fand, which hitherto, in fpite of all that could be done, has for ever been forming in the harbour's mouth.

In the church, at the bottom of the caftle hill, there are two infcriptions, one to FOOTE, the other to CHURCHILL. Poor FOOTE died at Dover in the Ship inn. CHURCHILL was buried there, having died at Boulogne. It was near the port, the firft corner, on the oppofite fide after paffing the Englifh Hotel. Mr. WILKES lived in the houfe; and HUMPHEY COATES, the Wine Merchant, unluckily happened to have the vaults under it. And there it was, between them, *acria pocula*, that CHURCHILL met his death. FOOTE fell through the villany of an infamous woman of quality, though the fagacity and eloquence of LORD MANSFIELD detected the confpiracy, and quafhed it; yet the effect of it was felt to the laft—FOOTE had a death-wound in his heart! and he lived only a little to linger towards his grave.—Foote's tablet was raifed by his grateful attendant, Jewel, recording fimply the day on which the public loft their favourite writer for the ftage.

Churchill's epitaph is in twelve or fourteen rhymes, of which it is eafier to comment the motive than the effect.

The PASSAGE TO THE CONTINENT is three times longer by

by Oftend than to Calais or Boulogne.—Of courfe the difficulties are trebled, and with them the bar againft home-bred folly clearing out fo many heavy famples to fhame us in foreign markets.—An advantage this, fhamefully overlooked, when wars are fo vehemently oppofed, and impolicy and inhumanity are the plea.

When a league or two from land, the view is interefting—it reaches from Folkftone to the Foreland on one fide, and the high lands of the French Republic on the other.—The fouthern hill, feen there, is between Saumur and Monkeuil—The height North of that is the point which predominates fo well over the whole department of Calais. The town of Calais is feldom feen in this run: but you often catch a glimpfe of DUNKIRK and NIEUPORT.

The time is from feven to fourteen or fixteen hours—and even that, fhort as it is, may fatisfy moft people, and make them glad to get even to Oftend. Such is the power of contraft when the change is from the worfe.

And yet bad as the town may be, it has been the caufe of one war, and the ftrefs of three others.

What the town then was, may in fome fort be computed by what it now is.—Geographical pofition cannot change—and by the fucceeding fkill and cares of man, the condition of the Port, &c. were likely to have changed, only for the better.—And yet, taking it as we find it, with the churches and town Houfe, which have arifen fince the laft bombardment in 1706, what compenfation do we find here!—What idea of apology hereafter, for conteftations thus fenfelefs and fanguinary, when on one fide or other, no lefs than ONE HUNDRED AND FORTY THOUSAND MEN were cut down, prematurely, to the grave.

In the fanatic perverfions of the time, horrid guilt like this, was, with effrontery, not fhort of blafphemy, referred, to the *firft great* caufe of all created good? And literally, medals were ftruck to commemorate thefe foul enormities!

enormities! Enormities, which the foe of mankind would wish to remember, to inflame the final sentence of the condemned.

Among these inscriptions, as elsewhere Puns are to be seen—and OSTEND-E NOBIS PACEM was their play of words even in their prayer thus,

> Two words make up the noise,
> Sports for Dutchmen, and for English Boys.

thus far, was Cowley exact in the local habitation of this folly? A folly, which in weak allegiance to bad fashion, even Shakespere tried, and ever but once tried in vain.

The town itself and the trade of it, small as they are, were yet smaller before the late salutary improvements of Joseph the second;—and even now, the population is not 10,000—and the port clearances are not more than 1,200 vessels a year.

A consideration on the state of Trade at Ostend may perhaps usefully be extended.——It is something more than a business of the counting-house and quays:—It is a moral epoch in the surprises of political perpetration!

For, when after two or three years well directed enterprise of a judicious individual (La Merveille, a Frenchman) the East India Trade first opened on the Netherlands—It became in the year 1722 a collective object for the community—and every eye rationally looked forward as to the hope of approaching good!—A good, unmixt with any evil, but the corporation spirit!—That spirit, by an effort perhaps disloyal to the indefeasible sovereignty of truth and policy, had pent up, by a patent, partially to a few, those independent indefeasible rights, those blessings of our common nature, which, dependent on the common elements, seem like them happily given, open, to all.

The Trade of the poor Flemings, little in itself, and thus made less, with five ships only, and with funds not more than six millions (of Florins), still was enough to act upon the jealousy of mean competition. It roused and scared the peddling politics of the DUTCH. And with an eagerness that explained the motives, the ministers of each contiguous monarchy, France, England, Prussia, Sweden, one and all, were immediately on tip-toe to make it a pretence for war! And, the affair ended as almost every contest must end, with no possible popular profit!—But instruction, for the enforcement of Peace! While, Government as in almost every instance of War, gained, proportionably, as the people lost. The IMPERIAL Government, with the *pragmatic sanction*, had the hereditary succession secured—and the Maritime Powers were fortified, by this new inroad, upon trade and navigation.

Thus the people, like their property, were transferred at pleasure! Thus they suffered themselves to be despoiled of their birth right! A birth right, unalienable, as long as winds shall blow and waters roll! So the trade began; and ended almost in its beginnings. Some temporary efforts have been made for the trade to struggle up again; and virtue, which in political manœuvre, as well as in private life, is the best policy effected, in two or three periods, not only pauses from decay, but advances towards recovery.—The best of these periods were, such as might be expected, when in the NETHERLANDS there were wit and virtue, enough, to escape a War, and other nations had the guilt and folly of committing it! In the NEUTRALITYS of 1733, and, again, during the ruinous madness of our AMERICAN crusade!

At present also, there is some trade in the port. And indeed so many vessels, *wisely* laden with money and stores, to be wasted on foreign objects, but all English, and with all these seemed such a wholesome stir, such an utter absence of all commercial distress, that the place really looked like a trading town in England, *before* the War!

But

But this, cannot be counted upon; it is a mere temporary flash, and muft finifh like the fulnefs in the tolls of Cork, at the end of the flaughtering feafon!

The prefent government of the town is reputable to the paffive virtue of the people.—For they amiably allow their chief magiftrate, the bailli, &c. to be named by the Emperor. Places in the magiftracy, have been, hitherto, thought objects, lefs of profit than of honor. But fince the late attempts have failed of revolution and reform, the Bailli's place has been £3,000 a year.—A profit rent, hardly conceivable by thofe who live and thrive, as we all do, in a fyftem, where not any appointment is ever called over paid!

As for the fubordinate objects of legiflation, there feems no great caufe of complaint. The courts of juftice, are never indecently clofed for any long recefs; and though the appellant jurifdiction, is not, as it perhaps ever ought to be, within themfelves, yet it is not remote.—It is at GAND and MULINES—and the temper of the people there is favourable to truth; for they are enlightened, and of courfe, properly eager to be free.

The misfortunes of men, fo continual every where from accident and from human violence, have no artificial exacerbation. There are no ftamp impofitions, upon law proceedings.

In Scotland, the lawyers are a tribe fo multitudinous, that their cloathing, black, is called the Edinburgh hunt. They over-run Flanders too. But their fees are fo fmall, that it is not better there, to give up a caufe, rather than pay the cofts.

The PORT DUTIES too, are a vexation, comparatively light. Imports are free. Of courfe, there is a fcope alfo free to the commerce of fpeculation.—On the inland vent of foreign merchandife, the duties are about ten per-cent.—

As there is no cuftom houfe at the port, ftrangers are unannoyed

unannoyed on landing; and escape those petty, but mortifying ills, of delay and depredation, from searching, sufferances, and head-money!

In the manner of a well known Irish rhapsodist, who sees, ad libitum, a structure, to be planned, upon the right, and the hope of some other future glory on the left, so the port of Ostend may as safely be commended, for what it *might* be, *if* the shallows were cleared and the pier was improved.—*If* the manufactures and exports of the country, were encouraged by skilful bounties! But where is there any bounty amidst the rage and ruin of war! Nothing can come of nothing. When an exchequer is empty, the sole solicitude must be to fill it! not to give, but to get!——With other instances of unexpected neglect, there is still wanting the first great necessary of fresh water. It is still to be fetched from far. Though, the fine experiments of SHEERNESS will prove, the power of perseverance, and that in regard to water, any body may have it who will dig deep enough for it—though through a quick sand itself, and even below the level of the sea.

On one of the days we were kept at Ostend, July 19, the colors were consecrated, for the French Emigrants, with such sapience, entertained upon our establishment. With English pay in their pocket, they had an English uniform upon their back; and in regard to sentiment and language, they were as perfectly English, also, as some late associations.—They were drawn up, in the great square, before the Hotel de Ville, and the regiment of Sir Charles GREY, was in a line, facing them.——It was an epoch for a man whose heart was in the right place, and who had energies to utter what was in it.

The Aumonier, of the regiment, analogous to our army chaplains, appeared. He sprinkled the colours with consecrated water. He then attempted to speak, but the attempt, like the Amen in Duncan's murderer, stuck in his throat.

throat. He might have profited on the very failure, and like the humane Lord, so very luckily faultering when he urged the necessity of council upon each process for imputed treason, He, the Aumonier, might have made his emotions current for their expressions—and the currency, like the paper of the American Republic, might have all at once mounted above par!

But no such matter—sine re et sine spe—he stopped altogether.

He might have burst forth into a glorious, heart-improving rapture! He might have hailed the dawn of truth, the rising hope of unclouded light, over the opinions and actions of men!—The blessings of freedom were all before him. He might have expanded, with the expanding bliss!—He might have looked backward also with approving delight. He might have gloried in the downfall of despotism,—certainly, in one region never to be seen again!—He might have risen on its ruins! He might have raised around him with the plastic promptitude of hope, every fine formed fabric, gracious, useful, venerable, and good; religion rational, tolerant, and reformed; the equal law of liberty, the free intercourse of truth.—He might have apostrophised the genius of RATIONAL REVOLUTION, as far as it had signally blest, the English, the Americans, and the Dutch.—He might have implored the aid of that power, which called light out of darkness, and order from confusion!—And fain to atchieve, some of those perfections which he adored, he might have closed his oraison, with reasonable aspirations after *universal good*—for PEACE upon earth, and good will to men.

The poor Aumonier had none of these things to say; instead of all this, he set up a puling cry, like a child's brazed trumpet at an old French fair, with gingerbread kings and queens! Steeped in the colours of his trade, he wailed over the passing pageant of a worthless court—and,

God

God forgive him, heaved a found, too like menace and revenge!

An officer, M. de C——— followed him, and rather in a ftyle above all this—but ftill not in the firft tone of military eloquence.—That, from its rarity feems the hardeft thing for a foldier to do. For, there may have been fome who have fought like Cesar, but which of them could ever talk about it, half fo well?

The fcene, however, could not but have fome impreffion,—as Titus fighed to lofe a day, as Xerxes wept over the doom, too probable, of his embattled hoft!

But many men, many minds. Other people enjoyed the fight, and particularly an army agent, a jew broker, a crimp, a contractor, and an outlaw for larceny, all were unanimous, and voted it d - - - - - - - - fine.—And one crazy fellow at the head of the mob, literally threw off his hat, and huzzaed! An Irifh ex-jefuit juft efcaped from St. Omers, clofed the conference, fwearing bloodily, that he wifhed well to all the world, and therefore that he wifhed them all to be at war. For that there was no fchool like the fchool of adverfity, no good like evil, and no joy like forrow.—That war made men too poor, to be meanly loft in common enjoyments of life!—That it prevented building, the bane of our great towns, ever fince Queen Elizabeth!—That it thinned the community, with the hand of a great mafter! And, that fooner or later, it muft keep down the price of provifions—at prefent fo diftreffing! &c. &c. &c.

Nobody could deny the laft pofition. His arguments otherwife might have had weight—the majority thought as he did.

The day thus far dedicated to truth, to ufeful truth, was happily ordained to end as well as it began, for the parade ending, we met with the following curious infcription upon the quays.—It is a column, not of brafs, but of wood—

erected

erected to commemorate the late events. when the forces of the French Republic, chusing to retire, the Austrians took their place—and the popular emotions is thus made to live, in expressions nobody can doubt there.

THE INSCRIPTION.

Ob Lætum Austriacum
Anno 1790, Reditum,
Studio et Amore prius Erectam
Dein ut Impiis Regicidisque
Salvetur Manibus Furtim Abditam
Sacriligiis jam Expulsis
Aquilam Hanc.
Ex Voto, Piscatores Denuo Posuerunt
Die. 18, Cal. Maii 1793.

The devices are as good as the inscription—For, besides the Black Eagle, emblem of comfortable power, fulminating on a tree, supposed to be the tree of Liberty—there are the fasces and the cap of liberty, the cock and the lyre obviously of no more use, all are in flames!

On another side of the post, are the words,

Semper Fidelis.

With three keys, a dog, and a whale.—Somebody talked of a tub to the whale, but it is not true: at least we could not see it.

Thus we departed from Ostend.

FLANDERS.

FLANDERS.

At Ostend, as in some bad life touched by our great poet, nothing is so becoming as the leaving of it! There is a canal, with a trechschuyte on it, always once, and sometimes, as in summer, twice a day.—Here, as elsewhere, this sort of inland carriage is delightful: as giving motion without effort, and accommodation with little cost.—The traveller is wafted for a couple of Flemish schellings, 14 miles to Bruges, where Stivinus, the flying chariot-man, was surveyor of the dykes—and from Bruges, he may get equally cheap and well to Gand—with a table d'hote on board, of two tolerable services and a little desert, with some intolerable wine, for three or four schellings more.

There are collateral canals to Nieuport, to Dunkirk, St. Omers, Lisle, &c.

There is a carriage way to Bruges; but it is six miles further: and except in dry weather, those six miles are made twelve; the roads are so infamously bad.—Of Bruges there is a record, municipium Brugense, as high as the seventh century! And the roads, from their condition, may be presumed as antique.

Apart from their ease and expedience, the canals of Flanders, are not an idle contemplation. For, they were begun so early as the twelfth century! That there should be better works of the same sort now, in Holland, in France, and in England, is not at all wonderful. For the ameliorations of art are decided; if, as Horace thinks erroneously, the advances of morals be not.

In the FORMATION OF THESE CANALS, it was fortunate that the difficulties were small, when the arts of vanquishing such difficulties were, comparatively, so small also.— There happened to be no complex considerations as to ground,—when excess in one spot, was to supply deficience

in

in another. There were no subterranean passes as in the tunnels at Bezieres in the LANGUEDOC Canal, or in the yet more memorable works of the DUKE of BRIDGEWATER. There was no obstacle to surmount, like that on the IRWELL; and of course, nothing so well wrought as the masonry there, to secure it. The fall was scarcely any thing. There was almost nothing to rise. There were no underwater sluices.

It may be a topic of reasonable regret, that the accounts and details of these canals are no where to be found; at least, my son and I were not able to find them.—Such a well preserved record of a great public work would have been, obviously, precious, both for curiosity and use.—It had been an amusement, not uninstructive, to have noted the changes and chances of time, as they affected the price of labour, and with all, the peculiarities of its value and application!—There must have been the elegant pleasure in giving well-earned unsuspected praise.—And so to have hovered over the BRINDLEY, the SMEATON, or the STAMFORD of that day—with any other names, with virtuous use distinguished, by personal sacrifice to public utility, or by ingenious art aiding the design, or the execution!—And if there could have been before, such a man as the *Duke of* BRIDGEWATER, such a glorious instance of complex merit, and useful success, there would have been in degree, kindred emotions of self-congratulation and of social good! to have hailed him with due celebrations, as the *first* CITIZEN OF THE time; the man of all others the most illustrious in the service of his country, for MAGNIFICENT ENTERPRISE, for sublime ATCHIEVEMENTS!

A name so admirably exalted, by adventure and accomplishment, must re-echo in every heart of the most remote posterity, and through unknown time. And for the perpetual encouragement of enterprise, authorised by skill; let it be known, that the duke of BRIDGEWATER's successes have been as brilliant as his purposes! That the work, by the multiplied surprises of genius, did not cost him above £1000 a mile! And that the clear profits of his last year, amounted to forty three thousand pounds!

The canals of Flanders, probably, cannot be decorated with any story so splendid. Like Languedoc, and other fine works in France, they have been the result of collective efforts, half by government, and half by the province, or in better words, all by the people!

And these are the works, in which they may rationally glory. For the advantages are obvious and sure. They are inalienable. They facilitate human intercourse. They circulate human good. They diminish animal labor. They augment vegetable blessings. It may be only Virgil who can make his clowns toss about the manure with grace, but it can be by canals alone (and by the by—the Romans marvellously had none)—that the clowns every where can have wherewithal abundantly to toss it!

The Flemish navigation, if made with every modern finesse, certainly would be more perfect. Their channels would have been more sloped on their sides. And the bottom narrower than the top. There had been more sure provisions against the two extremes, of too much or too little water—better apparatus for the contiguous lands, as they might needs either irrigation or drain.

The Flemish agriculture for want of this, is proportionably impaired.

The pasturage is not flourishing. The rains lie in puddles where they fall; and there is no artificial flooding, when there is none. The grass lands therefore are few; and till a better order prevails, there is no reason for wishing them to be more.

The arable lands on the contrary, continue fine examples of that adroitness and industry, for which they have been praised through three or four ages.—There are no wastes!

Every

Every bit of ground is well tilled. They give way to no fallows. By a variety of crops they clear the land of weeds, and give repofe to one ftratum of the foil, while they work the productive principle in another.—Thus, befides wheat, barley, and oats, they ufe beans, french-beans, turnips, artificial graſſes, radiſh, and rape.—The circulations of fome farms were,

    1 Turnips 3 Trefoil
    2 Wheat   4 Barley.

In others they fowed clover with barley and oats, with fuch fuccefs, as to make the clover pay all charges of management, of feed, and of labor; and to leave the corn crop a profit quite clear.—The artificial graſſes are mowed; and when not ſtacked, are given to the cattle in the manger. The clover, which is the red fort, endures two years; and then, after a very light ploughing, it is found fuccefsful huſbandry to harrow in wheat.

All the crops are fo good, it is hard to tell which looks the beft. The beft in profit which we heard were wheat, producing £17 per acre, and turnips near £5.

For ufe, implements of huſbandry, they may be profitably told, to get models from England; thofe of Flanders are more unweildy; particularly the plough, and it is not always that it has wheels.

In their ufe of inftruments, England may as profitably be leſſoned to imitate them. For, though they plough with two or more horfes, they are reined, a whip is faftened to the wood-work, and the whole is managed by one man!

It may be prefumed, that thus they plough well enough, becaufe, one ploughing is often found fufficient, though their furrows are ſhallow too; for they fay, and very fpecioufly, that if they were to delve deeper, the foil, artificially amended by manure, would become more apt to be forced from its place. The furrows are formed with the moſt perfect regularity, and at every 14 or 15 feet, trenches as many inches deep are dug, and well banked by the hand.

On Manures too, there are in each country, they who may read what follows, with mutual profit.—The Engliſh may teach them to marle their lands, and to mix with their light ſandy ſoil, what they have often at hand, a good fæcundating clay.—While we from the Flemings may learn ſomething on the doctrine of animal manures—for largely as they are uſed, they are never mixed with ſtraw, which gives more bulk and leſs force to the maſs.—The ſtreet dirt of their towns is collected and ſold. The ſcavengers in London and in Paris are paid. The latter in one groſs ſum of 400,000 livres a year. In the former, proportionate fractions for each pariſh. But the Netherlands can ſhew them a better regimen—for there the ſcavengers office is ſold—not as conferring nobility, like the executioner's place and other dirty work formerly in France, but as an object of obvious profit. At Bruxelles this office is ſold for 30,000 livres a year.

In Flanders alſo—difficile eſt dicere—they do not let even their houſe drains run to waſte. What they contain is collected, and found to be beyond all compariſon the moſt productive of animal manure—and, with a very encreaſed degree, when flung upon the land, dry and in powder.—It ſhould be mixed with fine mould, otherwiſe it is apt to be acrid and heating.

This object was lately, about two years ſince, fully proved before the Societè d'Acriculture at Paris. And I remember well, on ſure authority, before the confirmed directors and profeſſors of the experimental farm at the Ecole Veterinaire, M. Chabert and M. Flandrin, with the additional teſtimony of the Secretary Yvart, the M. Parmentier, and the Duc de Charrot.—The directors and profeſſors abovementioned, it were unfriendly to the cauſe of uſeful truth, to diſmiſs without ſpecific praiſe.—They were admirable men.

Their

—Their knowledge of animals, particularly thofe which man's domeftic care is moft interefted to provide for, feemed unbounded. On difficult appearances I have feen them decide, with a promptitude and with a certainty, exceeded by nothing but divination. If Buffon had written, what now we know, till they were given to him, he had never read, the fine anatomical and phyfiological materials for the firft parts of his great work; even his knowledge could not have been more copious. And for the fagacious ufes of what they knew, with complex acutenefs, oculorum acies et ingenii, I cannot conceive any obfervance upon animal economy more fubtle and profound, fince the unrivaled powers of Boerhaave and Linnæus.

The odd experiment, which induced this incidental tribute due to clever men, began, I believe in Flanders, on the canal between Bruges and Gand; and France has followed, with an eftablifhment for the like preparation, at La Chapélle, near St. Denis.

Befides what has been mentioned, and hand-hoeing, with a never ceafed activity that is wonderful, the agriculture of Flanders can have no more praife.—There are fcarcely any hedges. And where there are no inclofures, there can be no pafturage of cattle. Cattle indeed make no part, of any little charm there may be, in the leafy landfcapes of Flanders.

What cattle there are, are not worth mentioning; the fheep and horned cattle are below mediocrity, rather than above it. They are, like other foreign animals, not fo diftinct in their fpecies as in England; and not only fo, each fpecies feems bad, and bad is made worfe by evil treatment. When huddled together, in the hot foul air of clofe and crowded ftables, they muft have indigeftion, pulmonary and verminous complaints; and when, after long confinement turned out, if they efcape the fhock of fuch a change, they are more or lefs affected with the rot.

For,

For, the Flemish fens are more formidable than Romney Marsh, inasmuch as mere moisture must yield in mischief, to moisture stagnant and corrupt.—It is on the same principle, that, in all wet lands, as in Cambridgeshire and Essex, the dry season, is more morbid, than the wet.

At Paris there is a jurisprudence in their public markets as to the sale of cattle; to inspect and to guaranty, the buyer as to the health of the beasts he may buy. In London, a reserve, especially in horses, to a certain price, is implied; and there are returns, not quite irregular, as to the number of animals which are sold. But in Flanders there are no such establishments; and, therefore, such documents are wanting, as might yield no bad inferences on population, on the state of domestic living as to consumption, and on the state of cattle, their numbers, and their condition.

As far as they have any external trade in cattle, it is to this effect: They smuggle some sheep from England; and they have been accustomed to receive from France some sheep and oxen, which the Flemings thus fit up for sale, by leading them into marshy pastures, which give a diseased enlargement, and make them weigh well, however ill they may eat.

Flemish industry, thus subtle and active, is not directed to many objects besides agriculture.

About Ostend there are some windmills for sawing deals. As at Lisle, they have the same sort of mills for expressing linseed-oil. But Flanders does not profit, as it might, by other advantageous use of the elements—by working their wood into implements and materials of construction—by boat-building—by the manufacture of flour—by bleaching grounds—by bricks and tiles. In the victualling trade, they might rival Holstein, though not Cork. And in butter and cheese, in catching fish, and salting it, why should they not be more than a match for the Dutch? They grow a few hops (and the earth is mounded high up around each stem) and

and they try to make malt, and brew beer. But Thrale and Whitbread have no reason to be afraid of them there. There is a little cultivation of flax too; but it is the mere domestic refuge in bad weather: for making thread or cloth, it is of no collective account. Their lace-making is going—their tapestry is almost gone. Hat-making seems the only manufacture which is thriving; and that, particularly at Malines, deserves to thrive: for, unannoyed by any tax, hats are there 30 per cent. cheaper than they are retailed in London.

Arts, besides these, they have none; except it be the art to do without them.

Formerly, as every one may recollect, how the fine arts flourished in the Flemish school. And the churches of Flanders still boast of many a fine work, not only of Reubens and Vandyke, but Crayer also, and Van Hont Horst, de Vos, and Vervoot.

But, more unsteady than the Southern gale,

Painting is but a fleeting grace, dependent upon more fleeting trade; and, upon the vicissitudes of the people, the only patronage worth a word, able and willing to protect it.

Thus, the fine arts are doomed to rise and fall, with each corresponding attitude, in the circumstances around them! Thus taste becomes a barometer of the nation! Thus the English academy is enabled to sustain itself, without a single guinea from any patronage whatever, by the self-depending power of its own exhibition! And thus, in the same sort of medium of ease aspiring to elegance, and curiosity acting upon wealth, the Flemish school arose likewise, and like a gay meteor was admired so long aloft!

For, while Reubens and Vandyke were making an epoch of one kind, the tradesmen of Flanders had made another! Their towns were become the emporium of the universe! They were the chief to settle the exchange, to regulate the price current of Europe! Five thousand sail of merchant

ships

ſhips have been ſeen at once crowding their canals; and their port laboured with as many clearances in a day! The groſs produce of their out-lying commerce was called one hundred and forty millions, while their home-banking buſineſs was calculated to yield as much more!

At that time, one merchant, with at leaſt as much money as wit, is ſaid to have lent the prince a million ſterling, and afterwards to have burnt his bond in a fire—and in a fire of ſpices too, as if their pit-coal from Mons, or a common bavin from the ſide of their canals, would not have done as well. Thus, however, the farce is well made, as the impreſſion of the laſt act is the ſtrongeſt: for, when a fool of a fellow may have got a bad bond, the gay way of getting rid of it, is certainly the beſt.

But, incredulus Odi.—The whole tale muſt be received as a clumſy fiction; an unprovoked inſult upon good-ſenſe and common manhood. For Charles the emperor was a man of ſpirit, and a gentleman: he was above the vice of money; and if the loan had happened, we certainly ſhould alſo have known, why he deſerved ſuch magnificent bounty, and how he afterwards tried, elegantly, to repay it.

However there are, who ſpecify the very name of the merchant. And a revenue officer, on the miſcarriage of a lately propoſed loan, very gravely informed me, " That he " feared the race of the above-mentioned lender was ex- " tinct." A gay companion of ours replied, " No, Sir, there " are ſome, not a few, of the ſame family to be found, in " another country."

But, though the imitative arts may thus be doomed to fall with the fall of the trade which raiſed them, there ſeems to be equal reaſon why the arts, more uſeful and neceſſary, might not try to ſtruggle up again; and why a government, good for any thing, ſhould not help them in their ſtruggle.—Why ſhould there not be the commerce of education?—For obvious reaſons beſt adapted to places which are poor!—

Why,

Why, with fuch clofe contiguity to different countries, why are there not fchools for the three contiguous languages, and for the mechanic arts?---Why do they not make paper inftead of felling their rags?---Why is not the trade of books revived, as it has been fo fuccefsfully in another region, from whence the fine arts, as they are called, have fimilarly fled?---The printing eftablifhments of the Plantins family, with their twice fifty fonts of letters, are ftill heard of amidft the few fcholars that are left in Flanders---Why is it that they are practically to be heard of no more?

Such were the queftions, which occurred in the fame converfation; to thofe we had an anfwer, of which we could not tell the full meaning---" That there feemed to be a never-
" failing expectation of providential wars, and that then the
" common arts of agriculture, &c. could fuffice---That the
" Flemings could then double their dreffings on the land,
" and, in the fame proportion, multiplying the produce,
" raife the price of it 30 and 40 per cent."

Their trade, befides this, is but fmall.---From France and Spain they draw wines, brandy, and fome American goods; and they fend money only in return.---From England they have cottons, woollens, iron, hardware, Wedgewood's ware, fpices, dying drugs, tea, and lead, to the amount of a million, for which they pay in fpecie, except about a feventh part in verdigris, lace, thread, bees-wax, and rags.

In the town of Ghent the Englifh commiffary had an office, and there were vaft depofits of hay, ftraw, and corn. Large buildings, with no lefs wifdom, were alfo erected near Bruges, as bake-houfes for fome of the German troops! The virtue too, as well as the policy of this, muft be equally apparent to all! For what effort can be more meritorious than giving the hungry bread?

The fyftem of life, in Flanders, may be fuppofed to vary from our own, but, as it may be, for the worfe. The pleafures of the table are their beft refource; and they coft

E   abou

about four tenths lefs than they do in England.—There is a little mufic in their churches, and fuch confolation as carillons every quarter of an hour---The carillons are bells jangled out of feafon. There are no public amufements. There is a theatre in both Bruges and Ghent, with a troop detached from the company at Amfterdam; but a traveller has no need to go as far as Flanders to be convinced that there may be a theatre without any public amufement. In each town there is alfo a fubfcription-houfe (infcribed la Societé), where four or five pleafant rooms are opened, with good fires and lights, a library, and all the papers of London, Paris, &c. &c. The fubfcribers are about 200 in each town, and they pay annually a guinea each.—This feems to be the only external refource for collective amufement in the town.—For public libraries, philofophical lectures, fcientific affociations, there are none.—There is at Ghent an academy and a college of medicine; but, like a college elfewhere, they are content with felf-approbation, and unambitious after other applaufe—what knowledge they have, they are pleafed to keep to themfelves.—This college confifts of fix and thirty doctors, four and twenty accoucheurs, and forty furgeons.- -They follow the Bruxelles Pharmacopœia of 1671; and they follow little elfe; for the fee of a phyfician is but two or three fhillings a time.

The converfation of the Flemings is more liberal than fome of their neighbours. Referring to government, both in principle and practice, they continue as Cæfar faid of them fo long ago, *Horum Omnium Fortiffimi!* Thus far they are decided; and their decifion to an Englifhman muft feem juft.—They are vigoroufly prepared to contend for the popular part of every government, and they are active in approving the overthrow of defpotifm in France. And though Dumourier, perhaps even then a deferter, and wifhing to difgrace the caufe, by his abufe of it, extorted a contribution of 200,000 florins—yet the Flemifh are not fo abfurd, nor

froward,

froward, as to confound the principle with the perverfion; they ftill are fteady partifans of rectitude and truth—They admire freedom when atchieved by others—They feem properly ardent to atchieve it for themfelves!—

They are fond of talking hiftory. Grotius and Father Paul are very popular with them; and from them, of courfe, they are well taught to difmifs their former tyrants with the fcorn and indignation due to rapine and to blood. In regard to our hiftory, Elizabeth is the favourite theme; becaufe the antagonift of a gloomy barbarian, the flave of avarice and ambition, fhe aided the Netherlands in their natural zeal for the emancipation of reafon!—With the punctuality of dealing, which they have in common with the Dutch, they are fond alfo of enhancing the perfonal virtue of Elizabeth, who paid her father's debts, while fhe co-operated with all around her, to diminifh the debt of the nation!

In refpect to their own annals, the pacification of Ghent is a never-failing topic!—It was a toaft where we dined, and the gentleman who gave it, a fine fanguine man, ran over very ably the moral fame of the people, thus glorioufly perfifting till they righted themfelves —Till they difcharged their ufurper! When the harpies of oppreffion were put to flight---When exaction, for a time, was no more.

With the firmnefs and the minute honefty of the Dutch, the Flemings have alfo fomething of their external figure. And this rapid change in fpecific character from the French, without any phyfical term of feparation at all proportionate, without a great river, a mountain, or a fea, muft ever be in the traveller's way a problem, more eafy to admire than refolve.

The Flanders women alfo continue as we have been ufed to fee them in their large pictures.—They have not the enchanting graces of Vandyke, his minute fidelity, and the chaftity of his colouring; but it is Reubens all over, each piece in loose drapery, with great ideas and lavish freedom of design.

When Dumourier extorted the money above mentioned, ninety thousand florins of it were raised, literally, in fifteen minutes! An effort, this, impossible to any men in Flanders but high sinecure churchmen; for they, like certain vermin, contrive to dazzle from contiguous darkness, and still are suffered to flourish in the surrounding ruin!—One bishop has church rents to the enormous amount of 300,000 florins!— And yet, even he is not the primate!

The bad effect of money upon the human heart seems too fatally undeniable. It is not the ecclesiastical character, at least in Flanders, which can resist it. A character generally speaking every where, with some advantages from sustaining study, and from long-continued habits, for the most part necessarily good and holy!

Of the archbishops in France, before the Revolution, one, the archbishop of Paris, had £40,000 sterling a year; yet, when he run away to Chamberri, he left behind him a debt of two millions. Another French archbishop, too infamous to be mentioned, but in a criminal process from the jeweller whom he cheated, was plunged deeper in debt, though his revenues were £48,000 sterling a year!

The Flemish bishop, above-mentioned, was also in distress from debt, and was actually allowanced by his creditors to 12,000 florins a year.

The officiating clergy are very kindly kept out of temptation from all pecuniary excess. In Flanders, as in France, before the revolution, they are known rather by their labors than their rewards. There is no living, I could hear of, more than £100 a year—scarcely any are above half that sum; and the greater part of the parochial clergy have but 10 or £15 a year!

The Curè of Conflans, the residence of the archbishop,

the

the Lambeth therefore of Paris, had but thirteen pounds sterling a year!

Of the parochial clergy I am not qualified to speak largely.—I passed some hours with three of them.—They were fine-tempered men; and though not comparable to English clergymen, who, generally speaking, are for various knowledge, and for the powers of conversation, the first order of men that I have seen, yet they were sufficient:—They were not amusing nor elegant, but they were judicious; and what is perhaps the greatest rarity in the Low Countries, they were neither prejudiced nor dark. The clergy through all the Austrian Netherlands have great influence; and if they were all, like these men, they might deserve it, and have safely what they thus deserve.

Even the parochial clergy are, perhaps, too numerous. And altogether, regulars and seculars, they are certainly so; for, in the diocese of Bruges and Gand, I was informed, and I believe it, that they exceed a thousand; that is nearly one entire ninth of all the clergy in the 26 dioceses of England. In the diocese of Gand there are 161 parishes, under the jurisdiction of eight rural deaneries: the town has seven parishes: Bruges has eight. There are eleven abbayes, eleven chapters, and the canonries are about £200 a year.

The ranks in the Flemish church are these:

Archbishop (of Malines)

Bishop,	Arch-deacon (one in
Provost,	each diocese)
Dean,	Treasurer,
Grand-vicaire,	Canton,

In the cathedrals there follow two school-masters, ten priests, and eight penitenciers.

There is one archbishop of Malines, and bishops of Bruges, Gand, Ypres, and Tournay.

The abbayes, convents, monasteries, oratoires, chapels, are endless. Of these convents two are still English; and
what

what I shall have more difficulty and regret to make believed, they are yet filled with victims from England!

The remuneration of the clergy is from lands, from tithes, and from fees in thefe provinces.---Two-thirds of the landed property belong to the clergy. The tithes, a ſtrict eleventh, are taken in kind, and moſt frequently let to ſome exactor of a farmer.---The clergy, to do them juſtice, ſeldom are tithe-drivers.

The age for holy orders is the ſame as in England, and throughout the Continent:---the deacon muſt be 22 years---the prieſt 24---the biſhop 32.------The biſhops are generally noble---they are ſo now.---But there is no neceſſity, I believe, for this abſurdity---or if there is, that one deſcent may do, with other eaſy expedients, like bought nobility, by brevet, &c. as in the chapters of Liege and of Trent.---The cardinal de Granville at Liege was a memorable inſtance of this.

If the aſpect of the towns is intereſting; it is, like the moſt famed edifice in Europe, an intereſt only of dimenſions. Bruges is five miles round---Gand is fifteen miles! There remain the walls of near two hundred monaſteries! through the wiſdom of time, aided moſt by Joſeph the Second, ſome of them were aboliſhed.---There are large ſquares, gates, and bridges out of number, and many buildings in large maſſes, with gardens, which are large. The town-houſes are vaſt; and that of Bruges, a modern building, of Greek architecture, with a portico and dome, would be one of the moſt ſtriking façades in Europe, if the portico was a little larger, and the windows were a little leſs bad!

Yet, though there are theſe, and a great many private houſes of much magnitude, yet the impreſſion was diſpiriting. For it was the impreſſion of decay.

Decay, when the object is inanimate, ſeems ever gloomy. It may not be ſo, when there is animation in it---when it may be elevated by moral counteraction!

Thus, I can hardly ever recollect a more cheering call upon
human

human praife, than in the contemplation of that remarkable viciffitude, when a perfon fell at once from the top of life to the bottom---and yet continued, upright, firm, elaftic, capable.

He had been one of the firft men in the firft city of the world. He was a gentleman, and a fcholar. His fhop had brought him twelve thoufand pounds a year, and he had an eftate of eight thoufand more! He was not only thus enormoufly rich himfelf, but what muft be no lefs delightful, and more undangered, he had the power of conferring wealth on others!---For his patronage was more monftrous than that of the minifter in the American war!---He was befides not more a favourite of fortune than of tafte.---His villa was famed for its fuperior captivations---and the ufeful fplendour of his enjoyments, almoft flung all around them into fhade!

Of all thefe he had been at once, bereft. *Pauper et Exul.* With no more than a meagre two hundred pounds a year, and that a life-tenantry of his wife, he was caft upon the coaft of France—and doomed to a bare exiftence at a fifhing town in Piccardie.---There he had a dreary lodging at a boat-builder's on the beach. He had no companions to lighten preffures by dividing them. For external confolations he had none, but frefh air and a dirty walk upon the quay---and the walk, in confequence of the way, was confined to a few fteps between the pier-head and the town!

The people who remember him there, ftill exclaim about it with equal wonder and praife! For all thefe faddening vifitations, they went as they came!---They feemed to have touched him not—like dew-drops from a lion's mane!—He kept himfelf unaltered!---his fpirits and his powers never failed him!

I faw him for a few moments, when he had ventured to exchange thefe horrors for others, and was hiding himfelf,

half

half incognito, in a two-pair of ſtairs lodging at a hatter's in St. James's-ſtreet!

There, I waited below for my friend who had called on him. And there, as they came down the diſmal ſtairs, he trifled with charming vivacity! he ſmartly clapped my friend upon the back,—and gayly bid him " buy a hat of his hoſt " to mend his credit in the houſe!"

So much for any apparent decay, at Bruges and at Gand. And ſuch is one uſe which may be made of it.

> The ſouls dark cottage batter'd and decay'd
> Lets in new light, thro' chinks which Time has made
> Stronger thro' weakneſs,—wiſer, we become
> As we draw near to our eternal home.

THE GOVERNMENT OF FLANDERS.

It were well for every government, and for the people, on whose account every government is formed, if all were, as the Flemings are said to be, viz. the best citizens in the world, but not the best slaves.—That is, the best commendation, politically, for spirit on one side, and for docility on the other.

The chief revolutions of Flanders are well known, from their union with Lorraine, through the state of vassalage to their counts, and the three centuries following, when, without any consultation of the popular will, whatever, they were made either—the cause or the consequence, doomed, unjustly, to be visited with the infernal abominations of war. —While like a wreck, literally as if with no one living thing on board, they were banded about, from Spain to the Empire, from that to France, till at length, in the year forty-eight, by the treaty of Aix la Chapelle, the emperor became, as the lawyers call it, seized of them again.—He becoming their chief magistrate, and they as properly paying him for being so.

These payments, are, in each ordinary case of annual supply, what the prince settles at his good pleasure.

On extraordinary events and demands, it is requisite to have the consent of the states.

The states were, at first, represented by deputies, from the upper orders only—the tiers etat, the people, having only a right to deliberate, but not to act.

This decent system continued till 1754, when happily, as good is ordained to grow out of evil, the states and the government broke, and the people, partly by purchase, reassumed something like their right.

The Barrier treaty, another precious process, was the efficient cause of all this. The states were summoned to supply

ply their quota of fubfidy for the Dutch.—This, the ftates, properly, refufed—alledging that the " play was not worth " the candle—that the pretence for the war was nothing at " all to them--that they were to get nothing by the ulti- " mate iffues of the war—nothing by the incidental influ- " ence of it—this, though lefs falient, is generally the point " moft ftrong, in all fuch confiderations. And that, all " things taken together, they finally refufed."

The occafion was fo obvious, that the people could not help profiting by it. And recollecting the maxims of experience by which honeft men are faid to come by their right—they made this propofition—

" That if they were admitted to participate in the mea-
" fures, for which they were doomed to pay—if they were
" to recover their original and indefeafible right, not only
" to hear and to deliberate, but alfo to legiflate and to
" act—

" That then, they would fupply the fubfidy that was
" begged, a long as the other provinces thought proper
" to pay their quota, or fhould think there might be any
" juft caufe for any payment at all !"

To this his highnefs moft gracioufly condefcended. The people were reftored to their conftitutional right, the fame as the other conftituent part of the ftates—the people at the fame time paying the money they had bargained. This happened in the town, before inexpreffibly illuftrious, by the foundation of the golden fleece.

The imperial minifters, at the fame time, treat the paft eftablifhments as conceffions merely from Charles V.—and infer, that in the conftitution of Flanders, if a conftitution it can be called, the will of the prince is the law of the land; and this claim of the people, though admitted, was matter of favour only, and not of right.——A plea, this, not very welcome to the ears of an Englifhman—but, fenfibly lefs outrageous in a fyftem, where even the inauguration oath is

all

all on one fide, is taken by the people, and not by the prince.

To all thefe proceedings, before recited, there were remonftrances from the clergy, the nobles, &c.—But the clergy had loft all weight, by their fuperftitious imbecility, their proftration as to all manly character, and by their mean compliances—and the nobles, yet more weak, ignorant, and abject, had been long regarded as the mere dirty worn-out furniture of the ftate, in pageants and fports, for the court or for the chace.

The emperor, therefore, accordingly difmiffed them, (though in this inftance their refufal of the fubfidy was right) and rectified the edict in favour of the tiers etat, referving to himfelf, as became the monarch, a power to alter and enlarge it, as there might be need, for his fervice.

Such is the fundamental part of the political affociation in Flanders.

Another peculiarity, is that public offices are to filled by Flemings—that a foreigner, even from another province in the Netherlands, cannot come into place; unlefs the ftate to which fuch foreigner belongs fhall have firft enacted, that Flemings may in their ftate be equally employed.

The nobles ftill retain fome very proper privileges. They may plant on their lands by the road-fide—they may prefent to church livings, where they have them, on their eftates—and if they are touched with the wonted fenfe of hereditary dignity, they are authorifed to afpire to, and to obtain, a high pew in their parifh church.—But the more obnoxious impofitions of feudal times are made to ceafe. There are no game laws, the chace is open to all, and the farmer is no longer liable to lofe life or liberty, if he fhould eat a hare when he might happen to be hungry, or knock down another beaft that otherwife might down with him!—And the other abominations of the privileged orders, their exemptions, affumptions, and fines, will, we hope, be feen no more,

but

but as we look back upon the hideous objects of the dark ages—to mark the fine advances of civilizing liberty, to glorify the energies of her sense and spirit over the monsters she has subdued, and the horrors she has passed!

The divisions of property are unfortunate—not simply the inclosures, though hedges, by the bye, are wanting—but in what regards property in the land.—Of all the landed property in Flanders, two-thirds of the whole are the estates of the church!—The full impolicy of all this was known and felt, so long ago as our Henry the Seventh.—And from that time to this, the checks have been wisely multiplying, against the ills of mortmain, and unbroken entails.

Joseph II. with as much acuteness and more bounty, wished to do the same. But his life, alas! failed. And so there are still wanting, as in the better state of kings in England, those unmixed advantages to society, from a quick flux of wealth, from encouragements to actions, from invitations to enjoyment.

The ecclesiastical corporations, therefore, superserviceably rife, are still suffered in Flanders—they over-run it, in the worst way, with rapacity and sloth. And that extravagant and erring ascendancy in society, which even England endured before the reformation, yet usurps there uncontrouled! With political disparagement, no where more dispiriting, but under the Pope, in Portugal, and in Spain!

In ecclesiastical endowments, there subsisted till of late an interchange of patronage—reciprocally, admitting Frenchmen in Flanders, and Flemings in France. But this, by the late revolution, has ceased.—It was a regulation not extending to useful incumbentcy, nor to those preferments which gave a title, like our freehold, and a tenantcy for life.—It affected only, idle preferments without cure, removeable at will.—Even in Flanders, residence is punctual—and pluralities not allowed!

The magistrates in the towns of Flanders are a sort of resident

resident governors, as the marquis de Merode at Gand, a high bailiff, with a court or council of thirteen, over whom he prefides—and three penfionaries, who have about five and twenty fecretaries and procureurs.—Thefe, as ufual in almoft every government, manage with *little coft* to the public, all the moft important objects of neighbourhood and order, the police of ftreets and roads, buildings, markets, prifons, the arts, the hofpitals, external worfhip, and the poor.

Portions of thefe form the tribunals, civil, and military. —Thefe have cognizance and controul over all caufes, in firft inftances, and jufticatory proceffes. Gand is alfo the appellant jurifdiction of Tournay; though the laft appeal is to Malines.— In the more important cafes of appeal, to the ordinary judges are added fome of the council of Brabant and Hainault, and fome profeffors, the firft in the law-line, at Louvaine.

The admiralty court, for all that the Auftrians have of fea-coaft, confifts of the two penfionaries of Oftend, and one of Nieuport.

The rights and forms of the old courts of Flanders are ftill moft prudently preferved :—thus, if a farmer wifhes to build a bridge, or a citizen a houfe, nay, for a bow-window, or a balcony, there muft be an application and a fine. Thefe are fubject to a court—and the court are appointed by the prince. Our juftices in Eyre, is an ingenious contrivance we have not all to ourfelves. In Flanders they have judges of wood, &c. and to mend the matter, in Hainault they are hereditary—the Duc d'Urfel is the grand veneur.

Their town taxes on the neceffaries of life, les droits d'Entreès, the confequence of one order of woes are the caufe of another!—They fprung under Philip's wars, and they grew to be fubjects for feparate courts and judges—paid by the people, appointed by the prince.

The ecclefiaftical courts were well checked by Jofeph II. But they remain to be abolifhed.—The judge, called the official,

ficial, is aided by affeffors.---The appeal, whether in what ufed to be to the pope or to the metropolitan, is now better ordered to judges delegated by the country.

There are many fubdivifions of tribunal, of courfe, I fuppofe, not for the fake of patronage in appointments, but for their more effectual executions. The laws are not, as elfewhere, a remedy worfe than the evil; but they are cheap and undelayed. And yet there are no fmall numbers fed by them at Gand, viz. 230 advocates, and half as many notaries and attornies.---The fees of all are but two or three fhillings---and their pleadings are in Flemifh, and in writing.

The FINE ARTS had nearly been forgotten; and it is their own fault they have fo little worth remembering.

There are Libraries at the Dominicans, the Carmelites, and at St. Peter's.

As for Architecture, there are no novelties but new ftores, and bakehoufes building for the German troops!---and churches, &c. not of the reformed religion, applying to the fame wholefome purpofes.---They all are vaftly admired by the foreigners---and, indeed by all who have an underftanding in thefe curious things!

The military hofpitals of the Germans alfo might do the heart good! for they were admirably fitted to touch it with the right fenfe, as to the *glorious* confequences of war!---If the beds had not been wooden---if fo many fad objects had not been huddled altogether in each room---if there had been cleanlinefs and frefh air, there had been nothing to have faid of the hofpitals themfelves, and only a vain lamentation from humanity, that there fhould have been this caufe for any fuch hofpitals at all!

In the maladies and misfortunes of man, not derived from the violence of his fellow creatures, there are other hofpitals

in

in Flanders;—but thefe we faw had but few patients in them. And thefe, in large, but ill-regulated rooms, were folicitoufly attended by the medical people and the nuns:— but otherwife, ill and ignorantly provided, even in the Bruxelles hofpital. The air is almoft mephitic. The beds are wooden boxes. The curtains woollen. The prifons alfo are not ill-conditioned. The debtors have a fmall fupport from their creditors and the ftate—and if fick, are well fupported (at an expence of 14d. a day) by the ftate. The labour of convicts is fpinning, carding, weaving, net making, &c. And what they earn, is from three-pence Englifh to eight-pence a day. And if they labour extra hours, the profits are their own. If they labour lefs than ordered, they are punifhed with rafping logwood.

Of Painting, the prime object is the Reubens on the cathedral of Gand—it is the refignation of the Crown by Charles V. one of the few princes who deferved what he refigned—and in another part of the picture—another good act, St. Bavo giving alms—Reubens, and his two wives, looking on!—and every body, elfe may look on. Even, after the three chef d'œuvres of Reubens, in the great church at Antwerp, at the Luxembourg, and at Whitehall!—For, the head and grouping in each fubject are treated moft mafterly. With his combination of oppofite excellencies, bold drawing and fplendid colouring—the fullnefs of nature, and the artifices of his clear obfcure.

What is called Reubens, in the church of the Recollets, I fhould hope and imagine, not to be his.

In two or three other chapels, in the cathedral, covered alfo with curtains, which a few minutes, and a few fous will undraw, are a Sebaftian by Crayer (who by the bye, died at Gand)—and by Van Hont Horft a Madonna, and two children weeping over the crucifixion—the whole of thefe are much praifed—but it were fafer to praife nothing but the children.—One of them, fhows Van Hont Horft

to

to have had fine ideas of nature in her happiest forms, for the countenance is of the same captivating character as the Dutchess of D!

At one of the chief financiers, there is, as may be expected, a collection of valuable pieces.----Among them, at the bottom of the office, are the loaves and fishes, by Vervoot.

" Comme chez vous," said a shrewd Fleming to an Englishman who was in the room—" comme chez vous, " monsieur Anglois;" to which the English gentleman answered, " yes Sir, you are right—the great original idea, " indeed the finished sketch of that performance, the " loaves and fishes, has been in England a long while! cer- " tainly, before the American war."---The Flemish gentleman, with great gravity replied—he solemnly believed it!--- And then descanted on the execution of the great work in England—the handling, the clear obscure, and the knowledge of effects! Who does not know them all?

> Quis genus Œneadum, quis trojæ nesciat urbem
> Virtutesque, virosque, aut tanti incendu belli!

THROUGH

THROUGH ALOST TO BRUXELLES

From Ghent, is an affair of four or five hours, through thirty miles of gay road, well planted throughout by every land-holder on the road-side, and well paved by the people in 1705.

The agriculture, of so much general reputation, is the same as that before detailed so fully. Good where it is arable, bad where it is grafs—the cattle still but few—the hedges few, and of no effect, but as so many little lines of relief to the eye.—With so many plantations, in lines, clumps, and groves, that it is, literally, not possible, to see wood for trees.

My Flemish friend, who was in political character what we once in England knew as a whig, said of these trees, " That they were like a bad majority upon worse opinions!" (he had heard of, I suppose, in Brabant) " collectively a " covering for every thing; but separately taken, flimsy, and " not worth half-a-crown!"

The views are not so fancifully flung about, as near Armentieres and Bailleul, in the way to Lisle, where the road turns at every score of roods, and each turn is bounded by a church. But still the scenery is pretty;—tame, indeed, but not flat. The surfaces are for ever, gently, waving. Small dells also are frequent; and those with little uplands, are covered with woods.

The cottages and villages, extremely numerous, furnish the best charm in the scene,—for they imprefs ideas that are cheering, from neighbourhood and order; from independence, sufficiency, and ease.

The cottages are, usually, well placed, with good gardens round them, generally at good distances.—with gable ends to the road, or better still, often turning their back on it.

Who quits the world where strong temptations try,
And since 'tis hard to combat, learn to fly.

This, high if morally taken, and not low as a preference of taste, is a mode of building common through Germany. And a German lady married into the highest rank in England, but more ennobled by personal merit, (she is not living at present) used whimsically to praise Old Brentford for this, and to say, " that it always reminded her of Hanover."

The peasantry, added to their gardens, commonly have a few acres of land, which, with a cow or two, some swine and poultry, with occasional day-labour, when it is every most dear, and selling what in their produce of their little grounds may be superfluous or rare, enable them to struggle through, and make a hard and humble station, as happy as it can be in this life.---Unless it be, with a reserve, in favour of the local preferences of America, where, besides the blessings of peace and few taxes, every peasant is a landowner, and of course is doubly a citizen, in privileges and powers, from real possession, as well as from political rights.

As to tenantry, the state of the country is what England was formerly, when our farms were less, and the farmers consequently so many more.---The largest farm, that occurred here, was on the Tournay road, between Halle and Bruxelles---where the quantity was 200 boniers (or double arpents---312 of English acres) for which he paid 20 florins each.---His establishment was, 20 servants, 50 horses, 10 waggons (of course, otherwise employed than merely in the farm) 60 cows, 30 hogs, and 400 sheep.---The ground belonged to a convent. His markets were Halle and Bruxelles. ---Price of labour, 10 sols of Brabant to 18 and 20;---five sols of Brabant are equal to eight of France.

Going from Gand to Bruxelles, the only town upon the road is Aloft.---It has the advantage of the river Dendre--- and, like almost every morsel of land in Flanders, it bears the memorials of war---memorials not easy to be forgotten; for, after the battle of Ramilies, the works were destroyed, and the town abandoned!

It.

It has been the fashion to attempt talking up the French Court, with artificial emotions, not only of sufferance, but respect! as if the human powers when not dragged and debilitated to the door of death, could ever sink into oblivion, over their multiplied enormities! their unexampled combination of opposite ills, from levity and obduracy, from guilt in plundering the public purse, and wasting what they had plundered—in the everlasting guilt and folly of war, in battles without cause, in victories without effect!

Aloft, the town now talked of, is one out of twelve towns over-run in one summer, and laid low by the armies of French despotism! When not only the king, Louis XIV. was there, but the queen, with the gentlemen and ladies of the court, fondly followed to the war-feast! not like bloodhounds, from hunger, but unlike every thing but themselves, for sport!—Absolutely in pageant shows and revelry, amidst the infernal horrors they had committed in sieges and in battle, with rapine, ravage, conflagration, and blood! The utmost exaggerations of all-complicated woes! Miseries, of which, otherwise, there could have been no cause on earth, —as, certainly, as on earth there can be no penal consequence, but remorse, at all adequated either.—The existence of this savage pursuit, as the refined amusement of the court, is a melancholy fact, I fear, not to be disputed. " La " Campagne Rassembloit, plutot, a une partie de plaisir, " qu'une operation de guerre."—These are the words of a cotemporary authentic writer!

For all these deep-wrought lessons, of edifying woe, and useful inferences on the necessity and temper of the court, the country of Aloft was, like Bruges, Gand, and Brabant, honored with a place in the Barriere treaty, and obliged to supply their quota of subsidy to the amount of 500,000 crowns!

On obligations, like these, the Flemings fail not to express emotions, with no small profit, examplary to the less manly citizens of other countries.

In this shock of infernal war, not every thing was lost. A sketch or two of Reubens survived the wreck. And a sketch usually has, from obvious causes, more merit than works elaborately finished.

In the church of St. Martin, which holds these sketches, there are objects, which probably will not have so many admirers as the lower animals by Reubens. There are a dozen of canons, a provost, and a dean. The dean, however, is in some sort respectable; for he is at the same time the curè of place, the officiating parish priest. A name and office eminently high! and in every part of Europe I have passed, regarded with rational fondness, with well-earned esteem.

Besides the establishment of a chapter, a very dubious race, perhaps every where, there are no less than eight monasteries—as usual, blasphemously thwarting the benevolent destinies of man! Where, the guardian angels of our lot, labour and rest, useful business and innocent pleasure are superseded by the foes of our common nature, the abominable brood of folly and despair—by vain hope, and false fear, continual indolence, and continual mortification!

There is, however, some contiguous compensation for the mind, in the tomb of Martin, whose life, in happy opposition to what was last mentioned, was actively good, and useful!—He had enlarged the range of his intelligence by travelling, and on his return from Germany, he brought the art of printing with him.—Flanders, therefore, owed him much; but if it had been more, it would have been paid. For he was so happy, as to have the friendship of Erasmus, and his praise!

Thus, even in that country, dark in bigotry as it may be, there is incidental use, from the exterior of religion. And
the

the traveller, well difpofed enough to go to church, may hope to come back rather better than he went.

The chief magiftrate is a burgomafter, with a greffier and eight echevins.—Enough in all confcience to take care of themfelves. This they do here, as elfewhere, with never-ceafing zeal! And having done that, we would recommend to them, the care of the fick poor, and their petty gaol, as bad as it can be, from cruelty and neglect!—From foul air, dirt, darknefs, dungeons, and chains!

The people, however, not in the hofpitals nor gaols, now contrive to do pretty well. Like the fellows who made fetters under Nero and Tiberius, they fatten upon mifchief. They flourifh by the war, which, with becoming gratitude and good-humour, they fay, is juft and neceffary, and glorious to them. For their chief trade is felling corn. Which thrives proportionably to the number of good people, fo very fenfibly, going there to eat it!—Hence, the town, already, is enlarging, with fpacious rows of new building, flanting like Sloane-ftreet—and there would have been alfo, an hofpital for the foreign foldiers who are fick and hurt, but that the wifdom of the towns-people ftopped it—for they faid, very properly, " That it was fufficient impofition to hear of " fuch mifery, and to pay for it too—but as for any thing " more—they muft beg to be excufed!—to fee it, with " patience, was impoffible!"

BRUX-

BRUXELLES.

It is with men as with the herbs and plants they tread upon; they affect all the different aspects and soils that can exist between the Alpine, the rocky, and the bog.——Louvois, the man who first exacerbated the pestilent art of arms by magazines, admired, as a beast would do better, the flats of Flanders for their fæcundity in forage!---And Crequi, is said, for a different reason, to have cursed the country, because the people in it were too wise and happy to be recruits—and thus, in other words, to be shot at for something less than for a farthing an hour!

A traveller need not stir from home to be insulted with nonsense and barbarity like that.

As we approached Bruxelles we aimed at emotions and objects rather better than these.

The sun shone—in all the glow and glory of July! yet a sprightly, genial, wind from the north-west, acted as a cover from the heat. The hedge-rows and vistas, out of number, gave a quivering shade. The vallies stood thick with corn. And, if they who were at work in them, did not laugh and sing, the misfortune was their own—and the fault was not Nature's!

And to their Lord owe more than to the soil.

At Bruxelles, a town so old as to be named in a patent of Otho, 976, according to an historian very venerable, and not always childish, all things are at fixes and sevens.—" The " number of houses are twice seven thousand six hundred— " and seven times as many the people who dwell therein." —Of these, seven are pious houses—and, at least, more than as many not so.—There are seven tribunals, of course seven reasons for not going to law, with seven places, and seven gates, where you may hang yourself—if you do go to law!—The river Senne, rises seven leagues up between Trivelle and

Rœux,

Rœux, and you may follow it into the Dyle, &c. seven leagues down, if you will. Seven crowns were once seen, and felt, at Bruxelles—and what is not always the case seven heads were said to be under them!

But Bruxelles has something better than all this—viz. a square. The park, which is, in respect to the cultivated ground, and the woods and walks in the centre, the best thing of the kind in Europe! as the Palais Royal at Paris, and St. Mark's Place at Venice, are the two squares best built; and a rampart, where you may walk and ride amidst gentle scenery, with views over two hundred and twenty villages and woods (La Foret de Soigne), flowing up to the very walls of Bruxelles! The dryads here, the penates of Bruxelles, give them most of the wood they want to burn. They measure 16,526 arpents (an arpent is nearly 2 English acres),—and of these, a hundred acres are cut once in a hundred years—and so it is hoped, and believed, they may cut on for ever.

> Let their plantations stretch from down to down—
> Now shade a country, and then build a town.

The rampart itself, is in itself, cheering, not only that it is tolerably planted, and that it may raise a good natured wish, that it may be better kept—but, because, it presents another order of objects day by day, approaching nearer, than before, to the cause of what is true, humane, and useful.

Nunc campus, ubi troja fuit.

The fortifications are abandoned, and abolished—and all the grounds before wasted on such mischievous toys, as the angles and inequalities of gunnery, now are subject to the plough-share, and the pruning hook!—We saw fine crops of corn already waving over one part, and I trust, we shall have credit for the desire, that they may be seen withouth delay, in as useful triumph over all.

> " Rich harvests bury all their care had plann'd,
> " And laughing Ceres reassumed the land."
>
> Swift,

Swift, with proper fcorn, paffing by the laurel of the warrior, celebrates with due praife, the man who can make two blades of grafs, or two fpikes of wheat, grow, where there was but one before; what would he have faid to Jofeph the Second, who, in fpite of the prejudices, and evil accompanyments of his rank, was thus friendly and active in the caufe of man, releafing the towns from the miferable tyranny of gates and outworks—and fuperfeding the dirt and debauchery of a garrifon, with the farmers glory, with a nations blifs!

In good, as well as evil, one act with fure propenfity feems ever leading to another. With the food and accommodations for men; this encreafe of men were encreafing likewife. Before the war, which checked and blafted every human good, there were feveral plans for new buildings, and the fauxbourge were going to be included in the privileges of the town.—The circuit of the town is about a league and a half.

The population of the town, an object no where afcertained with the wifhed-for precifion, is lefs conjectural here, than in fome other places.—According to the beft documents which could be collated, the people average nearly, if not quite, to feven in an houfe, including in the calculation, the inhabitants of religious houfes.—A population that is very great, confidering the number of perfons thus unhappily wafted on monaftic vows, and the enormous collective ills, with which the town has been fore vifited! For, befides a peftilential epidemic, fweeping off half the people in the preceding century, within thefe laft hundred years, it has been eight times the feat of war! And as fuch, rent and wafted with all its flagitious horrors! Befieged; feized; evacuated; pillaged; bombarded; and burnt!

Amidft fuch ravages of mifchiefs, for the moft part unprovoked, and unprofitable, in the extreme; there have happened, now and then, eventual confolations. The Romans

mans left their roads behind them. America has thus had fome European arts.—Poor Bruxelles has nothing to brag of, but a fimple fluice, which prevents the river Senne from overflowing the lower town. And that the people owe to the French in the year 1747.

Of the population, when thus taken, as accurately as circumftances allowed, about twelve or fifteen years ago, the amount was no more than 7!,427—and the diftributions as follow—but the returns were lefs than the truth—there was an alarm of new impofitions, and new levies—many perfons for a time abfented from the town—and from the regifters, many more.—From 80 to 100,000, is a computation nearer the truth.

1 Of chief merchants, bankers, nobles, &c.
above - - - - - 7,055
2 Of church-men, regulars, and feculars, with
thofe of both fexes in convents, above 1,587

N. B. This is equal to one entire fixth of all the parifh priefts in England—and nearly half the eftablifhment in Ireland.

3 Infants, above - - - - 14,099
4 Shop-keepers, above - - - 9,883
5 Work-people of both fexes, above - 20,908
6 Servants, ditto - - - 8,443
7 Beggars! Ditto, above - - 1,974
8 Military, and travellers - - 2,474

N. B. The beggars are what are commonly called fo. The placemen come under the firft article—fee under number one.

The military and the travellers, are particularly variable as to number. At the end of the year 179:, when I was firft at Bruxelles, there were 3,000 French fugitives, and more than as many troops, the regiment of Bender, part of the Augfbourg regiment, and a corps of cavalry.—The mperial forces, in the Auftrian Netherlands, were then, according to the office returns, 42,000 men! Forty two thoufand men, at three Flemifh fous a day!!

There is the more aftonifhment and regret in this, becaufe, as day-labourers, in Brabant, they might have earned, with good to the community, from one to two fchellings a day! And for labour, at all ingenious, the pay is double.

The opportunities, however, of ingenious labor, feem alas! lefs and lefs. Formerly, there was a tapeftry manufacture, fcarcely lefs thought of, by thofe who could think of it at all, than the Gobelin and Sabloniere at Paris—in fine thread lace, before Mechlin and Valenciennes, Bruxelles was the beft—and, at the great fire, when 1,400 houfes were burnt, no lefs than 400 of them were prime manufacturers of cloth.—At prefent, with a little lace, and lefs tapeftry, they make a few woven cottons, and fome cloths and ftuffs—of which the camblets are the beft.

The town is tolerably well built, as to the walls of the houfes; but their windows, and doors, are after the fafhion of the French. The lower windows are alfo deformed with iron bars; offenfive, even beyond the eye—as implying fomething wrong in the place, either from real danger, or from falfe fear.

However, there may be hence a refource in thofe emergences, to which all ftates in their turn are liable---and when the beft of metals, iron, may be wanting, they may find it here. As one of our great brewers faid to a wretched nobleman, who had threatened to ufurp a venal feat, nay, though it coft him ten thoufand pounds, by mere weight of metal—" Tell the gentleman, like Zeno
" phon, to be diftinguifhed, by the retreat of the ten thou
" fand, that if his poor power can go no further than to
" £10,000—all the old iron fhall be fold off my condemned
" cafks—and I will thus beat him, at his own weapons."

The buildings at Bruxelles, compare in one point, advantageoufly with Paris. For, the houfes having

fewer

fewer floors; but three or four, generally have but one family under one roof.—There is none of that huddled abomination, Tigribus Agni, the human head under the ferpents tail, fo fhocking over fome of the moft fubftantial fhops in Paris—and which ufed to make the ftreets there, a jakes for morals, no lefs than for health.

In another way, the buildings at Bruxelles cannot juftly be denied praife. For, as one of the wittieft men in Europe faid of the things called modern comedy, " they " are moral at leaft, if not entertaining"—fo of the chief houfes here: they raife but little envy without, and ufually, the fpectator may be quite cured, if he will but enter within. The houfes of Aremberg, Tour and Taxes, de Ligne, d'Egmont, d'Urfel, de Hornes, with the governor generals, and the Imperial Plenipotentiaries, are the few, to be confidered rather highly.—We had occafion alfo to vifit a Princefs, on a commiflion from Lady I.—and we found her fo lodged, that in all qualities of fituation, fpace, convenience, and tafte, a man that knows how to go to market, would be better off, even in London, at a rent of 60 or £70 a year.

But *non quo fed quomodo*—in houfes, as in thofe who fill them, it is not how much, but how well; and therefore, it was a well judged compliment to our refident, then intellectually fit to reprefent Englifhmen, when the Duke and Duchefs of York left the hotel de Galles, and defired Colonel Gardener to invite the Court, the Arch-Duke and Duchefs, Prince Charles, M. de Lambefque, C. de Metternich, &c. &c. with all the Englifh fit to be feen—and they all met at Mr. Gardener's lodgings, in the pretty little mezzonines, fcarcely 16 feet fquare, at the Belle-vue.

The places for a traveller to fee, if he has time, are the Arch Duke's chateau de Schoemberg (in the village of Lack), and the villa of M. Walkiers, the banker.—They are not half an hours drive from Bruxelles, and clofe to one another; befides, the way, is through the Allee Verte, thofe beautiful viftos, of elms and limes, where the canal goes to join the Scheldt! Viftos, which the French fo handfomely refpected in the year 1746—but which, they would hardly have refpected now.—For, they were filled, with hay-ftacks and other forage for the army, in the moft fad wonder of profufion, from tree to tree, through a fpace perhaps of near half a league.

The Arch-Duke's chateau is a modern building, Ionic without, Corinthian within, with two fronts of 260 feet, the depth 150—with a central portico, at the entrance, and a bow in the centre behind.

The effect of the building at a diftance is gay, and impofing enough; when clofe to it, the effect is maimed by bad figures at the top of the building; and the pediment of the portico being filled by a clock, which feems fit only where the character of a building is appropriate, as at Inigo's church in Covent Garden, to fimplicity and ufe.— The gate of approach, loaded with bad ornaments, cupids and what not, is at once lofty and trifling, elaborate and dull.

In the internal diftribution, the beft rooms are forty feet fquare—a dining room 52 by 40—a chapel 27 by 22—and the ftate room a circle, 54 feet diameter—the dome is the cieling of this room; and nearly midway, between the bottom and the top, there is a fmall gallery on 12 Corinthian pillars.—The floors in the other rooms are inlaid mixture, angular fhapes of oak, mahogany, and petrified cedar. In the circular room, the floor is fhewy, formed of various marbles.---There are five windows, which fhould have had five looking-glaffes oppofite—there are but two, with three glafs doors, but not looking-glafs.

The looking glaffes are the manufacture of Venice. And thefe, eight feet by fix, are among the largeft ever blown
there

there. For that is the Venetian procefs; not by the mould, as in France and England.

There are few objects of art. The only pictures are four large ones by De Lance of Antwerp. They are mythological fubjects; of courfe the worft in the world.—The ftatues in the garden are by Godicharles. Le Roi of Namur fupplied the five feet whole length of the Virgin in the Chapel. It is not bad ftatuary: for it has, which is very rare, thought and emotion.. In every effort of imitative art, this is the firft attribute; and, of fuch fure avail, as to atone for imperfections in any other.

The architect was Montoyer. He built alfo the Vauxhall in the park at Bruxelles.—The houfe was began in 1782—it was finifhed in 1788.—A fmall temple, and the pagoda, the only buildings in the garden, are alfo by him.

The pagoda has eleven floors. And there, as at Kew, it may be confidered as a well-placed trifle. As giving artificial elevation to a flat; like letting a dwarf fee by raifing him on tip-toe. Yet there is comfort in them, and much amenity. And what can trees and villages do more?

> Whofe trees in fummer yield him fhade;
> In winter, fire.

The grounds the Arch-Duke keeps in his hands are between 2 and 300 acres.---There is an artificial water, fifty toifes acrofs, and a quarter of a league long---the lawn floping down to it from the houfe, with the uplands on the other fide, and the fine woody hill, form the prettieft fcene.

The ornamental ground may be fome of the beft out of England. The turf and the plantations are not bad. They only want fome gravel, hedges, fcythes, gardeners, and fheep. The kitchen garden does not vie with Welbeck and Clumber. There is but little glafs. But there is a roundabout

about as in the apparatus for second childhood at Chantilli; and orange-trees in tubs, but not as many, nor as old, nor as high as at Verfailles!——For there ufed to be at Verfailles a plat of three or four acres, covered with 1400 orange-trees in alleys, the oldeft the Royal Louis and the Bourbon, were thirty feet high—they were planted by Francis the Firft.—The French faid, upon the trunk of the Louis was, as they fay now of their republic, undivided and one—the Bourbon had four ftems.—Both were great curiofities—and greater ftill, the flowers ufed to be gathered every morning, and fent to the Thuilleries for the late wretched Louis to drink as his beverage at breakfaft.

Experimental hufbandry there is none. That, with each other ufeful rural grace, is to be found only among the philofophical beauties of Britain! Wentworth, Richmond, Oatlands, and, yet more, the duke of Newcaftle's Nottinghamfhire grounds, &c. &c. &c. all are thus honorably adorned, with the complex charm of curiofity and good-fenfe; of private pleafure working towards the public good.

> Varium cæli prædifcere morem,
> Cura fit, ac patrios cultufque. Habitufque locorum,
> Et quid quæque ferat regio, et quid quæque recufet.

The adjoining villa of M. Walkiers, the banker, is another more pretty building by Montoyer, amidft the fame little fertile fcenery. The architecture is Ionic. With a loggio throughout the middle floor of one front, like an Italian villa—the ground plan of the houfe is about 150 feet by 50.—There is a fmall grafs-plot before and behind, with fide walks, through very fmall trees, in half a dozen ftrait alleys:—not one of the trees are worth five fhillings. There is no gravel for the feet, no water for the eye—and the inclofure is a flimfy two-feet hedge, which a child may either pafs through, or ftep over.—And yet, this is the thing that has been compared to the Derbyfhire Ilam—a place of grand

grand effects, at least as far as English scenery is to be called grand—a place where mountains and uniting streams enforce attention, with the surprises of what is unexpected, and with the force of what is vast.

Such is the power of an active fancy influenced by good feelings more active—easily susceptible of sensations that are pleasurable; and with a temper yet more desirable, willing to please others.—Such is the liability to error the most veracious mind may feel; as the recollection becomes feeble in proportion as it is far. Thus descriptions may fail; and if they were ever requisite, thus refutation of them must become requisite also.

These are the houses most remarkable in the country.— As in the town, the late building for the assembly of the states, &c. in the Park, is the most shewy. The building, like its purpose, is imposing and heavy. It cost the city 600,000 florins. The architect was Guimard, who shewed much more skill in his other work, the Place Royale, and the façade of the Condenberg church, which well imitate the Place Royale at Nanci, in Lorraine—decidedly, one of the handsomest squares or places in the world. The Park has too the handsomest coffee-room in Europe—better even and more gay than the rooms at Liverpool, at Glasgow, or the Dublin Exchange—though that, on the outside at least, is a fragment of Palladio. And it may give another fanciful value to the place, as that here Charles V. built, and retired after his abdication, 1556.—Most of the large houses were built by abbayes of Brabant.

The theatre has nothing to recount which can improve our own, except that there are five rows in the hearing orchestra.—The shape is long and narrow, instead of being short and wide—in other words, the shape is so far as bad as it can be. It is five story high.

The annual receipts amount to 200,000 livres. The disbursement are about 180,000. The remainder 20,000 livres

livres is thought a sufficient profit for the manager. The nightly charges, exclusive of salaries to performers, are six pounds sterling---the admission three and four schellings.---The orchestra is numerous---thirty-eight performers; and there is a director keeping time with a paper roll. The performances are both plays and operas, and the last when we were there were not the worst.---At the carnival, the balls, &c. are here.

The theatre, as an estate, is among the most productive in Bruxelles. The building cost but 160,000 florins.---Having under the same roof, a coffee-house also, and a cabaret. The two last lett for 14,000 livres a year. The playhouse for 6000.

The foundations of the theatre are the walls of the old town---and they are, from the natural action of time upon good cements, and the tendency to induration seen in all calcareous sandy earths, excessively cohesive and hard.---The date of the elevation is 1700. Bombarde, an Italian, was the architect.---A plan for a new theatre has been proposed by Perrier; but this, like every thing which is good, has been ruined by the war.

The arts at Bruxelles have very few memorials left. The best pictures, as the Reubens from the Annonciates, and from the Jesuits, &c. &c. were bought by the Fifteenth Louis, are now in the collection of the French Republic ---The best picture which remains, is the Vandyke in St. Gudule---a head of Mary Queen of Scots, the hands touching each other as in an act of adoration.------The best morsel of statuary, is a head, undoubtedly fine, whether antique or not antique, in the collection of the Duc D'Aremberg.---Upon this head, much has been said! and as it is impossible to say more, it has been reported, though erroneously, the Laocoon itself!---That long-lost head, which, perhaps with his best success in this department, Michael Angelo so magnificently laboured to replace!

The

The collections, &c. which people frequent, are at duc d'Aremberg's, M. Danoots, and M. Walkiers,—the bankers ---but the beſt part of their collections are, the modern gold coins of their ſhop, evidently worth more than even the coins at Blenheim.

If public ſtatues be a proof of merit or of taſte, there has been at Bruxelles but little of either. There are no ſepulchral devices, to excite and reward any ſuch efforts as thoſe of Roubiliac or Banks---the ſtatue of prince Charles, unworthy the enthuſiaſm which raiſed it, Jan. 1775. Werfchufft, a workman at Manheim, has to anſwer for it. And as for the figure of the prince in the Place Royale, that is no better---who put it up, we know not; but the French, with their republicaniſm and eight draught horſes, pulled it down.---The important reſtoration of it was on a day no leſs important than the Feaſt of St. Charles (Baromeo) when four days were given to the celebration, and a hundred days indulgence, in a public advertiſement, offered by the prelate, to thoſe who would work at it for nothing.

Thus the ſtatute was raiſed again, upon a time-ſerving pedeſtal of wood, and the inſcription, as of the ſame material alſo, was in blundering Latin---" Optimo principi, " patriæ delicio."

Another ſcholar and courtier of Brabant propoſed, in our hearing, that it ſhould be delicto.

But lord Aylcſbury's fountain and inſcription are the moſt gratifying of the public works at Bruxelles---for they raiſe emotion ; and the emotion is fair.----It is inſpiriting to ſee a man tenacious of what he thinks the truth, when truth and intereſt chance to be aſunder ! It is cheering to ſee him, " mente ſolida," unembarraſſed and firm, redreſſing himſelf of accident and human violence, turning ſtrangers into friends, and making a foreign country look to him like his own ! It is venerable to look over the ſolemn lapſe of forty long years, and ſee a man, in protracted vigor, happy; and

I thus

thus to the laſt, with ſtudied bounty, uſefully kind to thoſe who made him ſo.

The inſcription is as follows:

THOMAS BRUCE
COMES AYLESBURIENSIS MAG. BRITANNIÆ PAR :—
HOSPITIO, APUD BRUXELLES 40 ANNOS
USUS, JUCUNDO ATQUE SALUBRI
DE SUO, PONI, TESTAMENTO JUSSIT
ANNO 1740.

ANNO 1750
PACE, UBIQUE TERRARUM FIRMATA
THOMAS BRUCE, THOMÆ HÆRES
ERIGI CURAVIT.——
FRANCISCO LOTHARINGÆ ROMÆ IMPERIUM
ET MARIE THERESA CAROL. B. F.
REGNA PATERNA, FORTITER VINDICATE,
FELICITER ET GLORIOSE TENINTIBUS
CAROLO LOTH. BELG. PRÆS.

The heraldry of lord Ayleſbury, with the motto " Fui" mus," is alſo there.—The ornaments, not worth mentioning, were deſigned by comte Calembert, and executed by Burge of Bruxelles.

Lord Ayleſbury's houſe was fronting the fountain, near the church.

Thus the ſecond James, though good for nothing in himſelf, unleſs the invention of ſea-ſignals be good, was the cauſe of good to others.—Thus Louis XIV. advanced beyond the oſtentation of his nature, became elegantly bountiful---and thus, this fountain was made.

THE GOVERNMENT

Of Brabant is mixed, and not altogether according to the Asiatic idiom, where the word mixed implies a concurrence and confummination of evil.

The monarchical portion predominates. It is vested in the governor general: who, by the Walloons treaty, (1574) ought to be of blood royal. His authority is supreme. In the form of sovereignty, and to the same extent---in the administration of old laws---in the origination of new laws---in a power, executive as well as legislative, equally uncontrouled. The governor general can also naturalize strangers, legitimate illegitimacy. And after all, he can undo what he may have done; for he is absolute over life and death. He prescribes the taxes; (sur l'entrée et sortie) the quantum of each imposition; and dooms where it may fall! He nominates all chief magistrates; and can cancel or continue the subordinate officers, who seem to be nominated by others.---He convenes the states: and, as he pleases, may preside in them. ---He appoints, with some reserve, to each ecclesiastical benefice---to all establishments, civil and military!---he can create officers, in addition to the immense number already, with such productive influence, created---and to crown all, he is chief of the golden fleece.

The power of the office reaches even beyond the grave! for it is absolute over opinion itself! at least as far as goes to the public profession of it in the everlasting interests of religion!

For all these great efforts and fatigues, as necessary as expedient, as just as they are wise, the remunerations are such as might be expected. He has a court. And two companies of guards, paid by the people. He has palaces and grounds in and out of town---he has the edifying satisfaction of having half a dozen ambassadors about him---with a million of florins annually levied in the low countries---60,000 more left by Maria Teresa---and 200,000 besides, furnished from Vienna!

The office, like certain popular prescriptions here, is created by patent---under the sign manual of the emperor.

The reserves and modifications of unlimited power are as follow :---The emperor reserves to himself the donation of bishoprics and abbayes---the creations of nobility---and of the dispensing power over lands in mortemain, to alienate or to exchange them. The modifications are not to change, whatever there may be of the lion's skin and the lions share, but to cut it up, and to divide it---not to qualify, but to appropriate the absolute nature of the Supreme Power---therefore not for the people, but for the prince.---Thus, the minister plenipotentiary from the court of Vienna to the court of Bruxelles is supposed to have, whenever exigencies urge, powers equivalent to the governor general---over property, life, and political opinion !---to convene assemblies ; to give places ; to remit punishments !---He has not, indeed, such authority by patent ; but he does it all on the foot of instruction, as it is called---and a grave and significant Brabanter added to us, " that there could be no doubt of the " minister's power too over the golden fleece."

The minister plenipotentiary is an appointment of modern date. Charles VI. began it in the year 1716. The Marechal Koneysegg was the first who filled the office. The present minister, M. de Meternich, is a gentleman of capacity and fame. That he is accessible, knowing, and polite, I can say from my own, short, experience.

The more material forms and constitutions respecting the governor general and the goverment, are these :

Though the legislative power is considered as being solely in the representation of the soveregn ; yet, the states are consulted, where the objects of a new law are local---and where their import is extraneous, they are referred to the superior tribunal, the council of Brabant.

For the council of Brabant, though in some sort reduced to a mere court of law, and by arbitrary alterations, as the introduction of foreigners, &c. may be very

sup-

suppoſeably impaired in its purity and power, ſtill, according to the Joyeuſe Entreé, retains the prerogative, that no law can be executed, without the participation of the council, teſtified under the ſignature of their ſecretary, and by the ſeal of Brabant!---A right, this, often very properly thwarting the plans of bad miniſters, who would miſapply the imperial juriſdiction over Brabant and Limbourg, with their dependant lordſhips of Dalim, Kolduē, Fauquemont, and Outre Meuſe.

There is the routine of a law paſſing which does not iſſue at once from the prince.---The firſt propoſition and plan, the bill as we ſhould call it---is ſubmitted to the privy council---when they have deliberated, it is communicated by the miniſter, to the governor general. It is ſometimes ſent to the emperor. The governor general paſſes the bill into a law at the council. The law is promulgated in his name, and bearing the great ſeal, which is affixed by the preſident.

Such are the characters eſſential to a law.

The ſtates of Brabant are formed of the clergy, the nobles, and the tiers etat, or deputies from towns.

The clergy are the archbiſhop of Malines, the biſhop of Antwerp (in right of two abbeys they hold) and eleven other abbayes.

The nobles are twenty-nine. They muſt have the rank of baron, at leaſt: with a qualification in manorial lands; of which the minimum muſt be according to the following rates:

  A Baron - - - - 4000 florins per ann.
  A Marquis - - - - 10,000 do. do.
  A Duke - - - - 20,000 do. do.

The proofs of ſuch property muſt be thus properly regulated.

1. If it be alledged to have been ceded by a parent, there muſt be a proof of the ceſſions being complete.

2. The vouchers, as to title, deſcent, donation, &c. muſt be equally exact.

3. To

3. To prove every six months that the lands, &c. continue with each member, and are not encumbered

4. The proofs and vouchers to be exhibited on oath---and the first deposition to be in six months after taking the seat.

5. The vouchers to be by exhibition of leases---by receipts for rents---by proofs from the neighbourhood that rents are not overcharged---by valuations precisely prescribed, viz.---of lands by the bonnu⁻, proving the mensuration upon oath. ---Plantations upon commons are valued at a fourth part of the rated value of the soil---in plantations on the road-side, each tree is valued at two sols a year.

Manorial rights are estimated at an average of ten years.

6. Finally, the rents must be proved to be three-fourths, clear of all impositions and outgoings whatsoever.

7. These, with the leases, title deeds, pedigrees (also attested on oaths) are to be deposited with the proper officer.

N. B. The lands must measure at least twenty-five bonniers, with a haute justice, or power of criminal justice, a village, and a church.

The further personal qualifications are these:

1. To be 25 years old.
2. Not to be in foreign pay.---Nor to have a foreign order of knighthood---for some minds in the Low Countries are so very weak as to be moved by a bit of ribband, as much as by amassed gold.
3. Not ennobled by the property of a wife; however that property may have on it a seignory in lands and tythes.
4. The pedigree to prove---first, the four quarters---viz. two on the father's side, two on the mother's.---N. B. the first ennobled, as is so often observed in other countries, to go for nothing.

Finally, to exhibit, including himself, seven paternal generations of nobility : that is, a father and five grandfathers.

And

And to regifter all this, fatisfactorily, before the College of Arms!—Which is conducted no lefs gravely within, and is refpected no lefs folemnly without, than a fimilar eftablifhment in another country!

In the province of Hainault, there is a fenfible improvement upon this, by a fpecification and proof (as every body fees it is conftantly with us) that the fource of the nobility was meritorious!—that the line has run on in legitimacy, undoubted, for 100 years! (another point equally our boaft) —And that where, unluckily, nobility has happened to be bought (which being fo unknown in England, muft be proportionably incredible and fhocking) that then, in the firft inftance, there muft be fix generations exhibited inftead of four!

A title, though of a lower order in nobility, if with more antiquity of creation, takes precedence of a higher title lefs ancient.

Such are the memorable peculiarities of the nobility.

The third order in the ftates, the tiers etat, are deputies from Louvain, from Antwerp, and from Bruxelles.---They ufed to be nominated at difcretion; and of courfe, were then, more numerous than now. They are now only the firft bourgmafter and penfionary council of Bruxelles, and the firft bourgmafter, firft echevin, penfionary of the other towns.---Thefe deputations are renewed every three years.

Thefe deputies do, as the Englifh reprefentatives ufed to do, on all leading difcuffions, refer to conftituents for their inftructions!

As might be expected, the prelates and nobles are not inftructed.

The tiers etat are chofen, not by univerfal fuffrage of all the people! but by the magiftrates alone!

To conftitute a refolution, the ftates muft be unanimous ---and when the clergy and the nobles agree, as unhappily they are too apt to agree, to a fubfidy, impofition, &c. the

exprefs

express compact of the constitution demands the concurrence of the tiers etat! The words are, " a condition que " le tiers etat suive, et autrement, pas!"

The sessions of the states are ordinarily in March and October. But they may meet at any other time—as when the sovereign wants money, &c. &c. So, of late extraordinary meetings have not been wanting.—To the honor of the states, such requisitions for money have oft been made; but were made in vain! The last memorable instance was in the year 1790!—and again, in consequence of the four millions and a half requested in November 1793!

The states have attendant officers, as a council, a greffier. The greffier assists at each meeting; states the cause of it; and may debate:—but he cannot divide.

The states have also a receiver general in each chief town. To him all other receivers are accountable and contributary.

Such are the chief characters of the states: their rights, and their powers.

As for the grand tribunal, the council of Brabant, that through a long period it was composed of a definitive number; and they all natives—viz.

The Chancellor,
8 Council in each chamber, 2 Greffiers,
6 Secretaries, 7 Translators,
8 Ushers, A Fiscal,
Receiver, Notary,
Chaplain, 400 Advisers.
50 Procureurs,

By late constitutions, the emperor has the power of augmenting the numbers; and of introducing foreigners, as two of the council, and two of the secretaries. Two of the council are ecclesiastics.

The oath of inauguration is to observe the Joyeuse Entreé.

Their

Their prime political prerogative, that of participating in the legiflative power, has been before explained.

Their more conftant occupation is, as a court of juftice.—They form the firft tribunal—to judge each infraction of the bulle d'or—to grant letters of emancipation—alienation licences to ecclefiaftics---and permiffion to will away fiefs.—They have the power of grand reverfion and appellant jurifdiction, from Flanders, Luxembourg, Namur.—And they judge in the firft inftance, all town officers, gentlemen, royal caufes, caufes upon feudal tenures, prelates, placemen, churchmen, members of the collateral councils, prince's houfhold, and what feems ever in Brabant the top of each climax, even the knights of the golden fleece—with all trials for coinage, treafon, &c.

The judgment of this court is pronounced by arret, of which, when deemed oppreffive, there is no reform by any other tribunal; no remedy but by the procefs called, in Brabant, the grand revifion:—on a propofition of error in the proceedings—to review them, within the year.—And that revifion is final. There is no further appeal.—On fuch revifion, to the ufual judges are added from eight to eighteen affiftants, and a law doctor from Louvaine, named by the chancellor.

The councils, juft called collateral, (from their being ad latus principis, and meeting in the palace till it was burnt, 1731) are the three councils, d'etat, privè, et des finances.—All formed by Charles V.

The firft, le conceil d'etat, was the organ of chief fway. The prince in perfon, fometimes prefided in it. When abfent, his reprefentative, the governor general. The other members were, the archbifhop of Malines, the treafurer, chancellor, fecretaries of ftate, of war, &c.— And all the prime objects of the ftate, peace and war, foreign treaties, home employments, finance, &c. all were under their controul. On hard queftions, and urgent need, the council were

were properly accuſtomed to call in and conſult other men, advanced to notice from known ſkill in the law, in the church, in trade, or in the ſcience of government. Their opinions being given as they pleaſed, orally, or in writing, they withdraw. Leaving the council, on ſuch documents, to deliberate and to decide.

In the time of Charles VI. this council fell into difuſe. The places became merely honorary, as they were called. And as ſuch, multiplied accordingly. Flung about, like the chamberlain's gold key through Germany, on every objeƈt about the court, to increaſe influence, and reward thoſe humble enough to obey it.

The ſecond of the three, the privy council, was alſo eſtabliſhed by Charles V. in the year 1531. It lapſed into difuſe: but it was reconfirmed in the year 1725. The board is formed of a preſident, ſix council, three ſecretaries, one receiver—all named by the ſovereign. The preſident is generally an eccleſiaſtic, or an advocate, graduated in law at Louvaine. There have been but few of the nobles in the liſt.—The members are appointed by letters patent.

Their objeƈts are, the matters of ſovereign authority, and of high political import; legitimation; naturalization; warrants; pardons; patents; the donation of each office, civil, military, eccleſiaſtic, in the prerogative of the prince, in which it is his buſineſs to ſign and ſpeak.—By a ſpecial delegation from the governor general, they exerciſe a juriſdiƈtion, independent, and paramount.—When in other tribunals the judges differ, in the privy council lies a power over appeal.—The applications for new creations of nobility are referved by the prince to be made to him alone.

This council has, at the leaſt, the rational praiſe of aƈtivity and diligence. They do not deafen the people who employ them with any ſuch inſulting nonſenſe as the fatigues of their ſitting; though, with a receſs of a few days only at Chriſtmas, they meet throughout the year every

morning

morning, from nine o'clock to half paſt one.—And in arduous caſes, they convene opinions, and confult.

It is the office of the prefident to make a report, daily, to the governor general, of all propofitions held fit to be refolved *(pour y etre refolu par elle)*.

The communications to the governor general are, properly, in writing. For refponfibility, in every government, cannot be too accurately preferved.

The third council (de conceil des finances) has continued from the fame date.—It is formed of a treafurer, feven council, two greffiers—and it is their practice alfo, as it ought to be the practice of every government, to confult out-of-door opinions; as good or better than their own.

There ufed to be fome receivers-general. But here, as elfewhere, they were found good for nothing, but to themfelves.—To coft much; and to profit nothing. They were therefore becomingly difmiffed. And in 1784, the general audit and receipt were adjufted by two common clerks, called for the purpofe " prepofès principaux."

The chief objects of this council are implied in their name. But, befides the taxes and fubfidies, they take care of the royal lands, &c. And as for the prefent council, it is faid that they do not take too much care of themfelves.—A reputation this, rather rare, any where, in men whofe trade is in the finances of the people!

The laws, fuch as they are, thus conftituted, are adminiftered as follows:

All proceedings are in writing.—Of this the confequences are good. Though not without evil.—Truth, certainly, is lefs liable to be difguifed and perverted: as the paffions are not urged to act againft reafon. But there will be lefs hope of thofe glorious, complex, energies, which conftitute eloquence!—Which, if always on the right fide, would make the occupation of our great popular advocate as enviable as his nature.—I cannot help faying that I had named him in the rough draft of this leaf. But my pen, I could not help it, now hurries acrofs his name! He knows, how unfeignedly, with what zeal, I refpect him. And I would have others know, how againft inclination or intereft, a writer, fhould refpect himfelf.

On the occurrence of any cafe, for which there may be no provifion, in the prince's edict; and no precedent, eftablifhed by ufage, it is, then, the practice of the courts in, Brabant, to follow the Roman law.—On queftions of trade, they are directed by the ufage of Oftend, Antwerp, Holland, and France. Their criminal law, is chiefly that, promulgated under the Duke de Alva.

The number of law practitioners, is, in Brabant, as in fome other places, perhaps, more than their value. In the court of the council of Brabant, the advocates are reckoned 400! The procureurs, are 50. The tranflators, are feven.

The tribunals, befides the abovementioned, are as numerous, as former governments could defire, or wifh there are.

1. A chambre des comptes, where all revenue caufes have their audit.--This eftablifhment began at Lifle, in the fourteenth century. In fubfequent periods it was transfered to Bruges and Bruxelles---and after a feparation, the jurifdiction of the two countries was again united in 1735.

2. A high feudal court (la cour fouveraine fædale) fupreme over fales, alienations, &c. &c. Every fief, not only in Brabant, but in Liege, Juliers, and Cologne.---This is the court, which at the beginning of the prefent century, was the arbiter over the territorial claims difputed by the Emperor and the King of Pruffia---and, the decifion had at leaft a fhew of vigor; for it adjudged the town of Turnhout to the latter. In this, and in other courts, the perfons who afpire at prefiding, muft make proof of certain

fpecific

specific qualifications. So that it cannot be there, that the good bishops apprehension is realised, of the bench being filled with the refuse of the bar!—The qualifications at first were, noble birth, and that, legitimate. But as it was soon found, that ignorance and folly could be equally well born; breeding also, was by degrees demanded—not only in common law reading, which in every country is little more than an affair of eye-sight and memory; but in other accomplishments, as moral science, and the languages dead and living, Latin, Flemish, and French.

3. A third tribunal called Thonlieu, presides over roads and rivers, forest lands, and royal demesnes.—In this constitution there are three assistants, who must have practical knowledge in hydraulics, in mill-work, and other water architecture, engineering, mechanics. This is rationally satisfactory to the people—and what must be equally soothing, to those who admire the influence of the court, they have contrived to make, even for this sole establishment twelve judges, besides greffiers, advocates, and procureurs!

4. A tribunal for the chace, &c. fisheries, &c.—with seven judges, under a grand veneure, &c. &c. &c.

5 A ditto—with cognizance of all causes, connected with the palace—like our board of green cloth—and perhaps, if possible, equally just and necessary, expedient and wise.

6. A mayor's court (here called *Drossard*), with controul over vagabonds, criminals, &c.

7. La chambre d'Uccle (from a village so named), with jurisdiction over all the manors dependent on the dutchy of Brabant. The district includes 100 bourgs.

8. Military causes, are subject to another set of judges.—And indeed, each regiment has an auditor.

9. There are also ecclesiastical courts, another bad remnant of dark ages, with official, fiscals, assessors, &c. &c. &c.

The court is usually held by Fiscal of Brabant, and a delegate of the bishop of Malines.—That offensive inroad upon natural and civil liberty, the imprimatur, is usurped by them. Without their licence, no book nor paper can appear!

In these, and some other yet more minute and insignificant presidences, as Aulic council, Heralds Court, the Mint, Mont de Pietè, Appeal or Customs, &c. the judges have their assistants (les jointes)—and all, so placed by the Prince, are, by him, removeable at his pleasure. And it is observed there is no want of complaisance. Of course, from sympathy—his pleasure happens to be theirs!

" For they who live to please—must please to live."

Not only the Amptman, the first civil and criminal judge, but even the first town officer, analogous to our Lord Mayor, with all his officers, deputy, treasurers, secretaries, are appointed by the prince. The chief magistrate must be a descendant, either in the male or female line, from one of seven families, still holding the ancient seignories! In Brabant, of three persons presented to the prince, he names one; and each nomination may be, if he will, perpetual. The chief magistrate, Amptman, has but 2,000 florins fixed appointment; the Bourg-maitre by casual perquisites, has the average profits, which are 6,000. He has a guard of four halberdiers. The mayor of Paris, at the revolution, had but three.—The salary of the echevins, is 650 florins.

The bourg-master, if the governor general does not supersede the powers, names new council from the body of citizens. And they, together, represent the town—keep the keys of the gates, &c. &c.

The citizens are distributed into 9 nations, and 10 companies; the master of each, as we should say, is with them called a dean. The bell calls them together, when any thing is to be got out of them as a subsidy.

Citizenship

Citizenship is a birth-right, where one parent is, of Brabant, born. The fee, on taking up the freedom, is 17 pistoles. But citizenship is not needed by every tradesman or manufacturer. He must be, only, of some one city company. And even that is not demanded, of bankers and agents.

The citizens formerly had town-sports—and the few princes worth mentioning, mingled in them, as Charles V. Alexander Farnese, and Charles of Loraine. But latterly, it hath pleased divers princes to sport with arms; and the good citizens, in their turn, have been called upon, liberally, to *enjoy* their share in the contingent supply.

" To enjoy is to obey."

The revenue of the city is 800,000 florins. Their annual expenditure upon foundlings is 100,000. The city debt is 2,000,000. The interest on it is $3\frac{1}{2}$ per cent. From their funds was the supply for building the council-house on the north-side of the park. It cost 600,000 florins.—There are other public objects, important, but not referable to any particular class.

The chief prison, Wilvorden, on the road to Malines; where the damps and foul air may do, what any casual mercy may have left undone.—The waste of money on this enormous building, was at the expence of the province.—It is however to be otherwise commended—for the prisoners, except when at work, at table, or in their chapels, are kept solitary—and even at table and in chapel, the men and women are apart. The cells are 992. And all the rooms, stairs, and passages, very spacious.—And yet these, for want of common precautions, open windows, cleanliness, fumigation, were offensive and unwholesome. The term of confinement, and the severity of treatment, are various. Some have been sentenced there for life. But the superintendance of the prisoners is strict and just—and it is not rare, on good behaviour, for their sentence to be foftened.—For any occafional acts which may be praife-worthy, there are indulgences and rewards—while there are penalties and reftraints for thofe which are evil. —The penalties are privations or forfeits, from a fous to a fixpence.---On that odious procefs, imprifonment for debt, even England, may have benefit on a comparifon. For at Bruxelles, a debtor may be doomed to loofe his liberty for a few florins. An Englifhwoman was in the prifon---and we were on the ftairs to fee her. But the gaoler gave us fuch an account, as made it improper for the perfon who was with me to proceed.

The lottery, a pernicious practice, we caught among other evils of the Dutch, prevails in Brabant alfo. But undebafed by any political corruption whatever; the object attains atonement from its ufe. It is an inftrument of charity, working with a judicious hand for policy, good manners, and human happinefs.—In the lottery, drawn every three weeks, are ninety numbers. They are given to the fame number of poor girls. For each number that is drawn, there is a prize of fo many florins---(150 or more) thefe accumulate as a marriage portion—and when the girl gets married, her number in the lottery is given to another.

In Brabant, as in Italy, the drawing of the lottery is not a job for fupporting fufpicious men in the humble fhape of commiffioners—nor is it inhumanly protracted, for the fake of inftigating vice, and profiting by the inftigation.—But three or five numbers are drawn; and of courfe, the drawing is difpatched in lefs than as many minutes!---It is but juftice to the French republic to acknowledge, that lotteries are abolifhed there.

The Mont de Pieté, a ufeful eftablifhment, which almoft every part of Europe but the Englifh have copied from Italy, has rid Brabant alfo of contiguous ills. With no fuch vermin as the pawnbroker, the poor muft be rid of one fpecies of oppreffion---and thieves fail for want of that neceffary accomplice, the receiver. In the two centuries through
which

which this foundation has flourished, it has done much good, and little harm. Active auditors of the accounts have been ever found in the leading officers of the time, the chancellor and the archbifhop of Malines---and the fpecific fuperindendant has been always unfufpicious, if not refpectable. The firft in this office was, the architect, Coebergher.---The intereft of money then (1618) was 32 per cent ! The Lombards never exacted lefs than 10 ! It is now fo moderate on the pledges as $6\frac{1}{4}$!---They muft be redeemed within twelve months.

Minors, an object of neceffary care under every government, are here likely to be governed well---to have the protection of the law; and at the fame time, to be protected from its abufes ! For the tribunal taking cognizance of them, is formed, half and half, of lawyers and of citizens. It is 150 years old: and there has been found no reafon to alter it.

The chief placemen, befides what has been already ftated, are the chancellor, who is the organ of communication, from the governor-general and minifter plenipotentiary; and the fecretaries of ftate and of war. They manage the correfpondence with the emperor from the governor-general; with all deliberations and decrees, appointments, paffports, &c. &c.---The emperor names thefe. But a power of rejection remains, with other remnants of freedom, in the ftates ---a power which they exerted ftrenuoufly in December, 1793; when they refufed admiffion to the propofed chancellor, Van-de-Velde !

The manners, converfation, and purfuits in Brabant, cannot have any very fpecific and prominent peculiarities, much varying from our own. For the law of latitude is uniform: and there may be more fad uniformity ftill expected from the political preffures which furround them.

Before the late difafters of war, few places were more gay than Bruxelles---more captivating to a ftranger !---and many a traveller, we were told, intending but a jaunt of a week or two, had ſtaid there months and years. The court, alike free from libertiniſm and hypocriſy, had freedom, vivacity, and grace. Hoſpitality too, not known, alas! in the courts of avarice and pride, flouriſhed there. The leading people of property, Duc D'Aremberg eſpecially, in ſpite of ſuch an affliction, as blindneſs, kept open houſe once and twice a week. M. Walkiers, the banker, lived alſo in all the uſeful affluence of vaſt fortune; dignifying, as being raiſed, fairly, by himſelf. The theatre had occaſional ſupplies of the beſt performers from Paris and Italy---and the carnival, as but in one part of Italy, was protracted to the firſt Sunday in Lent!

Their preſent amuſements are but bad farces in the theatre, and worſe in the field. There was no talk of any maſks, but when the congreſs was there. And as for any general feſtival, there ſeems public cauſe for none---but when St. Sacrement de Miracle, the chief ſolemnity of Bruxelles, inflames the people to burn their candle at both ends, and with ribbands and tapeſtry, to rival Venice with her doge, and London with the lord mayor.

Politics, however, ſeem to ſtand in the ſtead of all. And when they reprobate Vandernoot, a politician ſuſpicious from his poſition, and not only ſuſpected, but dull---or when they praiſe Vonki, the enlightened reformer from whom the party are called,---when, paſſing from their own objects immediately before them, they refer not a little feelingly to the politics of England, and the French republic and the American; in time ſo occupied, their converſation ſeems to paſs with animation and bliſs. All appears complete. Nothing is too much. Nothing is wanting.

Their own paſt hiſtory fills but little of a ſcholar's talk. Brabant, to ſay the truth, has not to boaſt of many eminent men. Except Spiegeleus and Veſalius, who in their time had general fame and merit, I know of none. For Breighel and Van Meulen, the painters, if worth one word, can

hardly

hardly have more than one.—And when you are told, that Arnauld is buried at St. Catharines, you hear it with the emotions which are due to what is singular as well as good! —a man illustrious for learning, wit, integrity, and truth!— a man who routed the Jesuits by the better force of Jansenism—and rose from thence, and raised others, even Boileau himself, to labour for the love of God.—Racine gave an him an epitaph for him; and Boileau wrote his eulogy while he lived. And yet ———— !

In the absurdity of unteachable ignorance and misapplied contempt, he was persecuted and proscribed by one of the dark and petty princes of Germany. The canonical warrant against him would not be worth mentioning, but that there are words in it, with precision, really ludicrous—literally the same, as in a state paper, not easy to be forgotten in our own time.

The fatal words are " ONE ARNOLD !"

Nos——For boisterous nonsense, like this, is fain to affect the plural——*Nos*, infra scripti, certiorati de coventicules, &c. quæ habentur apud CERTUM ARNOLDUM, (i. e. ONE ARNOLD) doctrinam spargentem suspectam, censemus D. Vicarum, conventicula dissipare, et prohibere etiam cumdicto Arnoldo conversationes.

Datum in Conventu Minorum (the meeting of the minors) hac 25 Augusti, 1690.

Such is the uniformity of evil, from the same evil source. And thus, must be the perversions of spleen and spites of hope founded—ill, and frustrated—worse !—However different the mind, the effects may be the same!

For General Burgoyne, except when he might have certain shocking instructions, probably never was at any thing like a meeting of the minors. Certainly no two things could be more asunder than he was, from the obdurate ignorance which then was so doomed to accurse the human race. Mr. Burgoyne had a full understanding: and his heart

was more valuable. He was moſt quickly ſympathetic---
and yet he ſeemed acceſſible chiefly to good emotions---
humane, beneficent, generous, elegant, kind.

Boileau's verſes on *his* one Arnold, are as follow---there
can be no harm in wiſhing juſt ſuch a man as Boileau to do
juſtice on the other.

>Mais des heureux regards de mon aſtre etonnant
>Marquez, bien cet effet, encore plus ſurprenant!
>Qui dans mon ſouvenir aura toujours ſa place.
>Que de tant d'ecrivans de l'ecole d'Ignace
>Etant, comme je ſuis, ami ſe declare
>Ce docteur toutefois ſi craint, ſi revere
>Qui contre eux de ſa plume epuiſe l'energie
>Arnaud, l' grand Arnaud, fit mon apologie!
>Sur mon tombeau futur, mes vers, pour l'enoncer
>Courez en lettres d'or, de ce pas, vous placer.
>Sur-tout a mes revaux ſachez bien l'etaler.

This is the part of their literary hiſtory, which ſeems to
pleaſe in Brabant moſt.

In political hiſtory, Duke Albert, as a popular favourite,
is in more frequent praiſes than Charles of Lorraine; than
Hercules Farneſe, or than Charles the Fifth.---Duke Albert
they mention, indeed with the reſpect due to a character
of perſonal virtue and public uſe! He was a man,
they ſay, who could reſiſt the temptations from the influence and the peculations of war! he wiſhed well for
to mankind! of courſe he never failed to wiſh well
a for peace! He was of too high, and of too pure
nature, to amaſs, ſo equivocal in princes, a ſecret trea-
ſure!---When his country received the foreigners whom
political viciſſitudes made fugitives from France, as Condé,
Marie de Medicis, and Monſieur, he did not meanly fling
them upon the bounty of the people! He formed their
eſtabliſhment, as even that dubious gentleman, Louis XIV
did for our ſecond James, from his own privy purſe!---Lip-
ſius, the profeſſor of Louvain, livedwith him upon proper
terms. Albert was not only his patron, but received his

leſſons

leſſons in return! Otto Veneus or Van Vein, the painter, was much favoured alſo. But a little colloquial familiarly, furniſhed a pretence to jilt him of his price.

The laws of moſt concern to individuals, families, and neighbourhood, from local police, perſonal regulation, from municipal orders, from marriages, births, deaths, wills and ſucceſſions, all theſe were with becoming zeal aided and advanced by Albert. For the wiſer and honourable prince well ſaid, " Theſe are the objects of moſt moment to the com-
" monwealth! theſe are the laws which produce conſe-
" quences of pure unmixed good! advantageous to all,
" and injurious to none! Theſe are the indiſpenſible parts
" of every civil aſſociation—they coſt nothing to the com-
" munity—the people, in general, can thus do what is
" wanted for themſelves!!"

The marriages of Brabant are by banns, on three ſucceeding Sundays. Their burials are the ſecond or third day after the death: and, very properly, a little way out of the town. The fees on burials, I think, are very trifling, and rarely demanded---but I cannot ſpeak preciſely, for I either forgot to aſk; or having aſked, my memorandum fails. On marriage, the fee is 12 florins, if both parties are in the pariſh—if in different pariſhes, 24.—On baptiſm there is no tax. The fee is optional.

The pariſh prieſts are named by a *concurſus*, or convocation, at which the biſhop or vicar-general preſides: after a probationary exerciſe, a diſcourſe in theology and morals. The three beſt candidates are preſented to the governor-general; who of the three, appoints one to the benefice then vacant. Among the uſeful officiating clergy, pluralities are forbid. The archbiſhop and biſhop hold abbeys in commendam. The abbayes in Brabant are enormouſly rich; one of them, in the late ſtruggle againſt the reform propoſed by the Vonkiſts, raiſed and kept a regiment of dragoons. When Joſeph II. ſo properly ſuppreſſed ſome

religious

religious houses, he allowed 400 livres to each of the clergy so reformed.—The clergy are for the most part disaffected to the Imperial government.

Holy orders are given at the same age as with us. The ranks and titles in the church are the same. The rural deans, that very ancient office, of whom a few remain with us, as at Battle, in Sussex, and Rippon, are numerous there. In Hainault, they are called doneys de cretientè. In every parish there is a charity school. In most parishes, some other eleemosynary foundation. In St. Gudule, they distribute 700 loaves a week—5000 florins a year.

The revenues of St. Gudule, the chief parish of Bruxelles, are 11,000 florins, and 1000 measures of corn. Besides petty revenues for altars and priests. The other eleemosynary establishments in the town, in all 53, amount to 222,000 florins a year.—Of these, 3,400 were for the use of travellers in distress—and 555,000, with 2,300 measures of corn towards an hospital for the sick.—But travellers who now want aid, must go another road to find it: for there is none any longer here. That charity is abolished.

The hospital is abominable for every thing but to shew what ought to be avoided---in bad air, wooden beds, woollen curtains, and difficulty of access. There are eighty beds—and the sick are huddled two in a bed.—There is a provision for foundlings; but, very properly, they are distributed in small numbers, and nursed out of town. A practice as succesful as might be expected here, in France, and in England. Where, in one district, it is ably proved by the archdeacon of Colchester, that out of 120 infants so nursed, not one had died.

There is a mad house at Bruxelles--where some patients pay—but none, without the magistrate's leave. The mode of partial payment has been long practiced in the South of France, and in the North of Italy, for all patients—and lately at York, for lunaticks only. At Milan there are a

few

few beds, fufficiently neat indeed, from 6 livres to 2. And at Lyons, among other odd inftances, there was a valetudinarian, who had lived for years in the Hotel Dieu there, on this eftablifhment of 5 livres a day, in the rooms fet apart for what they call les malades payants.

The propriety of the practice may be queftionable, in all cafes but lunacy alone; for, where the mind is not thus befide itfelf, why fhould it be bereft of what muft be moft precious, the foothing, the inftructive applications of friendly folace, of family endearment! Thus fhut out forrow from the world, and pain apprehended and felt, and you fhut out with them, fome of the beft inmates appointed for each dwelling upon earth, the charities of our common nature! The friends of man—who alone can feelingly perfuade him what he is! Who alone can exalt him to what he ought to be—in the gratifying capability of fympathy! With all its trials and triumphs, merits and rewards—binding up the broken-hearted—being eyes to the blind—and feet to the lame!

Of the health and difeafes of Brabant, it is not poffible to fpeak at large and precifely; for the documents, fo common in other countries, in this are wanting. There is no authentic fhew of any thing like a regifter—there is not even a common yearly bill—no enumeration of difeafes nor of deaths—nay, not a public regifter of the weather! Of courfe, without analogy, there can be no probability, as a guide to truth.

Other towns in the low countries are vifibly on the decline. In Bruxelles, population feems, and is faid, to encreafe. And yet longevity is rare. There are not many much above 60 years old—and, few, if any, above fourfcore. A hundred, is an age unknown.—One in 30, is ftated as the probable proportion of deaths; and yet, the population of the Netherlands, has been ftated at 188 perfons on every fquare mile! A computation, more than

double

double the ratio in England—near a fifth more than Naples! and exceeded only by the Dutch---who are called 193.

The diseases, such as come about marsh lands, where water and air are bad, are here as elsewhere, more in low places, than in high, and in dry seasons, more than in wet. For more moisture, though bad; by stagnation is made worse. Thus the ague and diarrhea are rife. And till lately, the small pox, unsubdued by the cold regimen, was formidable also. September and October, February, March, and April, are mentioned as the months, the most morbid. The worst winds, are thought to be the North, North-East, and East, loaded from the vast marshes between Brabant and the Meuse. The West winds, are stated as the best: and they prevail, not so much as in England, but more than half the year. The North and North-East, prevail in January, February, and April.

The dry days have been observed to be 180---most from May to September; the rain is calculated at two or three and twenty inches, though after the professed inaccuracy of our own transactions (see last year), who shall dare to trust any reported mensuration of rain, two feet of snow, and one foot of ice have been seen. The frosts are rare before Christmas, or after February.---Hail, thunder, and lightening are rare. The great wood close to the town, act as natural conductors, disarming each electric cloud. August 12, 1763, is the last of any mischief, memorable, from hail---mists, and fogs abound.

At Bruxelles, compared with London, the seasons, both in summer and winter, are pushed 3 degrees (of Reaumur) further, both in heat, and . in cold.---The barometer is rarely above 28. 9, or below 26. 9.---The mean height is 28. The mean variations, from 28. 5, to 27. 7.---Yet January 1, 1784, the barometer fell from 28. to 27. And the thermometer in the same 24 hours, fell 17 degrees, viz. from 3 above freezing, to 14 below it.---The thermometer rarely is above 28, of Reaumur, or lower than 10 below freezing. The mean height, is from 18 above, to 5 below freezing. But laſt July, it roſe above 30. January 1776, the cold dropped to 16.

The ſoil is for the moſt part ſandy. There is a little clay upon the hills. Some flints of all colours. And more lime. There have been found ſome ſtones, with a little iron in them; but without hope of any thing like a vein of iron ſtone; there is no ſign throughout of pit coal either, in the direction towards the pits about Liege, nor at Mons. They have picked up a few petrifactions, madepores, and ſhells.—The higheſt ground about Bruxelles, is 216 feet above the level of the ſea, the loweſt 54.

The agriculture, tenures, and value of land, &c. not materially differing from Flanders, have been deſcribed there. The leaſes are generally from 3 to 9 years. Their kitchen gardening is better than Flanders, but yet far worſe than about London. Their other manufactures, cotton, tapeſtry, linens, camlets, ſerges, thread-lace, though the chief, are not very important. In the book trade, they do a little: (for there are twelve printing-houſes)—but not ſo much as they might; from their better poſition, they might ſupplant the Dutch; and reprint, both from Paris, and London. In Brabant, as it is, 1,500 copies of a book, are thought a vaſt impreſſion. They make their own paper; and there are two founderies for types. But both manufactures ſeem at a ſtand: not at all moveable by any advances of the art, by any of the very fine printing, in Parma, Paris, or in London!

The roads are, as in England, properly ſuſtained, by thoſe who travel over them; there are two or three barriers in each ſtage, for which our chaiſe and pair paid at each place two ſous. Corveès, or arbitrary road-work, as exiſted under the old tyranny of France, there are none.— The town has had lamps, reflectors, ſince the year 1705.

M

Wine,

Wine, which is chiefly French, and water-borne through Oftend, is dear. Beer is the common folace of the middling people. It has a name, but it ought to be a bad name. It is brewed at Bruxelles with the river water, which in winter is turbid, and in fummer ftagnates and fails.---The manufacture of Louvain is better.—The water which fupplies the town is tolerably good; clear, taftelefs, with little fpecific gravity—and fhewing, on the ufual chymical trials, little impregnation of extraneous matter.—The refervoir is near the Louvain road; filled by an engine, the model of the well-known machine at Marli, and it flings the water up 140 feet, with fuch power as to run 2000 cubic feet by the hour.

There is a public library, with fome ufeful books in it, open three days in a week---an academy of belles lettres, who have publifhed fix volumes of tranfactions, if poffible, more dull and childifh than their neighbours---and a fchool of painting, with gratuitous leffons and prizes, where the mafters are bad, and of courfe the fcholars are worfe.

The fyftem of life, in regard to perfonal indulgence and domeftic fhew, is ftill fo fimple, and in fuch narrow compafs, that we were told, 100 to 200 louis d'or were enough for all the purpofes of a fmall plain family in middle life, who had three fervants.—This was before the war. When bread, in London twopence a pound, fold at Bruxelles for a halfpenny—when meat was threepence—and butter fixpence for 16 ounces.—A man ftill fells himfelf as a foldier, wonderful to tell, for three fols a day!

Such are the memorabilia of Bruxelles.

THE FOLLOWING TABLE
OF
RATE AND PRICES

In Flanders, was taken very accurately the end of November, 1793. With little variation, it may serve as a statement for Brabant also.

The price of freight—by land and by water.

By water, on the canals, is regulated by the last.—

The last of hay weighs	1000lb.
Do. oats	2300
Do. meal	4000

Of these by the last—

	flor.	stiv.
From Ghent to Bruges	3	10
Tournai	9	0
Oudenarde	7	0
Courtrai	7	10

On an average, it may be computed at three florins by the day, throughout the Netherlands.

The custom of the country allows six days for unloading—for each day after the six, there is a charge of six florins.

Carriage by land—

A waggon with two horses, per day	7 florins
A cart	3

Day-labour—

In summer	17½ stivers
In winter	14

N. B.—A florin is nearly 20 pence English.

A schelling	-	7 do.
A stiver	-	1 do.

Travelling post—3 schellings each horse each post---the carriage (when supplied by the innkeeper) pays as one horse—the driver is the same amount as another.

Price of provisions:

Bread	2 ſtivers—the pound—16 ounces
Coals	1 flor. 10 ſtiv.—ſack of two buſhels
Meat	3¼ ſtivers per lb.
Candles	4 do. do.
Charcoal	3 flor. 5 ſtiv. for two buſhels
Wood	25 flor. 4 ſtiv. or 1l. 16s. 4d. ſterling for a cord of 12 feet ſquare
A turkey	2 flor. 10 ſtiv.
A fowl	10
A duck	11
A gooſe	2 0
Snipes	12 ſtivers a couple
Woodcocks	24 do. do.
A hare	24 to 30.

As for taxes—

In Flanders—there is a land and houſe tax, by an aſſeſsment on the tenant, of the 20th part of his yearly rent.

Theſe, with cuſtoms before mentioned, with town duties on wine and ſalt, &c. defraying all the expences of government, as it is called, or local regulation.

In Brabant, the taxes are the droits d'entreè et ſortie—on the propoſed reforms, the land-tax was alſo deviſed : but the priviledged orders, with their uſual decency, refiſting, the idea was never executed.

The total amount of taxes, in the whole Auſtrian Netherlands, is 360 to 370,000l. a year.

The money and money trade of Brabant are as follow :
Bills of exchange, drawn on Bruxelles,

From Germany, are uſually	15 days after ſight.
Switzerland,	ditto.
England,	30 days after date.
France and Geneva,	do. do.
Dantzig,	40 days do.
Italy,	two months after date.

N. B.—

N. B.—Each draft, except when payable at fight, has fix days grace, Sunday always included—and when unpaid, is protefted the fixth day.

When drawn at fight, payment muft be made in twenty-four hours.

TO LOUVAINE

Through the Fauxbourg, where the German infantry, vaunted as invincible, fled vanquiſhed, and in the moſt vile diſorder, before the army of Dumourier, is the road to Louvaine.—Such was the confuſion and difmay, and ſo utterly complete the difcomfiture of that day, that there ſeemed no trace of any thing like a plan!—general orders for any poſition, there were none! There was no rallying point! To great part of the army, at leaſt, the very road through which they were to fly and to follow their fellows, was, on arriving at Bruxelles, unknown!—A young Engliſh gentleman, unfortunately then ſerving with the Germans, was among the firſt who entered Bruxelles; he was uninſtructed where he was to march! but getting a horſe from the ſtables of his father, long reſident among the moſt reſpectable people there, he was led by inſtinct, by fortune, or by knowledge of the country, to take the road for Louvaine! For ſome of the army wandered more to the north—and even to the weſt of the north.

And through the ſame route, four little months afterwards, did the ſame army of the French republic, ſold, too probably, at Dort and Maeſtricht,—certainly ſold on the Montagne de Fer, lamentably find it their turn to fly!—traverſing Bruxelles by the gate of Schaerebeck, to the road for Enghien and for Halle!—each ſide with nothing but a woeful balance of difaſter—with an equal wreck of happineſs and life!—with not leſs than 20,000 men hurled, unprepared, alas! to their untimely grave!

Such are the enormous, barren, miſchiefs of war! that infernal combination of every woe, ruſhing, relentleſs, from folly and from guilt.

And all for nothing!—to the people!

Each army, in their flight, feeling the ſame ſenſe of danger, took the ſame precautions to eſcape it. They perpetrated,

petrated what in the language of the trade are called abbatis. They difmantled the road they had paffed; and they cut down trees to fall behind them---an abomination, which fails of proportioned refentment, only from the emotions hurrying againſt more horrid provocations---but which generations may lament, and therefore in fome old tract, de ſtatu dæmonum, not ill put down as a violence worthy of the devil himſelf!

Thus the whole country, from Bruxelles to Louvaine, has felt the force of the fpoiler---a country that feems deferving a better fate from the claims of nature and of art—from labour well done, from plenty well enjoyed!

For the grounds, through the whole thirteen miles, chiefly arable, were ftill a model for the farmer. They were, as policy and manners delight to hear, divided into many holdings. There were fo many more fmall farmhoufes and cottages—and of courfe within them fo many more people happy!—Villages alfo, very flouriſhing, were frequent, and each village had its church. The ſtate of human nature, therefore, might be rationally rated high. Men, if enlightened and free, if not in bondage—to ignorance, nor pillaged by the impofitions of their government, might be fuppofed happy; nearly as happy as man in this life may be.

The country has fome pretty openings to the north, north-eaft, and north-weft, particularly on the hill a mile out of Louvain, (La Montagne de Fer)—and yet more from the rifing ground near Bruxelles. There the villa of M. Walkiers the banker, the palace of Prince Charles, the tower, the two fmaller temples, the floping lawn, the two fide plantations, the windmill, the old buildings at Anderlecht, the adorned cottages of many lefs great but as ufeful men, with good huſbandry in the fore ground, and not bad wood in the back, form together a fcene, which is very chearing —as what is chearing is alfo good!

As

As ill luck, or malignity would have it, thefe, the beft points, have moft fuffered from the havoc of war. The people are already trying to redrefs themfelves. They have began planting on each fide the road; and when the road is artificially raifed, they plant on each fide dell, which is below it.

Louvaine is as one who has feen better days—" go to " a fellow that has had loffes"—or forgot, as Bentley faid to the Dean of Norwich, forgot more than you ever knew.

It is a town like the pedigree of many a grandee, with antiquity probably great, and certainly greater than its merit—when times were fo abject as to deem it reputable to have defcended even from a ruffian of Rome, " Damnatus " et exul," a warrior or ufurper, Louvaine was fain to vaunt itfelf fprung from Cæfar. But as Cæfar himfelf is no longer of any likelihood but as a writer—*and there be many Cæfars ere fuch another Julius*—and as the town magiftrates have no intereft in preferving a preference fo little applicable to themfelves, they very fairly let Cæfar go as he came, and are content with tracing the genealogy of their penates to fome Dukes of Brabant in the twelfth and thirteenth centuries—what the man's name was it is obvioufly not eafily to tell—for as the Turin wit faid on the taxes there, " it is not poffible for the patience of man to " remember all of them"—or according to one of the court chaplains immortalized by Pope, it may not be decent to mention the condemnation before an affembly fo polite.

As for the Univerfity of Louvaine, the prime importance of the place—it was founded at the beginning of the fifteenth century. The firft leffon was given there in September 1426. And five years after, the Pope, God help him, *permitted* theology to be taught there!

It is pleafing to contemplate the declining progrefs of impofture!

imposture! A being, now, like the animal incognitum, (the monsters that have eat themselves out on the Ohio) once the terror and bane of all around, now scarcely known otherwise than by description! Worse even than this, are the marks of the beast at Rome! It is known only as an object of ridicule or pity—suffered to exist in foreign countries, but as they were dull and dark—in other countries, at all enlightened and free, as in Britain, long since superseded and flung away, with indignation and with scorn, and politically annihilated every where, but in Portugal and Spain.

The university of Louvaine, like the universities of England, is formed of several separate establishments. There are thirty-eight colleges at Louvaine.

13 of them are for divinity.
 1 for the Dutch students—founded in the year 1616.
 1 for the Irish—founded in 1623.
 1 for the Savoyards—established 1551.
 3 for law—one of them founded by Winchel, a physician, as it is said, in grateful remembrance of much practice he had among the lower clients, who were so sick.
 1 for medicine—founded by Bringel, a valuable physician.

The resort to this university, as to all others, has been different at different times. It is an event, resulting from some single incident, or from the fame of some particular man. While Boerhaave taught, no young physician thought he had any claim or chance for practice, but as he had attended for instruction at Leyden. When Blackstone read, Oxford had almost a similar vogue for law. Justus Lipsius gave the same attraction to Louvaine. During his time the pupils there were numbered at 4000.

Of late, the numbers have shrunk much short of this. The seductions of contemplative and monastic life, impose, less and less. While the pursuits of honourable and active business are followed more and more. The students, on the late political viciſſitude, ſhewed themſelves, with propriety, very friendly to a reform—and ſo far, no longer needing to be ſtudents, they proved themſelves fit for the momentous energies of practice, and the relative duties of neighbourhood and of ſocial order.

Thence the eſtabliſhment, no longer conniving at impoſition, was made to decline. It was light upon the deeds of darkneſs. Umbrage roſe from the bigotry of the prieſt-craft. Political ſuperſtition thwarted more. Soon after the propoſitions and purpoſes of the Vonkiſts began to ſway, the number of ſtudents at Louvaine were not more than two or three hundred.—That expectation failing, men think it allowable to fall into the old track; and, more majorum, they do, what other people have done.

Accordingly, the town and teachers are obliged to them—for the number of ſcholars are again reported to be near 2000.

Nor is this, abſolutely, to be regretted. For though there may prevail, in Brabant, a falſe philoſophy, with ſome unhappy ideas of practice, ſpeculative and ſpiritual over-much ---yet, there are not wanting to counteract them, qualities and purpoſes, rational and very manly.

The chief government of the univerſity is very juſtly elective, and periodically changed at intervals not longer than three months. An Iriſh gentleman, rather German in his principles or notions, ſeemed unexpectedly ſurpriſed at this, when a profeſſor met the objection with more unexpected force :—

" Short durations," ſaid he, " ſhort durations of any de-
" legated truſt, muſt be the beſt. For the delegations muſt
" be, obviouſly, either wrong or right---if right, they may
" continue---if wrong, they ſhould ceaſe."

" I am not an Iriſhman," continued he " I am not an
" Iriſhman---I wiſh I was. But ſtill I can feel for all. And
" it is both ſhame and ſorrow I feel at any people ſuffering
" their

" their beft rights, either through perfecution or corrup-
" tion, to fall away, under a fyftem fuch as their Octennial
" Bill!"

The univerfity officer, to which this profeffor fo ably alluded, is called the Rector Magnificus. He is chofen, by turns, out of the five faculties, and the choice is moft wifely thus renewed every three months.

The rector prefides in a tribunal, paramount, like our chancellor at Oxford and Cambridge, over each dependance of the univerfity. Next to the rector, the chief officers are, the Confervator of Privileges and the Chancellor. They are both of prime rank and power---in the college government of the place.

The town magiftrates, alfo of chief confideration, are two Bourg-mafters, two Penfionaries, and a Council of Twenty-one.

The people to whom they have to adminifter and ferve, feem to be gradually on the decline. They are now numbered at no more than about 12,000---whereas, in a former period, they were computed to be feven or eight times as many. It is recorded there were four thoufand fhops and warehoufes in the place, and that the manufacturers exceeded fifty thoufand. A great part of them diftinguifhed themfelves in the fpirited refiftance of the affumptions, by Winceflas, Duke of Brabant---and that refiftance failing, they left a land fenfelefs and abject---the grand art of weaving woollens, a ftaple now in Englifh commerce, then flying with them into England.

The prefent trade of the town may defy a viciffitude like this, " cantabit vacuus," almoft any change now, except in one, the fale of beer, muft be for the better at Louvaine.

Beer indeed is their main manufacture and trade. They brew it from the River Dile---and then that fame water wafts it to Antwerp and Malines—while each paved road finks under its weight to Tirlemont and Bruxelles.

This may, in some sort, explain the intellectual pretensions of the present people. For, as Bishop Warburton so neatly said to our great actor, then a boy dining with him at Gloucester, " they who drink beer, think beer."

Besides the brewers, there are few other tradesfolks flourishing, except it be they who live by the errors of the church. For, besides five parishes and the collegiate church of St. Peter, there are no less than eighteen convents for men, and thirteen monasteries for women—one of them, we are sorry to say, is for English women. In the collegiate church are eighteen canonries, chiefly for the university professors.

The privileges of the university seem sufficiently considerable. Graduation there is necessary to the practice of the three professions in the Netherlands. From the sixteenth century the patronage of certain church benefices is, during certain periods, ceded to the faculty of arts. This is the patronage, in the territory of Liege before that time, by virtue of the Concordat Germanic, exercised by the Pope, during his months, thence called the apostolic months, November and February.—With the other privilege, called " Jus Tractus," of referring to Louvaine, all the persons and causes of Liege thus mixing with the faculty above mentioned. The conservator of the university forms the tribunal.

In Tournay also, as well as Louvaine and Liege, the nomination to prebends is with the university.

And by an edict of the Empress Queen, not, as it should seem of the ages called dark, but of the present century, viz. 1722, Louvaine has a monopoly of what little mind there may be through all the Netherlands of Austria—. " Not any native of that country can, without a written
" allowance

" allowance from government, purſue philoſophy in any
" other univerſity."

The lectures are read in Latin, and in the language of the Netherlands. The rules and orders, citations, theſes, inaugurations, diplomas, all are in Latin. The hours when the profeſſors read, are from ſeven in the morning to three and four in the afternoon. The vacation, better regulated, becauſe leſs immoderate than elſewhere, is from the end of Auguſt to the middle of October.

The ſtudents, for the moſt part, are endowed—in different colleges, appropriated to each different diſtrict and nation. A ſtudent, though a foreigner, and unaided by any foundation, may ſupport himſelf, perfectly well, for 12 or 1400 livres (48 to 56l. ſterling) a year.

The lectures, and eſtabliſhments for inſtruction, are ſuch as recommend Louvaine, chiefly to the natives of the Netherlands. And to them pre-eminently only, in the law line, and for their theology. In antiquities, juriſprudence, and controverſies of their church and country.—For general philoſophy, for the belles lettres, for experimental ſcience, for medicine, a foreign ſtudent may almoſt every where be better—and cannot any where be worſe. The anatomical ſchool, the ſole chief conſtituent of the healing art, is here, next to nothing. The profeſſor indeed was dead, they told us; and they had failed to appoint another.

The library is ſupported by a ſmall fee, demanded on each graduation. It is not a bad collection: and it might be very good—if all the books, ſcattered through the different colleges, were concentered in this one place. The room of the library is modern; it was built in the year 1724. The Greek manuſcripts left by Juſtus Lipſius, and the manuſcript bible given by Cardinal Beſſarion, are to be ſeen as curioſities, the favourites of the place.

The divinity ſchool is divided into eight or nine claſſes.

The law schools into twice as many—medicine has ten or eleven—and philosophy almost twice as many more.

In divinity and law, obviously partial pursuits, and if of any use, that use local merely, the few intimations which might be wanting to the curious reader,—we, by an accident, are not able to supply.—In mathematical learning, Beck is the guide—in physics, Beuer—in the medical school, Gaubius, Boerhaave, Leber, Haller, and Cullen.----In polite literature, criticism, &c. J. Scaliger, Vossius and Grosovius, Grotius and Erasmus, as well as Putcanus and Lipsius, are cited, with allowable partialities, as authentic merit, raised on ground contiguous to their own!

The literary fame of Louvaine is, as might be expected, buoyant in the conversation of their scholars.—Though it seems difficult to point out to any epoch made, particularly prominent by them, in the whole compass of human learning. Such fame is theirs, as can be conferred by the two last-mentioned names, and by Goltzius, Van Helmont, Spiegelcus, and Vesalius;—by Sonnius too, who had conferences with Melancthon—by Murnix, the first renderer of the Bible into Flemish, and who produced the formulary of association against the ridicule and guilt of Rome, the inquisition—and by Baius, who successfully followed St. Augustin, in the strong and sure position " that the scrip-
" ture, only, ought to be consulted as the judge and guide
" of the church,"—and that no ideas could be more nonsensical and prophane than the Romish doctrine of man's powers and works, developed through the disgusting abominations of selling indulgencies, and fictitious transfers from a fantastic treasury, preposterously imagined to be filled with the merits of the saints!

This, indeed, seems to have been the meridian of Louvain splendor, for the controversy stirred a chief part of Europe!—Baius met with multiplied honors—with opposition

tion from the univerfities of Salamanca and the Sorbonne! His writings were accufed and condemned at Rome!—though the Pope, admonifhed by his predeceffors' vain acrimony againft Luther, dexteroufly avoided any perfonal ftruggle; but praifed the probity of Baius, while he rebuked what he called a perverfion of his fkill. " D'une probite et " d'une capacité reconnues dailleurs," were the words of Pius V.—And the book of Baius, otherwife not very reputable, remains to this hour among the multitude of better books forbid by the inquifition at Rome!—In another obvioufly useful effort, the publication of claffical books, fo commonly remarkable in almoft every other univerfity, Louvaine feems alfo wanting.—Whatever at any time may have been the individual or collective powers of the place, they have fcarcely ever, if ever, been fo applied.

Of the prime and moft neceffary claffics, Greek or Roman, the editions, with fome memorable peculiarity, are very numerous. Homer 31 editions—Horace 38—Livy 25—Ovid 40—Tacitus above 16—Cicero above 90—Juvenal and Perfius 28—Xenophon 18, &c. &c. &c.—yet no one of them all, except a Juvenal and Perfius, in a gothic letter---this is the folio, 1475, by Joanne de Weftphalia, iffued from Louvaine. Even their own Bible, edited by the divines of Louvaine, was printed at Antwerp ---and the editions, with the notes of Lipfius himfelf, as Seneca, Tacitus, &c. were printed at Paris, and Amfterdam. The only books of any general character printed there, were, befides the abovementioned Juvenal and Perfius, fome of Puteanus and Ger. Voffius, Artis Rhetoricæ Method, 8vo. 1571.---Neither Spiegelius, nor Vefalius, though both Louvain men, were printed there!

The deficiency was fomething more than mechanical. For that is every where eafily fupplied. There were printers enough, as may be feen at the bottom of Breviaries and the petty Latin fchool-books of the time, as Flavius, Mafius,

fius, Dormatius, Livius, and others. And what could thefe want but pecuniary encouragement and intellectual correction, to make Louvaine follow, at leaft, if not lead, the printing fame and trade of Antwerp, Leyden, and Amfterdam?—Such men as Elzever and Plantin may be rare, but where, with any fpirit, can be the difficulty for an univerfity, to find or to make fome fuch man their own? Perfpicacity and toil, the praife by Lipfius upon Plantin himfelf, " oculatiffimus ac labori maximo," are, furely, poffible to all!

The refort to Louvaine univerfity is chiefly from the Auftrian Netherlands.—The foreigners who were ftudents have been commonly from a tenth to a twentieth of the whole number. Of them, the moft have come from Liege and Cologne, and the contiguous diftricts in the north-weft of Germany. French Flanders, before the war, ufed to fend a few. And fewer ftill were contributed by England and Ireland.—In the records of the univerfity, perpetuating the names of the ftudents at all diftinguifhed, who had done any thing fit to be written, or written any thing fit to be read, there appear not a fcore and a half of our countrymen, taking Scotch and Irifh altogether. And of them, the greater part, were Non-jurors and Non-conformifts, emigrating on the reformation and revolution. And further, like the fugitive French in the prefent day, working upon pity by the fame untenable pretences, and precifely in the fame language; " Hæreticis pulfi et per " peftilantes inceffores," &c. &c. forced away by the Apoftates and the Atheifts they had left behind—viz. in the Peter Martyrs, the Cranmers, each the hero, and worthy of the time!

Such was then, as it is now, the high untenable tone f effrontery and impofture. At prefent, indeed, it ftains only the venal publications of the age. But then, truth was thus blafphemed even in the fanctuary itfelf.

The

The following is a literal copy, from the church of St. Peter's at Louvaine—where all the Proteftant clergy of England, an order with merit of fuch force as to compel praife even from Voltaire, are branded with imputed prophanation! Where the reformation itfelf, is called " the " confummation of iniquity," (fummum nefas) and each Non-juror is juftified, by calling conformity, guilt.

<blockquote>
In impias eorum leges,
Jurare conftanter renuebat!!
</blockquote>

THE EPITAPHS

ARE AS FOLLOW:

Hic fepultus eft
Eximius D. ac magifter nofter
Thomas Stapletonus
Que Ceceftrix in Anglia, nobili loco natus
Et literarum ftudiisa parentibus addictus
Cum in collegiis Wiccamicis, Primum Wintoniæ deinde
Oxoniæ
Eum in artium liberalium
Difciplinæ curfum feciffet
Ut magnam fui exfpectationem
Apud fuos excitaffet.
At ipfo fuo urbis epifcopo accitus,
Ecclefia cathedrales canonicus inftituitur.
Sed paulo poft
Profanis hominibus
Omnæ Totius Angliæ ecclefias
Per fummum nefas (the reformation) inadventibus
Eo quod ille in impias eorum leges
Jurare conftanter renuebat
Loco cedere, et fibi fuga

Ut poterat confulere coactus
In hac regiones concedens,
Duaci primum conftitit, ubi catechiften ad tempus egit:
Donec tandem ad fupremam
Magifterii dignitatem
Et cathedram erectus
Sacras fcripturas publicè
Summâ cum laude interpretatus eft
Inde Lovanum
A fua majeftate Catholica evocatus
In hac academiâ
Sacræ theologiæ profeffor Regius
In hac D. petra ecclefia canonicus
In collegio Hilharibecenfi
Decanus exftitit
Demum poft 42 annos in exilio tranfactos
(Quos fera prælectioni
Aut fcriptioni, omnes impendit)
Ceffit e vita
Relictis laborum fuorum monumentis
Partem Anglice ad fuos
Partem Latinè, in commune
Totius reipublicæ bonum defcriptis;
Quæ, quanta fureit ejus induftria
Quanta animi pietas,
Quam accenfum veritatis Catholicæ
Propagandæ ftudium
Omnibus en lecturis!
Teftatum facient.
Lovanii tandem in Brabantia
Sanctiffime diem fuum obiid
12 Octob. 1598—Regnanti in Anglia Elizabethâ.

The aforefaid Mr. Stapleton wrote a few tracts of a fpiritual tendency, and fome upon church hiftory, and high church

church authority:---among them also was a brief, and feeble, life of Sir Thomas More.---They were printed in octavo, 4 vol. at Paris.

But to do justice to the muse of epitaphs, if any such muse there be, this sort of literature is in general not so bad at Louvain.---There are some inscriptions, with becoming energy and awe by very venerable men, who have done it for their own burial! There are some, with no less simplicity and strength, composed by others. The most eloquent and impassioned modern writer upon the Continent, praises, not unjustly, the ancient epitaph. Which mournful and didactic, is therefore abrupt and brief.---Yet, his instance:

"Sista viator---Heroem Calcas."

Good as it may be, is not better than the following at Louvaine:

"Lege, viator, et luge."
And,
"Expectat hic
"Viam universæ carnis, &c."

In the more diffuse style also, as upon the tomb of Garetus, there are lines, not, indeed, with such consummate beauty as in the fragment upon Danae, by Archbishop Markham, but yet with no small correctness, fancy and taste.

The following are the inscriptions, which seem to be the best:

Can. Reg. Ord. August.
Memoriæ
J. Garetti---Qui mortem obiit---1571
Superis reflorescit.

Rectæ perpetuo tenore vitæ
Et constanter, & ad perennitatem
Doctos qui coluit, pios et omnes
Non ipse impia, que nocere possunt

Sectatus studia, eruditus ipse,
Hanc Gariteus urnam habet, situsque
Hic est. Cum aonidum choro. Vel ullum
Si commercium habes, deum preceres
Exhorter, monloque te, viator.
Ejus denique, carne qui solutâ
Humanas animas laboriosis
Viventum* præcibus docet, juvari.
Ne gravare pios juvare manes
Lectis et violis rosisq, casta
Illius venerare busta, fama
Qui notissimus, editisque libris
Indelebile prorsus obtinere
Nomen, perpetuis meretur annis.
Et si vermis homo cinisque fiat
Morte, & palliduli cadant ocelli
Nullo unquam, Meliori qui per orbem
Vivit parte sui, interibit ævo
Dum clari Phario solo colossi
Stabiunt, nomen erit Garetianum.

Justus Lipsius---bur. at St. Francis---written by himself two years before.

Quos hic sepultus, quæris? Ipse edisseram
Nuper locutus, et stilo, et lingua fui
Nunc altero licebit. Ego, sum Lipsius
Cui literæ dant nomen, et tuus favor;
Sed nomen. Ipse abivi, abivit hoc quoque
Et nihil hic orbis, quod perennet, possidet.

* One of his printed works, 1564. De Mortuis Vivorum Precibus Juvandis.

Vis, altiore voce me tecum loqui?
Humana cuncta, fumus, umbra, vanitas—
Et scenæ imago, et, verbo ut absolvam
  Nihil!
Extremum hoc te alloquor
Æternum ut gaudeam tu apprecare
  Justus Lipsius,
 Vixit annos 58---mens. 5,
 Obiit Ann. Christi, 1606,
  10 Kal. Apr.

The following is the inscription on a marble sarcophagus.

  Justi Lipsii,*
 Quod claudi potuit,
  Hic Jacet.
 S. P. Q. Antwerpiensis,
Incliti viri famæ, orbi notæ
Virtuti cœloque recepti,
  H. M. P.

    On
Alardus Amstelodamus---by Erasmus, at Louvaine, 1544.†

Lustra decem numerans, studiis impensa juvandis,
 Impendens et adhuc, talis alardus erat.
Excepto quod erat surdaster: Cætera Felix
 Lingua satis pensat, quod gravat auriculas.

---

* Moretus published all in six volumes. 1 Critical, 2 Epist. and Miscell. 3 Hist. and Antiq. Admiriande. 4. Polit. and Philos. 5. Tacitus. 6 Seneca.

† His works were Theology, Philology, Comments on Erasmus, and Translation of part of Hippocrates, Epist. ad Damasetum de Atra Bile.

            Ant.

Ant. Sanderus,
By himself.
D. O. M.
Antoninus Sanderus,
Presbyter,
Piis fidelium precibus
Me commendo
Et a misericordia Christi,
Exspecto.
Donic veniat immutatio mea.
Amen.

He was Regius Professor of Theology. And this short inscription, in the true temper, may leave little doubt, that he strove to practice what he taught.

Lupus,
Reg. Professor and Provincial---by himself.

Hæres peccati, naturâ, filius iræ
   Hic jaceo, dignus nomine, reque, Lupus!
Indignus, non re, sed solo nomine, doctor—
   Verbis, non factis, me docuisse fleo,
Perdocuisse alios, et non docuisse se ipsum
   Quid juvat? O Mundi fumus, inane, nihil!
Agne deus---patris doctrina---redemptio mundi---
   Hunc, tibi prostratum, commiserere, reum.
Et latro, et meretrix, gratis, tua regna subintrant,
   Gratia peccatis, fiatet ista meis.

The seventh and eighth lines may consecrate all the rest. There is the strong expression of a contrite heart. That must be felt by all. They who can imitate it—happy are they.

The inscription upon Mich. Baius, eminent as he was, is not worth repeating: it is nothing but dates and titles through

through fifteen lines, reg. profefs.---head of his college, dean, confervator, and chancellor---of no fmall confequence at the time, and to himfelf---but ever after mere duft in the balance.

Infcriptions in any language but Latin, are rare.— Throughout the Netherlands we faw but one in French, and one or two in Flemifh, viz. at Bruges, on Raerfdorp, the phyfician to Charles V. Rickius and Lipfius, are the names which appear to have contributed the moft.

There might be, for the credit of the place, a memorial to Goldfmith, who, with Sam. Johnfon and Dr. Darwin, raifes the poetry of our time to the high level of Pope. For Goldfmith's degree, M. B. was conferred after fome fhort ftay at Louvaine.

The reform of the eftablifhment at Louvaine, which made fuch a ftir, through Europe, in the year 1787, and which was among the projects of Jofeph II. the moft meritorious and the leaft fuccefsful, was in the following diftribution.

A fpecial commiffion was appointed to form for the Pays Bas, a fyftem precifely fimilar to that prevailing in the Emperor's hereditary dominions of Germany, upon church government, the ordering of public ftudy, and the licenfing of the prefs.

The bafe of this operation was to be the preceding practice at Vienna, by the commiffion, (aulique) lately for the fame purpofe, created there. But in all extraordinary cafes, in the deviation from any former rule, in the creation of any new principle, fpecial reference was to be made to the Emperor himfelf.

The minutes of each meeting, before confirmation or revifion, " *Avant la mife au net*," were regularly to be fent to the minifter plenipotentiary, and through him, at his order, were to undergo the alterations of the council.

Such

Such was the act, made by Joseph, under the adminiſtration of the Miniſter Belgioioſo.

On eccleſiaſtical concerns, M. Leclerc, Baron de Fultz, and the Prevot Dufour, preſiding, theſe were the ſubdiviſions of them.

1. Canon laws—in public eccleſiaſtices—their illuſtration, change, abolition.
2. Biſhoprics and arch-biſhoprics—their coadjutors—whether there ſhould be any new dioceſe? Whether any of the old ſhould be ſuppreſſed? To define and limit their power—confiſtorial or official—which was held a chief ſource of abuſe.
3. To be definitive alſo on every object, hitherto, held at all liable to the Court of Rome. Extending this, even to the prohibition of ſending any money to Rome—or to any religious eſtabliſhment, out of the country. With all reſervations, ſuperiorities, patronage, and pretenſions whatſoever. The whole of which are in effect, very properly aboliſhed.
4. Pariſhes—what to be aboliſhed? If any new benefices wanted? Their patronage, endowments—with the propoſed diſpenſation with vows, ſuppreſſion, indulgences, proceſſions, pilgrimages, images, &c. ſuppoſed miraculous.
5. To determine the church ſervices, in each place, according to the population.
6. The appointment to any benefice to be by election.—Concours, as it is called—this is as before ſtated. The clergy, after proof exhibited of character and talents, to nominate three perſons to fill each vacant benefice—of the three, the prince to name one.
7. The ſtate of convents and monaſteries—their exceſſes and diſorders. To limit the number of ſuch buildings and the numbers in each—and their endowments. Penſions

sions to the monks and cures who were abolished (they were 400 livres)—and other applications of property in the religious houses suppressed.

The same people were to fix the general plan of academical study.

In the detail, the arrangements being under these professors—

Divinity, Abbé Stoger.
Law, M. Vanderheyden.
Medicine, M. Melly.
Philosophy, M. de Meyer.
Humanity School, M. Des Roches.
The Hospitals and Eleemosynary Foundations, M. Burha and M. Vanvelde.

FROM LOUVAINE TO LIEGE.

And memorife another Golgotha.   Shakfpear.

For thus, alas! the road had it through St. Tron and Tirlemont from Louvaine to Liege! Had all the amateurs of war been prefent, there was enough of the fublime, &c. to have fatisfied the moft fanguine of them all!

It was now many a mournful month fince the dire mifchiefs had been firft bewailed! And yet through many a long mile, there was the cry of havoc ftill! Heaving forth from every object around.

Through a main track, almoft every houfe was pierced through and through. In each poor clay wall, there remained the hideous ftigma of every cannon fhot! Of many houfes, battered and burnt, there was not left one ftone upon another! Of the few ftraggling trees, that continued on the way fide undeftroyed, not one efcaped, unftained, from the abomination of fpilled blood! The bones of horfes and of men were fcattered over every field! the fragments countlefs, as when one heweth wood upon the earth! entire fkeletons were yet to be feen—not yet dry, nor denuded quite!

Every face was in fadnefs—every heart feemed faint! The father bereaved of his children—the widow and the orphan, through aftounding forrow torpid, in filent fupplication for bread!

Calamity and death, at any time, in any form, cannot but be full of awe! Yet human violence, more fell than accident, feems to make difafter doubly dreadful!

One poor fellow, a farmer of the beft life and converfation, fell in his own houfe in the laft folemn duty of the day. A cannon ball rufhed into the room—and killed him! his wife and children alfo at their devotion, kneeling all around.

around! An excellent young man, but the day before a bridegroom, was another victim! He was coming forth from his chamber, when a random shot struck him. He dropped down dead!—and his bride, young and beautiful, her swelling heart literally burst!—she shrieked out, " O " God !" and never spoke more! A brave boy, not fourteen years old, was in the field—a dæmon, in the shape of a hussar, furiously assailed him and roared out, in broken French " Grace? Grace?"—Questionab'y thus—

The poor boy, either did not know what was meant, or disdained if he did. He replied " Et pourquoi, Grace?" when instantly, the ruffian let fall his sabre, and the boy, from his head, down, was cleft in twain! It was in another such scene of horrors, conjured up and perpetrated from the storehouse of all ill, that our gallant countryman, Colonel Eld, had a picture, which he wore hanging about his neck, driven into his heart! It was a miniature of a lady he had left in England—who had his plighted faith!

Horrors like these, too hideous to be born, were most rife and raging about St. Tron and Tirlemont, in the following villages, Driesche, Vissecot, Tirhaegen, and Roere—about Overwinden, and between Neerwinden and Landel.

There, it seems, after the best information, scarcely possible to doubt, that the army of the French Republic was finally sold! For M. Dumourier made the attack at Neerwinden, suo ex motu, altogether—without the customary forms of deliberation and council. There was not even any formal reconnoitering of the enemies position! Though the enemy were posted with manifest advantage of the ground! Though their force, 52,000 effective, far exceeded the force of the French. Though they were fortified with artillery more exceeding still!

The engagement, the first day, lasted but three hours, viz. from three to six o'clock, and in that short lapse of time above three thousand men were murdered!

If traditions are at all true, the difmay and difafters of former wars, do not fade away, on comparifon with thefe three days of horror, between Liege and Louvaine! This was the very ground, chiefly between Neerwinden and Landen, where a century before (July 1694), there was another dire confummation of the infpired poet's worft imagined curfe, " the people being fold for nought"— when, the Marechal Luxembourg bought, with fuch prodigal guilt in blood, the barren honours of the field.

We were fhewn the place, by a divine old man. He was a fubftantial land-holder — venerable in hoary headed ftrength! but more, from the ftrong wifdom of age!—with all his ideas and wifhes juftly bent upon good will and peace.

" There," faid he, ftill fighing heavily from his inmoft heart, " there is the fatal fpot---there---there---now, near
" a hundred years are paft, fince the earth was thus blafted
" by the defpots of that time! Then, thirteen of my kin-
" dred, I have been made to know---thirteen were doomed
" in one day to die! God help their endangered fouls!
" I hope they had no mifdeeds, as to the death of
" others!"

The excellent old man broke from us in filence, and in tears! We found, after enquiry, he had a frefh grief too—but that, why we know not, he was too proud or too fore to tell. We looked after him as long as we could, with ftrong emotion! emotion yet foothing too! for it was fympathy additionally ennobled by every preference, rational and good, by pity and by efteem!

The country in this route, continues productive of every growth, but anecdotes and inftruction. For almoft every object, artificial or natural, roads, foil, hufbandry, habitations, &c. have no fpecific differences, from thofe mentioned in the preceding chapters.

Tirlemont, three leagues from Louvain, is a paved town, which

which has been large; but is shrunk and shrivelled by age, by fire, and by war. It once was of prime political consequence; and had that fourth rank in the assembly of the states of Brabant, which is now held by Bois-le-Duc. But now, like the ebbed finances of one out of place, every thing seems to hang about it lose and empty. There are no longer houses to fill the walls: nor people enough to fill the houses.—There is a spacious open area in the middle of the town, with a good church, and a better inn.—The church, however, twelve or thirteen persons, probably, think well enough;—at least, if it be in the power of so many canonries and a deanery, to make them think well.

These are in the patronage of the chapter of Liege.

There are, moreover, no less than six convents for men! and seven for women!—But no other trade or factory was stirring when we saw the town—except that dubious craft of turning human creatures into hulans!

At the inn, we had a gay table d'hote; with some foreign officers, and an English gentleman, of vivacity and of taste.—He said, " he had been told, by people probably " disaffected to England, maliciously and eager to defame " it, that the new levies were for us."

" They are, said a Hanoverian leader, " they are in the " service of Great Britain!"

" In our pay, rather than our service, Colonel!"—was the dexterous replication of our companion.

" They are called the *legion* of Y---k"---continued a walloon.

" *For they are many*"---said our whimsical countryman.— Our lively friend, we found, had been no slight traveller. And was then on route, as we understood, to mix in the hunting parties of the English Viscount B——, in the electorate of Cologne and Westphalia.

He had been also at the Duc d'Aremberg's establishment for the chace, in the neighbourhood of Louvain. This, he
described

described as being very ample still---100 dogs---200 horses ---with keepers, riders, &c. &c. in proportion.---Stags and foxes were the usual hunt. But now and then, more ambitious, a wolf and a boar.

The chief misfortune in Duc d'Aremberg's life, the loss of sight, is well known.---It was thus in a shooting party, that the sad accident befel him. The party with him, were, his father, and our former engaging ambassador at Bruxelles, Sir William G———. The ground they that day meant to go over, they divided, as usual abroad, into equal parts, each person going on in an appointed drection, and knocking down all before him. Sir William and the father advanced through the woods with more speed than was expected. The son advanced with less speed. He was by some accident delayed. Embarassed and deviating from his direct line. As he was thus pushing on, as well as he could, through a very close and dark thicket, the rustling, most unfortunately, came to the old duke's ears as the approach of some *gross gibier*, as it is called, some piece of large game. And with the sudden heat of a keen sportsman, he urged Sir William, who was next the place, to fire. ---Sir William, alas! did so. And the loading, luckily not a bullet, lodged in the young duke's eyes! A disaster, like this, happening to a son, on the importunity of the father, and by the hand of a friend, made up an enormous mass of hideous woe, at first hardly to be borne! And such are mere corporeal ills, and specifically so light, when compared with ills upon the mind, that the loss of eyes, though so grievous in the extreme, seemed the least sore predicament of the three! literally, less dire than the agonizing thoughts of those who had, though unintendingly, inflicted agony upon another.---Time too, the chief assuager of all harms, seemed likely to be more active for the former than for the latter. Be it as it may, the Duke, then young, bore his calamity like a man; who, in the perfection of moral

thought

thought and action, derives his principles from the best appointed source.

Indeed, privation of this sense, seems, with much less effort of moral energy, supportable more readily than in another. For social comforts, the strongest stay of man, come, through hearing more potently, than through sight. And even for mere self-preservation in the abstract, conversation, preferably to all that books can do, offers aid much more constant and complete.---It is easier also to find substitutes for vision. Memory, and the other powers, all proportionably more alive and active, are found to join their forces, and among them to do what is wanted, astonishingly well. And above all, the blind, free from dejection, the symptomatic torture of the deaf, the blind generally have gay spirits, which never fail. All this has been, very cheeringly, seen in recent well-known instances. In a late prime minister's undiminished flow of talk---in Mr. Stanley the musician: who with memory admirably apt, even beyond his art, used to play well at whist, and carry his visitors about to the prettiest points of scenery, near his villa on Epping Forest---and again, in Duc d'Aremberg, who, like our young Lord D. still has got on horseback, and with a long leading-rein, has even followed the chace.

As to the chace, thus incidently mentioned, it is but fair to say, that it does not here, as in some other parts of Europe, offer the same violence to just and civilised feelings.---The chace is open. Each owner or tenant may do what he will with game, as with any other vermin, or good produce upon the land!---Nonsensical violence there is none, like *droits de chasse*, thwarting nature, and perverting justice ---with resentments beyond all possible provocation, straining right into wrong, and to objects so insignificant as a hare and patridge, sacrificing that most solemn trust, the life and liberty of man!

Abominations,

Abominations, such as these, ended through France, with the Revolution!—

Italy also, through decency, or through prudence, has already vouchsafed to amend in this point of duty, lessoned by the near amendment of their neighbours. The farmer may be at length allowed to reap freely where he may have sowed—and if invaded by the boars and foxes, he now may rid himself of his invaders—" To give the devil his due," said one of the most enlightened noblemen in Italy—" To " give the devil his due, we do owe this change to the " great changes in France—! Till then, there was less " danger of human punishment in Italy from a farmer " murdering a man, then if he armed his hands to get rid " of a wild boar!!!"

Such misdeeds, enormous transgressions of what is human and divine, were perpetrated formerly in France by every puny monster with a lordship or a manor! But the tyranny was perhaps no where so outrageous, as in the systematic wrongs of the H—— of Condè.

The game establishment at Chantilli, has at different times, condemned, terrible to tell, near a thousand men to the gallies! Many hundred peasants, it is now well known, fell murdered by their keepers! Literally hunted down and shot! And the bodies of the dead were thrown into the next ditch, or hid under a little mould, grubbed up in the park!—Such were the abuses, when each power and privilege of man, were superseded and overborn by the beasts of the field, the birds of the air, and by—vermin the most vile—as those who could execute the extremity of tyrannical abuses for a trifle, so insignificant as a chace! abuses which now, thank God, are no more—but which only a short interval past, really raged, with no hope but in the melancholy virtues, to yield any thing like refuge or mitigation.

Αυτους δε Ελωρια τευχέ, κυνεσσιν
Οιωνοισσι τε Πασι!—Διος δ'ετιλειτο βυλη!

Apart

Apart from this, which properly moving to indignation every juſt and virtuous man, ſhould have had a chapter in Beccaria, the recollection of Chantilli may not be inacceptable.—For Chantilli was the moſt extraordinary eſtabliſhment of the kind in Europe!

The following long liſts were copied from the houſehold regiſters there!—And, what ſeems unaccountable, they never were printed before—not even in France!——The copy was taken in the year 1788, and the gentleman who kindly aſſiſted me in tranſcribing it, is of all cotemporary Men but Doctor D—— moſt fit to perpetuate by an ode, the viciſſitudes ſo extraordinary in the place. This ſtatement, as an object, in natural hiſtory, is no ſmall curioſity! And as ſuch, it is philoſophically intereſting!—But it intereſts much more and edifies, when referred to a political conſideration. The neceſſity which urged for French reform in that department of life; and the rational approbation wherever reform can be wholeſomely effected.

THE FIRST LIST

States the total groſs numbers of game killed at Chantilli, year by year, through a ſeries of 32 years—beginning with the year 1748—ending with the year 1779.

FIRST OF THE GAME.

54878	33055	26371
37160	50812	19774
53712	40234	19932
39892	26267	27164
32470	25953	30429
39893	37209	30859
32470	42902	25813
16186	31620	50666
24029	25994	13304
27013	18479	17566
26405	18550	

Q   BIRDS

BIRDS AND BEASTS.

Their bill of mortality—The numbers in detail of each, specific defcription, thus regiftered, to have been killed at Chantilli, in the above-mentioned feries of years—

Hares	77750	Buftards	2
Rabbets	587470	Larks	106
Partridges	117574	Tudelles	3
Red, ditto	12426	Fox	1
Pheafants	86193	Crapeaux	8
Quails	19696	Thruflies	1313
Ralles (the male quail)	449	Guynard	4
Woodcocks	2164	Stags	1712
Snipes	2856	Hinds	1682
Ducks	1353	Fawns	519
Wood pigeons	317	Does	1921
Lapwings	720	Young Does	135
Becfique (fmall bird like our Wheatear)	67	Roe Bucks	4669
		Young ditto	810
Curlews	32	Wild Boars	1942
Oyes d'Egypte	3	Marcaflins (young Boars)	818
Oyes Sauvage	14		

GAME KILLED IN ONE YEAR.

By	Pieces of Game.	By	Pieces of Game.
M. de Cayla	460	M. Vaupaliere	75
M. de Canillac	953	M. Loftanges	247
Comte d'Artois	553	M. de St. Hermine	29
Duc de Bourbon	403	M. Belinage (three of the	
Duc d'Enghien	9	fame name)	10868
Prince d'Henin	170	M. Damezega	522
Duc de Polignac	330	M. St. Cloud	29
M. de Roucherolles	93	M. Boazola	471
M. de Choifeul	195	M. Goulet	10
M. deTremouelle	86	M. Brieux	62

M. de

By	Pieces of Game.		By	Pieces of Game.	
M. Balli de Crufol		196	M. Sarobert	-	78
Abbé Baliviere		54	M. Bateroy	-	6
Baron de Chatelie	·	26	Mr. Franklin		119
M. de Valou	-	8	Mr. Franklin (his fon)		198
M. Nedouchel	-	16	*** No other Englifh gen-		
M. Mintier	-	770	tlemen are in the lift.		
M. P. de Tallemont		17	Stag hunts	-	90
Conte d'Autheuil		403	Boar hunts	-	207
M. d'Autheuil	-	822			

The prince's name does not appear in the lifts 1779---That year the prince did not fhoot. —But from the years 1748 to 1778, the archives of Chantilli, with all due dignity rehearfe—

That, the pieces of game, killed by S. A. R. Monfeigneur le Prince de Condè, were in number 65-524.

That the nine pieces killed by the late prince's grandfon, the Duc d'Enghien, were all rabbets.

That the pieces killed by the Duc de Bourbon were thefe,

Pheafants	1451	Partridges	1254
Hares	1207	Red ditto	143

And by C. d'Artois, thefe

Pheafants	978	Partridges	1109
Hares	870	Red ditto	115

The eftablifhment was alfo thus extraordinary throughout! viz.

  21 Miles of Park! 48 Miles of Foreft!

The Horfes, when the family were at the place, were above 500!

The Dogs, 60 to 80 couple.

The Servants, above 500!

The Stables, are well known to be called the fineft and beft in Europe.---They are called fo by thofe who know not what is good.

As a building, it is, in the French ftyle, fuperb—As a · ftable, stable, it fails in the first requisite, fitness and accommodation!—What does it signify, that there may be 136 places for horses to put their heads in, if those places are scarcely five feet wide, and subdivided only by swing bars?

Stalls, enclosed on each side, there are but 40—and they are scarcely six feet wide in the clear. The heigth and width above 50 feet each, and the space in the centre, are the excellent parts of the building. This central space, an octagon of 80 feet diameter, and almost as high, is the place where the king and queen supped with music in the gallery, and jets d'eaux, about the statuary of the horses.—Some of that statuary is not bad.

In this part of architecture, as in every other, as indeed in all the arts and actions of men, the pretension to positive good, must in some sort, be adjudged by each comparative approach to it.- -It is not how much, but how well.

Thus analysed, What is this boasted building of Chantilly?—With all that lavish waste and ornament, basso-relievo and statues can do for it (and the very fanes are horses heads)--- Yet what is there so pretty and complete as the small stabling at the Duke of Queensbury's, at the Meuse, or Lord Milton's?---In skilful contrivances for use and comfort, Lord Fitzwillam, Lord Egremont, the Duke of Bedford, with their loose rooms, all exceed Chantilli!

It still remains to say- -that the Duke of Devonshire's stables at Buxton, are the best in Europe---the best in plan and execution for accommodation and effect.

The Duke of Orleans has the only building, of the kind, an Englishman could think complete in France.---It was at Paris, opposite the Palace Royal.

The Dog houses at Chantilli, are also far inferior to what we have in England---particularly at the Duke of Richmond's in the park at Goodwood, where there is a good characteristic façade, from a grey, grim stone-work, in Doric, making an object to the house and grounds---While

within,

within, the arrangements of diſtributing the dogs, their rooms for eating, ſleeping, airing, &c. when ſick and well, with running water and underground drains,---the whole ſhewing as far as can be ſhewn on ſuch a work, both humanity and ſkill.-- And there is pecuniary magnificence too---For it is ſaid to have coſt five or ſix thouſand pounds. Dante in the Inferno, uſefully figures the lower limb of one man, eſcaping uncondemned; ſaved by one act of caſual bounty, having once kicked a ſtray bone into the reach of a poor chained up dog!---After this we hope to hear no more of the Suſſex Squire's flouting at this atchievement, as inexcuſeably flung to the dogs.

After this, without ſome little diſtance and bar of ſeparation, like the ſpace above, it ſeems not eaſily poſſible to ſay much of St. Trond, which can ſay ſo little for itſelf--which is a little dirty town, with a dirty inn---one pariſh, with a dozen prebends, and a deanery!

The magiſtracy, made up of two bourg-maſters and ſeven echevins, are named, half by the Prince of Liege, the other half by the Abbaye of St. Nond.---To ſhew that the magiſtracy, have not always been what they ought to be, there are half a dozen convents in the town, humble and ſcanty as it is.

In the ten leagues from Tirlemont to Liege, the three large, rounded, graſſy mounts near Tirlemont, are the only noticeable appearances in the way. They are evidently artificial, and leſs likely to have been a funeral folly of any Roman, than a device to commemorate a triumph of ſome Goth.--- But if the reader has a mind to make a queſtion of this, it will not be debated---he may have it which way he will.

Aperere procul montes, ac voluere fumum.

We muſt haſte away to the hilly ſcenery, with the mines and manufactures of Liege!

For popular politics, as well as pit-coal fires, a rival to Birmingham itſelf!

LIEGE.

LIEGE.

BRACTON, the Judge of Harry III. in his work De Consuetudinibus, lays down the law upon stray sturgeon, that the king may claim it all. But touching a whale, he opines, and most people must wish the same, that the king may have a head, and that the queen may be well pleased to take up with the tail.

De sturgione observetur quod rex illum habebit integrum—de balena autem sufficet, si rex habeat caput; et regina caudam.

These are his words—and the reason is, from due regard to the wardrobe of the queen, that her august and sacred person may never want whalebone. Which, by the bye, proves the ugly use of hoops and stays to have prevailed among the deformities of the 13th century.

Now the city and country of Liege is like the sturgeon laid down by Bracton. The prince would have it all—head and tail, inside and out, body and soul—civil and ecclesiastical—temporal and still when time shall be no more.

The people, however, happen not to be altogether of the same convenient way of thinking. They have got up a rude notion, that all can look after one another, and that each may take care of himself. And in the mere spirit of trade, they seem loth to pay others for what they vainly fancy all men able to do for themselves.

Hence they have been at different times, of late, rather refractory and rude. They grumbled, forsooth, at such trifles as the taxes! And when the prince only wanted to bring in a successor, in the shape and title of a coadjutor, they, shocking to tell, put themselves on the defensive, and resisted!

resisted! As much as protesting in downright political blasphemy, they would not perpetuate the breed.

No, they could not be prevailed upon! Not even when the Prussian army, with their usual beneficence, marched into the town. Not even when they were offered the nephew of the late Emperor. Nay, not even when his late Serene Highness, Monseigneur Le Duc d'Orleans, equally ambitious of doing good, had graciously condescended to prevail upon his half brother, Abbé St. Farre, to have submitted to the toils of the high office. Still amidst all these offered blessings the people, fye on them, seemed insensible —they and their town magistrates, Cheftret, Fabris, &c. persisting to say, nay!—For the language of this part of Europe is, according to Steevinus, beyond all others fruitful in monosyllables.

Such was the very uncouth state of things, when they conspired with the French. And parting with their prince, would fain have formed a government upon the plan of, if not in union with, the French Republic. And when the consequences of a republic were urged—and their dangers to liberty and property, the hardy Liegeois disdained to answer at large, but called upon their fellows to look at Genoa and Geneva, at the Swifs, the Americans, and the Dutch! It was manifest there was no talking with people such as these.

So the allies, as they are called, with logic of a stronger sort, made the people know what they thought should be done! Dumourier insensibly let fall the wreathe, which amidst theatric captivations, wit and beauty had placed upon his brow! The French, however favoured, were forced to fly. And all the blessings were restored, of a Prince-Bishop and Chapter, Canons, Convents, Masses, Indulgencies, and Processions!

And finally, that the towns-people might know when they were well, and to make them remember it, the Prince
of

of Cobourg made a levy upon the town.—The amount of the impofition was half a million!

How the French loft Liege, or as they there were too apt to fay, how Liege loft the French, is a fact that will make no great figure in hiftory. For it was by a device as far afunder from fkill and prowefs, as a mere bargain and fale!

Hence the whole economy of the campaign! Hence Dumourier, quite unprepared for what he pretended, without an army at all adequate, without even the charts and plans for the route, M. Dumourier wafting time and ftrength at Williamftadt, at the Moerdyck, and at Dort. Hence the refufal of reinforcements, (10 or 15,000 men) urged by Miranda and by Bournonville. Hence the fiege of Maeftritcht unfupported and abandoned. Hence Lamorliere and Champmorin were left with force ill matched to their work—to keep the Pruffians in check, and to cover the left fide of the Meufe. Hence Valence, when he ought to have been aiding the army of obfervation on the eaft, was fuffered to lofe himfelf fo long at Liege. Hence Lanoue, not able to difpute the paffage of the Roer—was attacked on the right and left, driven from his cantonments, and his pofition after it, evacuating Aix-la-Chapelle, and retreating to Hervè. And hence the 35,000 men who were thus let pafs at Wyck, had all their fubfequent fucceffes, in the attack upon the retreat, ere the junction with Leveneur—in the attack at Tongres—in the enforced retreat to St. Tron—and fo on, at Neirwinden, La Montagne De Fere, &c. to the flight through Bruxelles, and the final evacuation of Flanders and Brabant!

Yet the French Republicans, retreated and retreating, continued formidable all the while. And in the laft great action near Louvaine, they would have finally defeated the Germans, but for a corps of Emigrants, who had fallied out of Maeftricht. The Emigrant regiments of Saxe, of Bircigni, raighn, of the French royal allemagne, were the men whofe prowefs turned the fate of the day.

Among the many wonders of this extraordinary retreat, the conduct of M. Yhler, a French general, in faving the laft detachment of ten thoufand men, was the moft rational and the beft. In value as well as number, it was a counterpart to Xenophon's ten thoufand. M. Yhler had to collect his men from all the out-pofts, piquets, and advanced guards, pofts of obfervation, foraging, recruiting---and fuch was his fpeed, his fkill, and his fuccefs, that he collected them all, and conducted them, without lofs, to the main body of the army at St. Tron.—Though the laft fix battalions had to repulfe and route a corps of cavalry, that purfued and harraffed their rear!—and though they had to make their way through Liege, the head quarters of the enemy!---the French, led by M. Yhler, marched through Liege in the night! And the army of the enemy, either were not aware of it, or dared not to difpute the paffage if they were!

The confequences of this to Liege, muft appear and be felt heavy by all!— for, added to the caufe of reform, thus obvioufly, to unknown time, deferred—there have arifen interruptions to free intercourfe and fecurity.—To pay the German impofition, there is a houfe-tax, now collecting, from door to door!—While, what is worfe than all, there is a large diminution of the people to pay it!—For, no lefs than 18,000 inhabitants of Liege departed with the French, in their retreat!—And all thofe people, loft to their native fettlement, continue adding to the population and to the welfare of France. Some, indeed, in the army; but the greater part in the mine works, in the founderies, and in the factories of fire-arms, fo rapidly augmenting by the French!

For at St. Etienne, near Autun, on the weft between Macon and Lyons, a prime eftablifhment for fuch work; it has

has been much extended and improved fince the revolution. When the work began, it was neceffary to have aid from England: our firft mechanical genius, Mr. Watt, of Birmingham, had been confulted before—but on this occafion, being otherwife occupied, the French applied to another chief artificer of our's, Mr. John Wilkinfon, whofe fkill has made the names of his furnaces, Burfham and Brofeley, every where known and refpected.—There he made the firft cylinders for that of St. Etienne, for Paris, &c.—but at prefent, fuch is the fure creative power of neceffity, the French truft no aid is wanting but their own. A young man of Lyons is the chief engineer now; and has already difplayed a genius able to advance his very ufeful art; and accordingly, the works are fpreading in all directions,—in the mine and fmelting furnaces; but moft in the founderies for cannon.

In fuch a number as 18,000 perfons thus leaving Liege, there muft have been many viciffitudes, very violent! many a fortune, by the fhock of accident, thus going to the bottom!—Poor Fabris, was among the moft remarkable of thefe. When I faw him firft at Liege—he was in the fullnefs of municipal power. The bourgmafter there. He had mixed in politics with the Pruffian adminiftration: and, indeed, had been received at Potfdam with little lefs than the vain pride of embaffadorial fhow.—He is now, I hear, keeping a ginguette (a fort of fuburb hop and cakehoufe) in one of the Fauxbourg's at Paris!

Yet, notwithftanding all this change, by accident and human violence, and in fpite of all this lofs in the population of Liege, the politics of the place remain unaltered! They are highly popular, and feem to wait only for a convenient feafon to give their government a radical reform!

For the people of Liege would be independent in the extreme. They affect to be too plain, they pretend, indeed, to be too poor, to bear the taking indulgencies, the

winning

winning splendors of a court.—They object also to the mixed constitution of the person they employ for their chief magistrate; and assert, that the ecclesiastical part of the character seems hurt by it.

This objection we repelled, as might be expected from Englishmen, in due allegiance to truth. But in vain!---for we were asked immediately, where is there such another family? All of such equal consideration--each as virtuous as wise!---Reference was then made to the very authentic annals of Liege; and they were stained, undeniably, with infamy, not seen in any other list of bishops, that we could recollect.

So long ago as the tenth century, Huduin, afterwards archbishop of Milan, came with money in his hand, as avowedly to corrupt the election, as a perjured candidate would be in a rotten borough—if there could be such a candidate, or any borough ever rotten. In the eleventh, Reginard got into the place, by money, to Conrad the Emperor! Some little time after, another prince-bishop was a convict, on the complicated guilt of selling canonries in the church! He was tried, cast, and condemned! The man's name was Alexander: the date of his reign 1130.--- In the same century, two of them were cited to Rome, on a charge, little less than of privately stealing!---viz. having made away with, to the count of Flanders, some lands about Malines, belonging to the church of Liege!

Another abuse, enormously oppressive, and from which it is impossible to separate, justly, clamour and resistance, is the *monstrous number* of ecclesiastics !---draining the country into the veriest inanition of poverty; and yet more, if possible, spoiling society, by the bad example of plunder, wasted often by ignorance, always by sloth! &c. &c. &c.

The number of churchmen, like the number of any other men, applying to collective life, must be an affair of relative expedience; ascertained by rules derived from the

R 3   propositions propofitions of each community to which they apply.—Though a great political queftion, it is at once made very tractable, by arithmetic and analogy.

The population of Liege has been much over-rated, when called 100,000.—Before the late diminution, 80,000 might be the fact. Yet the ecclefiaftical eftablifhments are as follow:

A bifhop. He is a fuffragan of Cologne—and alternately with Munfter in the imperial college of princes.

A fuffragan bifhop! The firft fuffragan was in the 13th century.

> Eight grand deans!
> Twenty-feven rural ditto!
> Two hundred and one prebendaries!
> Thirty-two parifhes!
> Seventeen monafteries!
> Eleven convents for women!
> Twenty-four fec. abbayes!

With provofts, treafurers, chancellors, officials, chaunters, &c. &c. out of all number.—The archdeacons are feven.

All this in the town, merely!—And, tantum fuadere malorum, making the ecclefiaftics to amount altogether to 8000! That is, within a ninth or tenth part of all the clergymen in England!

For in the territory of Liege, little as it is, no more than 105 fquare miles, three are 1500 parifhes!—With two or three priefts to each parifh—and to every chapel and convent, almoft as many more—the canons, alfo, are above 800—the nominal population of the territory, never more than 200,000—and now, probably, may be lefs.

In Weftminfter, fo far exceeding the population of Liege, the parifhes are but eight—the prebendaries, happily, no more than twelve.

The bifhop, elected by the chapter, is confirmed by the Pope, and had inveftiture from the emperor.—But that is now difpenfed with---and the bifhop only does homage for his fiefs.

He has the prime authority---he can iffue edicts and ordinances, for ordinary regulation and police---he convenes the ftates---their refolutions are prefented to him---and when revifed by the privy council, are fanctioned by him---in his name they are promulgated, and affume the commanding character of laws; to which, in his name, obedience is enforced. He names military and ftate officers; who take an oath to him and the ftate. He can coin; but the new money muft be according to the fixed denomination and ftandard. He is, moft wifely and ufefully, reftrained from levying any new tax, from making war, or even any alliance, without the confent of the people, teftified by the ftates.

Three-fourths of the land and houfes, through the whole diftrict of Liege, are the property of the church. And tythes are exacted with a rigor and minutenefs, which Englifh clergymen, in general above fuch enormous meannefs, do not know; and would difdain to practice, if they did. There are many hops about Liege, and the harpies abovementioned, however inconceivable, decimate the poles! There are fome vineyards too; and though hardly worth a word, there alfo the fame nimble exaction is at hand, and tythe is taken, fometimes of the grapes, and fometimes of the wine. Of trembling contributions, the prince bifhop has one from a fmall chapelry! It annually pays him, why, we know not, 80,000 meafures of wheat!

The revenue of Liege, about 1,200,000 florins, refults from a 60th levied on all merchandize paffing the Pays de Liege, by land or by water, a light duty on wine, and a petty impofition on land. Of this 1,200,000, the bifhop modeftly fwallows, for his fhare, 800,000! Each canon has about 200l. fterling per annum. A deanry cofts the people about a double canonry. The parochial clergy are

paid

paid not with the fame difproportion as in England, and in France before the Revolution---we heard no inftances of infufficient income, as in our eftablifhments, mocked as it were by cruel mercy, in the tardy augmentation of Queen Anne. Their provifion, in general, is from 60 or 70 pounds fterling to 120 or 130.---There are fome churches which produce more: but very few indeed, if any, above 300 or 350l. fterling a year. And this is ample for celibacy; and in a country where life is accommodated for half what it cofts in England!—No man holds two livings.

The appointment of the prince bifhops, in diftant periods, occafionally ufurped by the emperor and the pope, is now vefted in the chapter—they name the coadjutor too, who fucceeds, of courfe, on the bifhop's departure.—The prefent fuffragan, after all the compofitions abovementioned, is M. Stockhem, a fon of the baron, whofe anceftors have been fo often archdeacons of Brabant, &c. and who have been honoured with fubfcription monuments by the chapter, even at Calais and Bologne.

For a canonry in Liege, proofs of nobility are generally demanded.—Though in fome inftances the cuftom is not enforced, as particularly in the admiffion of Granville (afterwards archbifhop of Malines, cardinal and prime minifter of Charles V.) He was, un homme nouveau, without any hereditary diftinction whatever!—And again, in the cafe of Wazon, in the eleventh century, who was not only a canon, but the prince bifhop, elected unanimoufly by the whole chapter.—And he had been a finging boy in the choir!

Where the pedigree may be imperfect, they prop it (like a crazy joint-ftool with a bit of wood under it) with a certificate of college refidence—five years in the lawline are fuppofed to do; and in divinity feven!

The patronage of church livings, chiefly with the bifhop and the collegiate churches and abbayes, is not, we were told,

told, fo well adminiftered as by the *concurfus,* or election, properly eftablifhed by Jofeph II. in the Netherlands.— By the privelegium tractus, the univerfity of Louvain prefents to livings lapfing in the month of November every year, and alternate year in January---the emperor and the king of Pruflia, and a few other poffeffors of manorial rights, claim, here and there, fome patronage---alfo purchafed.

Another virtuous regulation of Jofeph II. the abolition of *dotes,* or receptions into convents, is, we have reafon to fear, eluded! The emperor prohibited the abufe: but we heard of its being done fecretly.—And we could not but feel the more regret, as fuch a perverfe payment had been made for the facrifice of a fine young woman from England—Mifs ———, the niece of Lady C———! 12,000 livres was the money paid for her!

The fhort ftory of Mifs ——— was interefting. She was beautiful, highly accomplifhed, and very good.— Among other admirers, whom fhe could not help, was M. le ci-devant Duc de M———. His duchefs was only at Maeftricht; but, as the devil would have it, fhe was fhut up with the fiege.

The duke was no difgrace to the late French court---or to his plan of action, which was furprife!---fo there were none of the impediment a virtutis; no time loft in reflection, no morbid fenfibility, no falfe fhame!

The lady, however, received him as infignificance and guilt ought to be received.—She brufhed him off directly —and left him ridiculed and failing—

" Flagitious, and not great."

Her affections, manifeftly worth winning, were then fairly ventured for, and won by a young man---not only of her own country, but who had merit alfo like her own.— But foon after that, they were feparated.---He had left her for a journey of a few days---but, alas! they never met

more

more. He was doomed to go, where no traveller returns. He died fuddenly!

Thus the poor girl was given over to grief!---Aftonifhed with the ftroke, fhe had no ftrength to rally!---and they who fhould have rallied for her, feemed alfo ftruck ftupid in their turn. In the thick darknefs of a bad perfuafion, they carried her to a cloifter, and laid her in a cell!

Not four months after, error was glutted with another victim! From the fame family, another victim to the veil!

Such are the feductions of romance, however dull and monftrous.---Such the poffible triumphs of nonfenfe and barbarity, overbearing humanity and truth.

The details of the pious fraud, it was not poffible to hear without aftonifhment and difguft---yet an eccelefiaftic that we met, praifed them all---and complimented his order on the activity of their zeal!---" Comme elles etoient eveil" leès! Bien! divinement bien!"---were among the leaft extravagant of his words.

Shakefpear's " Divinity of Hell"---may be among the words of the reader.

LIEGE.

LIEGE.

THE government of Liege is placed in the States, viz.
1. The Chapter.
2. The Nobles.
3. The Tiers Etat of Liege, and from the other towns in the Principality.

They meet apart, or altogether by a delegation from each of the three conſtituent corps, viz.
4. Canons.
4. Noble Gentlemen.
4. Private Laymen, for the Tiers Etat.—Half of theſe are choſen by the Walloon towns, half by Flanders; with two Bourg-maſters, and two Subſtitutes, who in the abſence of the Bourg-maſters may vote.

The Prince alſo has a power of ſending three or four Deputies, but they have no power to vote—with a Greſſier for each Etat, and two Receivers.

On each occurrence exceeding the power of the Delegates, then there are the general meetings of the States *.—They met for inſtance, at the end of 1793, to authoriſe an impoſition on each houſe to repay the money ſeized by the Auſtrians. They are convoked by the Prince.

The two Bourg-maſters and Twenty Council who form the town magiſtracy, have been, ſince the year 1648, nominated every year, half by the town and half by the Prince. The town here, like the definition of the world by ſome clever writer, is a ſmaller circle within the greater. The town, here, means no more than that part of it which have the elective franchiſe, viz. The City Chambers and

* From Liege, as from the reſt of Germany, the final appeal is to the Court at Wetzlaer.

Corporate Companies, each of which confift of thirty-fix—and who draw lots, divide and fubdivide, as they do at Venice, and with the fame effect; to thwart, intrigue, and to make corruption yield to theto the lefs odious dominion of chance.

What armed force is in Liege is paid by the States, and therefore moft properly appointed and officered by them. They were but five or fix hundred men, at 5 fols a day, (4½d. Englifh) and were no more offenfive than fo many conftables in red. Their annals have not to blufh at any barbarous treaty for troops. Though a town perfectly mercantile, they have no fuch trade as dabbling in human blood!

The Councils and Tribunals are not, as they might better be, elective, but are named by the Prince, viz.

1. A Privy Council, generally, but not neceffary, of Canons and Nobleffe, from each baillage. Other perfons may be appointed. The number is ten. The Chancellor prefides. This court has an appellant power—it revifes propofed laws, and propofes them upon criminal punifhments and taxes.
2. Chambre des Comptes—the number indefinite.
3. The Tribunals, Civil and Criminal, viz. 14 Judges, properly named, not by the Prince, but by the States---and to them
4. Appellant Jurifdiction---a council of nine---felected as they fhould be, from each order.
5. A Feudal Court---fifteen members.
6. Allodial Court---thirteen members.
7. Tribunal de Vinty Deux---has an inquifitorial power over every court and office---fometimes it forms a court of police, and fometimes occupied in external negociation —as with Louvaine, they formed the privileges cum tractus mentioned before. Very properly they are renewed every year. Of thefe 22, each order fupplies four judges, and

each

each of the outlying towns, as Dinant, Tongres, St. Tron, Thuin, &c. one or two.

The Prince, like every other citizen, is amenable to some laws---and when he may be suppofed to escape, they attach upon his ministers.

The advocates, the prolocutors, and procureurs are here, as elsewhere, enough in all conscience to take care of themselves, and to do their client's businefs. The first, like the first never-failing riflemen in America, are numbered exactly at one thoufand. The last are two hundred and forty.

The administration of law is in faint imitation of what has happened elsewhere, a little costly and slow. The courts, with great tendernefs to the judges, are closed for a quarter of a year. But there are no such fine doings as a stamp tax on each law proceeding---nor any benevolencies, like sinecure places, from the perquisites of the court. Thus, therefore too probably, the love of law may rage unchecked by any controul, and certainly there cannot be any encouragement hence ingenioufly as virtuoufly derived, for the poor in spirit, nor any premium to foster opennefs, to conviction---and talents for filence.

The judges are paid by the States a settled stipend---but they are allowed also fees upon each pleading of every caufe. Of course, there result a gain from this confequence like the former, and equally good. There never can be a dearth of hearings upon every caufe. It cannot be doubted but that the judges are accessible and candid---with the most easy compliance, the most winning promptitude, to revise and to re-hear.

The stipend to these gentlemen is four thoufand florins. But by fees and dexterity they can make the thing mount to six or eight thoufand more.

That I believe is the utmost ever got. It was one of the judges who told us so---and he added, " that his profits,

" from the place, both fees and falary, never amounted to
" more than fix thoufand."

But a friend, who was prefent, rather fhrewdly reminded
him—" that he was but a young man--propofiti tenax, and
" a little hard of hearing."

It is required of each law ftudent to have paffed feven
years in ftudy, before he can be called to the bar. And
from thence, without any definitive demand for more years,
he may rife to the bench. The judge, with whom I was
in company, was but twenty-fix years old. But, vivere bis,
by double diligence he had lengthened his days---and like
the moft lamented judge in another land, who funk under
fomething like fubornation of perfidy.--He was in temper
as well as accomplifhment, much older than his years.

As to the execution of the law, the capital punifhments
are various, viz.—For murder, the convicts' limbs are
broken, and a coup de grace given to his heart! for high-
way robbery, the offender is ftrangled. At the revolution
the malefactors were condemned to be hanged at the lan-
tern. The woollen manufacture is the hard labour, when
that is the punifhment. For fimple theft, the penalty is
banifhment.—The torture is ftill inflicted, and with a barbarity known only in ftates of the vileft defpotifm and fuperftition—medical people attend, as at fome militarypunifh-
ments!

Infolvent debtors are imprifoned—and for the fmalleft
fums. The creditor is forced to keep the debtor, and according to his rank, ten days. Then, if the debt fhall be
unfettled, the debtor is formally committed to prifon; and
the claim upon the creditor is only for the goal allowance,
of bread and water.

There are privileged places, as in Italy and Spain, where
the guilty can efcape the laws. This protection, manifeftly
infamous, is exhibited to the natives only—but for debt and
for every crime except murder. The revolutionary fpirit
has

has been excepted alfo! But with none of that whimfical folemnity fometimes feen elfewhere of interdict, " as men " muft fear eternal vengeance, and the difpleafure of the " ftate"—like the well known anti-climax in Hudibras—

<blockquote>
The God of War,
Lieutenant-Colonel to the Earl of Mar!
</blockquote>

The final appeal to Wetzlaer, may alfo, in one fenfe, be claffed under the criminal law of the country, and among the efforts of capital punifhments. For the caufes now before that patient and long fuffering court are more than 180,000! We could not help afking how old any of them might be—and we were very properly referred at leaft to the dark ages, if not to the creation of the world. Compared with this, our own chancery, though hitherto thought fuperlatively grave, and ftaid, muft reluctantly give up the palm. For we have, I believe, not often heard of any fuit as old as the revolution. And it was thought a thing to wonder at, when a late chancellor, who had practiced in that court twenty years, ended literally with a decree upon the identical fuit in which his pleadings had begun!

<blockquote>
And in pure equity—the cafe not clear—
The Chancery takes your rents—for twenty year!
</blockquote>

The prifons in Liege are a difgrace to fociety confcious of any thing like refponfibility to God or man. The ftairs and walls, which led us up to the door, were almoft impaffable with the moft hideous filth. Nothing but humanity or curiofity can get over it!—while the noife of a fierce watch dog was almoft equally irkfome to another fenfe.

The goaler came flowly on the ringing of a heavy founding bell, and, with fome difficulty, let us have admittance! The defcent to the cells is down forty or fifty ftairs—the paffages are pent-up, narrow, and dark. And the cells themfelves, not quite feven feet fquare! of ftone, ill-wrought

on

on every surface but the door! without any light! without any external air! with nothing like a window, but a small hole (six inches by four and a quarter) opening into the passage. The stagnant water from the old fortification, and its drains and ditches, oozing through the walls!

The prisoner is bereft of every thing. He can have no provision against heat or cold. Common cleanliness, the possibility of it, is denied him. He has a little straw, and there he may lay his head. He is in chains. He is without spiritual consolation. And rye bread and water, a few ounces of each, are all his food!

And this in a country where the chief power of government is with ecclesiastics!

As to the other great objects of human care, which should be human health and the art of healing, these are some of the chief circumstances at Liege.

Medical school there is none. The students who would thus qualify beneficiently to turn science to profit, generally go to Leyden, Paris, or Vienna. Vienna was beginning, under Joseph II. to promise accomplishments of the best order. An hospital, rather magnificently planned, and an anatomical school, in which, at least, there was a magnificent adventure of expence. For the preparations in the museum at Florence were all copied, and conveyed, not in carriages for fear they might shake and spoil, but by horses and by men!—And so, they actually traversed the whole laborious route, over the Appennines and Tyrolese Alps, from the Arno to the Danube! But since the loss of Joseph, this hope seems to have been lost too—almost the whole has fumed away in projection—there survive only a few transactions—one very moderate quarto volume, and no more! The professors, Frank and Scarpa, contributed to those transactions—and our prime anatomist, Mr. Cruikshank, decorated the establishment by becoming an honorary member.

The

The reputation of Vienna is accordingly lefs than Leyden, little as that properly is. And Paris, when acceffible, is the place German ftudents all appear to prefer.

They have a pharmacopeia of their own; in the year 1740, compiled from Paris, from London, and Vienna, from Etmuller, Fuller, and Bate. They alfo apply to the beft foreign works of the kind. Thofe of Edinburgh and London, are well known there, as the beft.

The chief phyficians and furgeons, are fuppofed to get no more than from 250 to 300l. a year—which, comparing the Liege fees of two efcalins with the London fee of a guinea, proves the labour to be equal to Englifh practice of five or fix thoufand pounds a year. Humble as that requital feems to us, it is found ample for the neceffities and comforts of life at Liege! For the country is plentiful, and taxes, only, are fcarce. And, accordingly, it is thought worth contending for! The number of practitioners in each department are exactly thirty-one.

The hofpitals teach a traveller nothing but the evils of neglect, in the chief requifites of cleanlinefs and air. One of thefe eftablifhments is for 350 people of the town— the other for 120 ftrangers. I hope it will be thought that we enquired after any Englifh that might be there. We did. And luckily we found there were none.

In a fociety like this, where, if government in any part fails, it is not for want of paying.—Where there is a court of clergymen, indeed nothing lefs than a legion of finecure ecclefiaftics, and of courfe a great quantity of book learning, and not a little intellect too, may be thought to be floating—it is monftrous, that the whole feems on all fides running to wafte!—that there is no one eftablifhment of ufeful fcience—not a fingle effort of mind to work in the moft ordinary way for the public good—no philofophical regifters, no ephemerides—not even what London has annually from the parifh clerks, a bill of mortality.

Con.

Consequently there must be a want also of each inference authorised from thence on health and sickness—upon life and death.

The local ailments most rife and fatal are rheumatism, palsy, and diseased liver.—-The first comes from vicissitudes of weather being very sudden and strong.—The two last, from hard drinking, which is a popular failing of the place.— Many pulmonary consumptions might be expected; but there are not many.—Notwithstanding the pit-coal fires, the large use of tobacco, and such wide-spread multiplied labours upon metallurgy and in mines.

The trade of Liege is active, ingenious, and comprehensive of much variety, viz.

Iron works	Watches
Steel	Black lace
Copper	Tanning
Coal mines	Paper
Alum	Woolens
Copperas	Soap
Lapis Calaminaris	Aqua Fortis
Verdigris	Hats,

and perhaps printing too should be mentioned; for the Liege people pirate, and not ill, the publications of France and Germany.

Their muskets and pistols are much cheaper than the English. In the barrel they bore a little better. In the lock they are not so good.—Some people however prefer them altogether, to the English manufactures at Sheffield, Birmingham, and Wolverhampton! And accordingly, a commissary, with a salary, Mr. ———, was sent to Liege last summer as a contractor for 50,000 muskets!

The French Republic managed this matter more adroitly; and drew better use from the gunsmiths of Liege. For near a moiety above one third of the best workmen, have been induced to leave Liege; and are settled some at Charleville,

but

but moſt at Paris, and at St. Etienne.---We ſaw very well looking pocket piſtols, for three crowns the pair!

The alum is as good as any in the world. The French think it the beſt.

In the Nail-trade they deal very largely. It employs 12 or 14000 manufacturers. The Dutch prefer them to our work, and they have almoſt a monopoly alſo, at the Hans Towns, on the Danube, and the Rhine, with the contributory rivers of courſe---the Moſelle, the Nekar, and the Mayne. The iron ore from Luxembourg, is thought better than that of Liege.

Their Watchmaking, in common with the reſt of Europe, yields in ſolidity to the Engliſh. It yields alſo in fineſſe and elegance to Geneva and Paris. For Paris furniſhes ſome very fine work. The moſt of it is fabricated at Geneva and in Switzerland. The beſt gold watches at Liege are ſold for 10 and 12l.

Their manufactured gold is, very wiſely, coarſer than the ſtandard. To that, like the Swiſs and Genevois, they have to work upon a metal more tractable than ours; and conſequently can finiſh with more ſpeed, and with leſs coſt, and indeed with more luſtre too.

This improvement, by encreaſing the alloy, was ſome time ſince ſuggeſted for the trade of London, by Lord Stanhope. But the people he addreſſed, I mean the craftsmen, had not wit enough to underſtand him. And ſo, the ſtandard, impolitic as it is, continues. And the Engliſh, with all the advantages of capital, cannot cope with the Geneveſe workmen in the market.

The ſilver and gold, manufactured at Liege, are authenticated by a town mark.

The Hats made at Liege, as at Malines, are of the low priced ſorts, far better than in England; and they are cheaper in the proportion, as eight or nine are to fifteen. The materials are better; there is leſs cotton uſed in them and more hair. The fine hats, the manufactured cottons and fine woolens are not so good as in England; their coarse woolen cloths, serges, &c. are better. The sheep, which are small, and well flavoured like the Welch, excel also in their wool. Those from the country about Hesbage yield the strongest wool. Those about Campane the finest. The bow strings for the manufacture of hats, Liege has from the French. England used to have them too. They are now made by our own people, urged by the all-instructing lessons of necessity! That necessity, which has made our former customers the French, already independent of our markets in the grand articles of fire-arms, gunpowder, bread-corn, and woolen-cloth.

Let us hear no more on the unbalanced mischief of the war, and that many millions have been wasted on the people in vain! It is not quite true. The people have got something, if not as much as they could expect.

They have learnt to make a few bow-strings for the hatters!

The Coal-mines, which have been six centuries at work, continue very considerable still---Added to their own consumption, they sell into other countries, to the amount of 250,000 crowns a year.

The Price at the pit is 10 florins for 2800lb. weight. In selling the smaller slack, bought chiefly by the bourgeois at Liege---the colliers give at the same price, 400 weight more.

The Mine we examined, which was that of M. Braconier, an advocate and a gentleman, who is applying this pursuit, so much better than the jargon of law, the powers of a large and lively mind. The local circumstances and modes of working are as follow:

Discovered to the augre. The mine had 7 veins.

1st	16 inches thick		5	2 feet thick
2	24 ditto		6	
3	7 feet		7	} 16 inches.
4	4 ditto			

The

The beft vein is the 4th---which is 80 to 66 toifes from the furface. The prefent pit, in the 3d vein, is 32 toifes deep.

This is a new work; on the road to Maeftricht, the firft water was drained by horfes; and when they could do no more, a fire engine was raifed---the cylinder 6 inches diameter, was made at Liege.

For a further and cheaper drain, a tunnel (as at the Duke of Bridgewaters, &c.) is now forming, 18 toifes from the furface; to iffue into the river Meufe. The tunnel to be 4 feet wide, 3 feet 6 inches high.

At the pits, which are walled throughout, they draw not with ropes, as with us, but with what is lefs hazardous, with iron chains---the whimfie (as they call the upper cranework in Wales) being all under a cover of wood.

The lands at top, and confequently to the bottom too, are fubdivided among different owners. The royalties on the mine, which in England, are from a 5th to an 8th part of the produce, are at Liege no more than a 24th. Where the tunnel, or underground canal paffes, there is a payment to the landlord of a 60th more.

The colliers wages are three efcalens for fix hours. The colliers, in all countries, earn hardly, a good deal. But being proportionably voluptuous, they are thence in a great proportion too, diforderly, unhappy, and poor. It is fo in the coal countries of England---And I was told it was fo in Liege. Accordingly we looked for it, but really did not happen to fee it. And indeed I rather think, it is an appearance lefs and lefs to be feen. The poor at Liege, as at moft other places, God knows may be unhappy, but not diforderly, for they are deeply now, and immoveably, devoted to political fpeculation and reform! And politics feem to be our firft confolation for the poor; not only from the moral chaftifements of difafter, but as they form an object, filling the whole mind, and except religion, agitating it, beyond all others, and perhaps better too.

At Liege, some of the old mines are working under the Meuse, as the Newcastle mines are under the Tyne, and at Whitehaven, under the sea itself!

As for Foreign Trade, Liege is a customer to France for wine, brandy, oil, and silk—to the Rhine and the Moselle, for wine. Draperies, cottons, drugs for dyeing and for medicine, they draw from the English and the Dutch. On these there are import duties; that on wine is 25 or 26 florins the ton.

The Landed Property, a prime object of skilful curiosity every where, is thus circumstanced in the Pays de Liege.

The Rent of Land, by the bonier, (a measure equal to four acres English) is from six crowns to 70 livres a year. The leases, not long enough for any stretch of agricultural improvement, are often for less than nine years: and seldom for more.—There is a partial land tax, incompletely laid, and worse collected.

The Soils are various—black mould, clay, sand and stones.

The Husbandry;—In the best arable lands so invariably, wheat. The price of corn, from the confusion of measures, was not to be ascertained—but the price of bread amounts to the same thing—viz. The best white bread six sols 5lb.—brown bread five sols 4lb.—the price was but half as much before the war!

In the lands of inferior value, the rotation of crops is, barley the first year,—oats the second year—wheat the third year.—The 4th year is fallow.

The intermediate crops, are potatoes, and cabbages.

The Grass gives two crops—sometimes, but very rarely, there have been a third —Hay before the war 100lb. weight sold for two escalins—since the war the price has been doubled.

The

The Grazier's Art, fo admirable with Mr. Bakewell and Mr. Chapman, is not unknown here; the mutton is not inferior to any in the world.—The black cattle alfo are very vigorous. And the dairy farm very good.

Duc d'Aremberg, Baron d'Aigremont, the family of Cherette are the chief owners of the land, of which the church is not feized.—As the churchmen too, vulgarly huddled together in towns, are moftly abfentees; agentcy is become a trade—And at Liege, as elfewhere, agents make themfelves thrive, while their employers are kept away.— With fimilar ingenuity, the Emigrants and Auftrians were haraffed in their flight. Their little property, like that of the poor French Princes when in Holland, fold for almoft nothing!—One fharp fellow told us that he had made in this war an amazing profit upon 800 horfes!—" Though" added he, fignificantly, " Though, after all, what was that " to the horfes of Heffe?"

The precious effects of the prefent difaftrous troubles have been felt at Liege, in all directions!—And among others in the money-trade.

Before the war, the merchant and the manufacturer could borrow any money he wanted at 2 per cent!—They now muft give $4\frac{1}{2}$ and 5 per cent. for it!—That is the higheft intereft allowed. And here, as in the Netherlands, every loan muft be regiftered.—And they flight the fagacity of Englifhmen, for confining that fecurity to two fifty feconds of the nation, Middlefex and York!

In the Police of Liege, there is the humane difcretion to protect the poor, from ufury as it were—that monfter of the deep! who pervades and actuates the plundering of a wreck!—Accordingly, the town Connives was not at fuch a dubious being as a pawnbroker.—There is in lieu of it, a fubfcription eftablifhment, a Monte de Pietè—where the poor man goes in his diftrefs, and where with as little mifchief as can be, the poor man is relieved.

There

There is a director and an estimator, both of approved repute—with 13 clerks.—They attend every day, and all day long.—On each pledge that is produced, they lend two thirds of its value; at an interest, for many years past, not more than 5 per cent.—But now, since the war, and its horrid impositions, &c. raised to 7½ per cent.—The pledges are kept fixteen months; and then if not redeemed are fold; and the owner receives any furplus there may be upon fale.---The fales are public; and constant---every four months; and of the property left unredeemed the corresponding anterior three.

While the late troubles raged, and while a foreign army were approaching, the establishment lent in a few days, less than a month, 65,000 florins, chiefly upon trinkets, watches, &c.---When one of the subscribers told us this, an emigrant officer was in the room---and he exclaimed with much earnestness " Would to God, we could have done so too, " when some of the allies took fuch care of our moveables, " in the retreat out of Champagne!"

This establishment was religioufly refpected by the army of the French Republic. Long as they were at Liege, there was not for a single moment, any thing like violence or fear.

The subscribers, who form the fund, are incorporated, and receive a stipulated interest of 4 per cent ---The remaining one per cent, (and it was no more before the war) is enough to pay all the charges of management, clerks salaries, sales, &c. &c.

In the town of Dinant there is a Monte de Pietè, a dependance upon this. Those at Antwerp and Maestricht have no longer any connection with it.

The Insurances from Fire, are the fame as through the Netherlands; viz. at Antwerp and Amsterdam.---The latter, when common buildings, is a quarter per cent.

When

When such a vast multitude of the citizens, hastily left Liege with the French, it should have been specified, that all the civil officers, constituting the municipality, were among them.---And when they took the final farewell of their friends---they said with affecting fortitude---

" Freedom is our object. We hope to find it in France.
" But if not, alas!---We will follow it to America."

" America, thank God, is open---and with blessings---
" ample enough for all mankind!"

For architecture, painting, and statuary, Liege has little or nothing to say!---The princes we suppose, have been disciples of that philosophy, which impugns the fine arts for emasculating the mind!---And so, they too, " have " never built a pigeon house!"---Notwithstanding their wealth, and the rich scenery on the Meuse, to boot.

When Dumourier was there, he lived in the old palace---when the wreath was put upon him at the play-house, he was opposite to what in London is called the King's side, the first box from the stage!

There are libraries at St. James and St. Benedict.

Of other memorabilia Liege is but bare.---There occurred but two inscriptions at all worth copying, one on the seminary, the other on the tomb of our countryman Sir John Mandeville, the physician, who, multo jactatus, after three and twenty years travelling, settled at Liege---and there he died.---His inscription at St. Jaques, is this---

Hic Jacet
Vir Nobilis
Dominus Joannes de Mandevile
Alias Dictus ad Barbam Miles,
Dominus de Campdi,
Natus de Angliâ,
Medicinæ Professor
Devotissimus Orator,

Et

Et Bonorum Largiffimus Pauperibus Erogator,
Qui toto quafe Orbe Luftrato,
Leodii, diem Vitæ Suæ Claufit Extremum
Nov. 17, 1372.

As Voffius has thought the journey of Mandeville worth mentioning, any body elfe may do fo too. It was written by him in Englifh, French, and Latin. Voffius fays, he had feen it in Italian: and knows it to be in Flemifh and German.

There is alfo a tranflation of it in Spanifh, viz. at Valentia, 1540.—Prior to that printed at Venice, viz. in 1534. The Flanders copy was the firft, 1483.---And what is remarkable, that of London was the laft, viz. 1696.

On the Seminary

Founded by Chapeuville, the Vicar General;---the infcription is by Poletus.

Salve Clara Domus, Studiis Sacrata Juventæ!
Salve iterum Venerande Domus! Tuq. Inclyte Pubes
Quem Præftans Chapeuvilleus amet. Ubi, Candidus, ille
Divinas Referabit Opes, et ———*
Strenuus Incumbens, Plena ad Subfellia Pandet.

The following alfo may be interefting, as it keeps in mind the pofition of the Englifh, living at Liege, in the moft important moment of its annals.

Liege 21, Fev. 1793.

Le general, au Citoyen le Croix, Commifläire de la Convention National, Deputè pres l'Armeè de la Belgeque.

* The word obliterated—They who wifh for more minute intelligence, refpecting Liege, may I believe find it in other books. I afked one of the Judges in the court of Liege, and he told me Louvrex was the beft authority on their conftitution.—Though fome years ago, at one of the Paris fales, there was a manufcript chronicle of Liege, beginning with the Siege of Troy!

Afin.

Afin de vous mettre à porteè, citoyen, de connoître precisément les motifs qui m'ont déterminè à avoir égard à la demande du comité de furveillance de Liegè concernant les Anglois qui fe trouvent dans la ville, Je.joins ici copie, tant de l'ordre que j'ai donné au Général Thouvenot que de la lifte de ces Anglois. La correfpondance que la plupart d' entr'eux entretenoient, foit avec les émigrés, foit avec la Garnifon de Maeftricht, a rendu néceffaire cette mefure de précaution, tant pour eux-mêmes que pour la chofe publique.

Lifte des Anglois dènoncés par le comitè de furveillance de la ville de Liège.

B. Grainger, fur quai d'Avroy, fa femme et une demoifelle.

Partira feul jeudi par la diligence. (N'eft point parti).

Madame Tailla, femme d'un Médecin Anglois, logée aux Dames---Angloifes, quoiqu-elle ait une Maifon à Hocheporte.

B. Dallman, la mere et une nièce, au fauxbourg Saint-Gilles, maifon de Conna.

Partiront enfemble Vendredi. (Ne font point partis.)

Milady Cliford et ces deux filles, maifon de Madame Pechat, quartier Saint-Jaques, logement refervé pour le Général Dumourier, maifon de Chanoine Leuvreux.

Stanhoppe avec fa femme, Garde-National quartier Saint-Jaques, Maifon du Comte Lannoy; ou en rejund.

B. Cearel, fa femme et enfans, grand ami de l'Envoyé de Hollande, logè chez Bolen Inprimeur, quai fur-Meufe.

Partira avec fa famille judi. (C'eft parti pour Bruxelles.

Milady Fitzgerald, avec une nièce, que l'on dit grande amie du nonce; fon frère fa foeur. Hôtel de Flandre.

B. Richard avec fa famille, Maifon du Tréfonuer Bonhomme, fur Avroy.

Partira jeudi à hiut heures du matin, avec fa famille, avec des Chevaux de louage. (Eft partipour Bruxelles).

U Madame

Madame Ryau, Convent Sant-Claire.

B. Pourès, Irlandoife, Manchande, au coin de Place venant du Palais.

Partira avec un fils, par la Diligence. (N'eft point parti.).

Certifiè par nous, Maréchal-de-Camp, Commandant dans la Ville de Liège, le 21 Fevrier 1793, l'an fecond de la Rèpublique.

Signè YHLER.

N. B. Ceux qui ont la marque bà côté de leurs noms, ut été plus particuliérment dénoncés comme fufpects.

TO AIX LA CHAPELLE.

The charm of scenery, that safe and elegant delight, is to be had rather in high order through the environs of Liege---in the common road to Aix la Chapelle, to Chanfontaine, and to Spa, and in the water-passage on the Meuse, each of Nature's ingredients, inequalities, wood and water, are in good proportions, and are well mixed and combined. The river is full, the hills are large, and the plantations frequent.

The Meuse, though when we saw it rather discoloured, is very interesting. It goes freely, and spreads well; the curvatures are sweeping, and the reaches are long—the views from it are full of space and animation—the banks open; and the hills are flung about, in all attitudes and aspects; with woods in fine varieties, to improve their shapes and pretensions, and with objects to adorn them.— Till the lands flatten about Maestricht, the landscape-traveller will find it worth his while to see the Meuse. And when left by him, the historian and the moralist may take their stand upon the ground—a ground that seemed for ever wet and tainted with tears and with blood! A ground they may make to yield its proper produce, some pabulum and prophylactics of life!—to strengthen man's heart, and give him a cheerful countenance! Instead of the fools-cap and the laurel—with which entire nations, infatuated, have made disguises for those monsters, who browze and feed full upon corruption and woe!

The roads to Aix la Chapelle, &c. are upon high-grounds, and ridges—not unlike that fine track (which is called the Hog's-back) between Guildford and Farnham. The lands also here fall and open upon each side—with fore-grounds of boundless amenity, and with distances of unbounded space.

The ideas of grandeur predominates. But it is from expanſion, cultivation, and uſe—paſtures, cattle, hay-making, corn-fields, hops, manufactures, roads, villages, churches, thickets, groves, woods, and ſcattered trees, all are in great abundance.

About Spa, like the Derbyſhire Matlock, the character of the country has more captivations, from wildneſs and irregularities—the idea of grandeur there may be, prevails from what is rough and miſhapen, from ſharper edges and ſtronger lines---from ſurfaces more broken, falls more precipitate, wooded rocks, romantic water, deeper hollows, higher hills!

Indulging a little leiſure in one of the moſt enchanting ſcenes about Chanfontaine, ſome ſcattered trees, which always ſhew to more effect from the top of a hill than the bottom, diſcovered, with uncommon minuteneſs, each ſingularity in each; of age, of colour, and of growth. The analyſis was made at once---how much the vigor and beauty of a woody ſcene may be aided here and there by deformity and decay. A Swiſs gentleman who was there, recollected well the good-ſenſe of the Pope, on the power of contraſt and the doctrine of final cauſes; but the eloquence of Pope was unknown to him---for he quoted not the fine verſes themſelves, but the tranſlation of De Cronſaz, in flat, cold, proſe.

At the bottom of the plantation, were a few young thriving oaks---clinging together, and precariouſly holding up a crumbling ſoil. The impreſſion was very delicate. For it aſſociated with the idea of a riſing family, that could ſuſtain their falling ſtock---the ground, from which they grew!

Aix la Chapelle may now be entered without any neceſſity of leaving your chaiſe; or, probability, of its being broke to pieces, and ſo leaving you. Formerly, indeed till laſt year, the road, for ever dirty, crept in a bottom between

two

two high perpendicular banks—and it was so narrow (not seven feet wide) that carriages could neither turn nor pass. The horn, therefore, (necessary also on other roads of Germany) was kept constantly at work by one postillion, to prevent meeting with another!

Now, parallel to that road, but on the high ground above it, another road is made—as wide as Knightsbridge at Hydepark-corner—and dry throughout as any road may be that has convexity and air. Different princes have been talking of this almost from the time of Charlemagne. The army of the French Republic did it! on their march! in a couple of days, though dark and short as in December! and though the work was a league long—though the road stuff was to be fetched from some distance—though they had a wood to clear—to *level hollows*—to fill them up with facines!

A clever partizan of the popular politics, giving this a dexterous turn with a strong hand, made us the more observe this—" they *filled the hollows*," said he, " but the hill,
" as here, wherever sightly and wholesome, was not lower-
" ed an inch!—As the late Duc de Penthievre, &c. &c.
" each honest harmless man, never lost a shilling of his
" estate; but only the weeds and vermin on it—(he meant
" the game) feudal usurpations, the tyrannical impositions!
" —the tenants were his; but they ceased to be his slaves!
" —They had their rents to pay, as before—but no more
" corveès, lots-et-ventes, droits de chasse, droits de change,
" tous les droits de diable!"

The French certainly did this good work. And good works, whatever they may be, are, as certainly, seldom to be done in vain. For, if their new road was a point to them in their rash advance to the Roer—it was of ten times the value, when they were forced to retreat!

God forbid that any man should be suspected of exulting in the successes of despotism. Trash and iniquity, like that,
must

muſt be openly ſoon, as it is tacitly now, in juſt abhorrence and diſdain, wherever men are men, with hearts in their boſom, and an atom of any thing like wit and judgement in their head.

And God forbid, too, that, at exceſſes from the oppoſite ſource, the averſion ſhould not be equal!—Nullo diſcrimine. No matter from whence it comes, Rapine and ravage ſhould be reſiſted by all. The French had no authority, from rectitude, to inveſt Aix—becauſe, unlike Piedmont, Flanders, and Liege—at Aix the people did not wiſh it.—And becauſe that wiſh not expreſſed, as through ſome other countries undeniably it had been expreſſed, the French attempt ſunk into the deep enormity of an invaſion! and therefore, unequivocally, it was abominable; upon every principle of reſponſibility to God and to man!

Accordingly, when the people at Aix relieved their town, I felt, as every independent mind ſhould feel when in joy, at hearing that there is relief from the oppreſſor.

And the people there, as they may have every where if they will, had the honeſt well-won ſatisfaction of thus relieving and righting themſelves altogether! For thus the peaſants took up arms! or rather, they made head againſt the French—for many of them had no other weapons but ſticks and ſtones! and with theſe, and theſe only, they encountered the troops, even ſuch troops as the French!—They received the firſt fire—and then ruſhing on, in a maſs, overpowered the French before they could fire again!—taking two pieces of canon! and driving all the troops before them out of the town!—In the ſame manner, on the ſame principles, and with the ſame ſucceſs, as the Marſeillois, ſeized the two canons in the Carouſel court of the Louvre, againſt the laſt active conſpiracy of the Swiſs troops, with the army of minions who were within!—in the ſame manner as the tactic-mongers, the moſt hackneyed in the trade, have been, at once, driven from the field, by men—

ariſing

arising from the less shewy, but the more honest arts of making clay-moulds, and minced pies!—By men, however, with the unconquerable will, on Nature's sole advantage-ground, and raised, as by a voice from Heaven, to arm in self-defence! instinctively to combat for liberty and for life!

This success of the popular spirit at Aix—when the town was rid of its invaders, was on March 2, 1793—the day after the defeat of Valence at Aldenhoven, the first defeat of the French.—The women of Aix have behaved with as much fine decision as the men—for when different despots have tried to entrap a corps of recruits from thence, the perpetration of the mischief has beeen stopped by the sense and spirit of the women.—" Why," said one of them to a foolish fellow who seemed desperate for a cockade, " Why,
" what would you cease to be a man?---are you tired of
" having a house over your head—a dinner upon your
" table—with a wife and family, and friends, to put you
" in good humour, and help your appetite to eat it? Go
" and be a vagabond and a slave—and be knocked on the
" head as soon as you can!—for your destiny can doom
" you to nothing but a short allowance of rye-bread, and
" a bit of a blue rag upon your back, and five sols a day
" in your pocket."

The foe of mankind could get no such abettors from Aix! But at Aix, as in most other places, he contrives not absolutely to lose his market altogether.—His trade is a pretty brisk one!—and with the fore-hand of the fox, he continually, perhaps, has got not less than the most enormous share of the lion.

They are a company who are imped with him. Four of whom are oftensible, at the card tables every night, in winter and summer, as bankers or dealers!

The games are rouge and noir, trente-un, and birabis—they have no games but what are adapted to all capacities, not of skill, but of chance.—Hazard, with great gravity, is forbid.—The time of the play is till midnight; the two last hours, a half-crown may be staked; but till ten o'clock nothing lower than a crown can shew his head.—At any time, whether of the gros jeu, or the petit-pont, there is no limitation upwards—you may be ruined as fast as you please—you may stake what you will—the bankers are expected to cover it.

Formerly there used to be very deep play, both at Aix, and at Spa. But since the holy war (indeed thence alone probably called holy) the gamesters have been, in all senses, shallow.—The few times that we happened to be looking on, a few louis-d'or, never more than fifty from one player, could be seen.—And generally, at every deal, more silver than gold.—And the coin, of both sorts, was all French.—The resort formerly, too, used to be very different from what it is at present—and the records of the rooms, sti'l vaunt the princes who have been there—as in some stables of Spain, they regularly commemorate each most egregious ass they may have had come from Castile!—Among these, the princes to wit, there have been not only the common figures of courts, the Navarres and the Valois, your grand-dukes, and your infantas, but those rivals in romance, the King of Sweden and the Czar!—The inscription touching the latter is as follows, at Spa.*

Petrus Primus, dei gratia, Russorum imperator, pius, Felix, invictus, apud suos militaris disciplinæ restitutor, scientiarum omnium, artiumque protosator—validissimâ, bellicarum navium, proprio marte constructa classe—auctis, ultra finem exircitibus suis! Ditionibus tam avitis, quam bello partis, inter ipsas bellonæ flammas in tuto positis—ad exteras se convertet, variarumque, per Europam, gentium lustratis moribus per Galliam ad Namureum atque leodium, has ad Spadanas aquas, tanquam ad salutis portum pervenit—salaberrimisque præsertim Geronsterici fontis feliciter potis, pristino
robori,

robori, optatæque incolumitati reſtitutus fuit anno 1717— du 22 Julii, reviſis dein Batavis, avitumque ad imperium reverſus, æternum hocce gratitudinis monumentum hic apponi præcepit—anno 1718.

At that time the Geronſtere ſpring, about a mile out of the town, had more vogue than the Pouxhon ſpring—indeed was taken as the beſt.—There is a trade ſtill for the waters of Aix and Spa; but it is, and probably will be, gradually leſs and leſs.—For what are the waters without the change of air, the change of ſcene, and the refreſhing gaiety of the jaunt?—Whatever they are, it is obvious they may be had wherever chymiſtry can be had, with fixed air and foſſil ſalt, with ſulphur and ſteel. The Engliſh and the French uſed to be the chief buyers of this folly—but if ever there ſhould be a peace again, and any body have more money than they know what to do with, they had better give it to encourage firſt-rate uſeful parts in their own country, to ſuch men as Pearſon and Black, Lavoiſier and Fourcroi, than mock expectation with bottled vapidity from the waters of Weſtphalia—febres diſcutere calculorumque vitia, &c. is the praiſe of Pliny, and therefore enough to paſs, well diluted, through the puffs, to the end of the world, of the lodging-houſes and the dippers at the wells—but who has ever found them ague-proof—or, what would be a more ſignal bleſſing, deed, a ſolvent for the ſtone?

Their power as a diſcutient, can be only over gold, and over gloom—for it is hard indeed, if in the fuſion of ſo much money as ſuch a journey will coſt, ſome quantity of bad ſpirits will not fume away.---Curioſity, and the love of change, both natural emotions, are no doubt inſtructively occupied on foreign travel, when their objects are becomingly, the mind and the manners of men—but apart from theſe, whether right or wrong, there is nothing at Aix or at Spa, that an Engliſhman cannot have better, dry-ſhod, without ſtirring from home.—Bath has no competitor in Europe, for the combined captivations of town and country—and for mere fcenery, it is not Germany, at leaft in this part of it, which can be mentioned, with the more exquifite perfections of nature, on the Devonfhire rivers, if not upon the Hampfhire coaft, upon the Severn and the Taaffe, the Wye and the Dee!

Vos patriam fugituis—vos, dulcia linguitus arve.

Of the martyrs to diffipation, that is the gaming-table only, at Aix, too probable no bad little book might be made.—But, as the artift faid to the prince, Heaven forbid that we fhould know thefe things as well as thofe who are doomed to live by 'em!

The French fugitive nobleffe are now the chief fupport of the place.—Of courfe, any traveller may go in boots; and fome, they faid, were there in linen, which was the colour of them!—And to ingratiate with thefe gentlemen, in the anti-room adjoining the faloon, there are frugal luxuries as they are wonted to defire, of tarts and fmall-beer, of Dutch cheefe and gin, ennobled with a little fugar, as liqueurs!

Of two among thefe wretched beings, the gaming-table-wreck we faw—one of them at the table put fifty louis d'or in his bafket!—at the firft deal of rouge & noir he put down twenty-five! and he loft!—at the fecond deal his ftake was fifteen. The deal went round, and he loft again!—at the third, he rifked at once the remaining ten louis d'ors! But—while the betts were collecting, and the cards fhuffled, he feemed to recollect himfelf—he felt in his pockets—firft one, and then the other—and with a quick fhort action of his left-arm, pulling out two great French crowns and a little one, he looked at them on both fides, and then, after a fhort paufe, defperately ftaked them alfo!

The fellow who kept the table had covered the ten louis d'or—and now, he anfwered alfo, to the laft forlorn hope

of

of the two great crowns and the little one! It was, for all the world, like the refponfe of echo on defpair.

An accident prolonged the deal—and, in that moment, it was impoffible not to think of a fimilar fatality in poor Goldfmith! who looking over a whift table, and, feeling in his pockets as if to count all the little money he had there, leifurely offered a bett " of five pounds feventeen and fixpence upon the odd trick."

At length, however, the deal came—and at the ninth card, it was determined. The laft ten louis, the two great crowns, and the little one went, where their fore-runners had gone before! The poor fellow, who was twirling his bafket, inftantly dafhed it down! He ftarted from his feat, and forcing through the circle, where he overturned two chairs in the way, he literally tore his hair!—and with horrid blafphemies, burfting through the folding doors in the middle of the room, he departed, and we never faw him more.

Another, who was alfo an emigrant, and had feen better days, had arrived at Aix, in the utmoft need—pennylefs— without hope, but in a friend. His friend did not fail. But his friend's circumftances did. Poor himfelf, in every thing but fpirit, he could not, as he wifhed, relieve the poverty of others. He could, with the utmoft effort of privation, part only with a few crowns.

With thefe, the new ftranger entered the great room at Aix—and getting upon one of the rufh bottom chairs in the outer circle at the table, and making a long arm, he toffed two crowns upon the board. Winning that, he doubled the ftake, and won that too. So he went on, encreafing at each deal; till, actually getting fifty louis, he was fo daring as to venture them!—His venture, yet more wonderful, profpered, and he got one hundred louis d'or in one evening.

He had the wit to cut a winner—after opening the laft

last rouleau to see that there might be no mistake, he let all the money glide gradually over one another into his pocket!

With many a bout
Of linked sweetness long drawn out!

He buttoned up, hurried by the centinels down the great stairs, and went with impatience, not unamiable, to tell the glad tidings to his friend. And though gone to bed, he knocked him up!—They talked the thing over, as may be thought, with sufficient energy, rapidity, and glee. Till at length, sobering into purposes more composed, they rationally looked forward, and reckoned on the hundred pieces of gold as one reserve and sure refuge sufficient, certainly in Germany, to make a man, if that man is a Frenchman, impregnable against want for two or three long years! He made a solemn resolution, if not a vow, never to game again.

To have made all sure, he should have left the town, but, as the devil ordained, he did not. He went next night to the redoute, but with no other purpose, but to take some little refreshment, to talk away an hour, and return.

Insensibly, however, he sauntered by the table of rouge & noir—till, looking on, he became giddy, and fell in! Fortune failed him! And he followed her till he was fleeced of all that he had won!—We actually saw him borrow a livre or two, to pay for his petty refreshments in the rooms!

Indeed, of all the emigrants who were here, we could hear no instance of any endeavours that were cheering! No activity in the pursuit of skill, no labourious industry in any study that might sustain them. One of them told us he had tried to apply himself to printing, but stooping for an hour or two in the day over the types, had made his eyes ach—and the ink, from the press ball, had, he feared, indelibly discoloured two or three fingers of his right hand. Another we found, quoting some prince for an example, with talents to be a mechanic, and had given his mind to

turning

turning—and indeed he had given five louis d'or too!—
But, ferre recufent, his arms after attempting it a week,
were too tired to proceed—he forfeited his money, and
would not practice any more!

In fuch a number of fugitives, and fome few of them, no
doubt, in the honourable predicament of fuffering for opinion, there muft be men of merit, with mafculine fpirit,
with plaftic powers, with mental refources that can never
fail. With two of thefe I have familar intercourfe. They
are virtuoufly and ufefully occupied in teaching languages—
and they know, I hope, I prize them, as all men muft prize
manners, intelligence, fortitude, and fkill. The one was a
Vicaire-general in the north-weft of France, the other a
Procureur des Communes.

There is a third, of whom I have been afcertained, and
of courfe muft wifh to know, who has learnt gardening
fince he has been in England, and now is in a nurfery earning ten fhillings a week! which he wifely and honourably
prefers to an eleemofynary fupport, very manfully offered
him by a farmer of a fuperior nature in Norfolk. This
gentleman, who, capable of fuch high action, cannot in any
circumftances be called unfortunate, is to have the firft
fmall farm from Mr. C. of Norfolk. And for the fake of
both, every one muft wifh it to be foon!

Yet, what are all thefe to the more marked viciffitudes,
to the more fignal merit in furmounting them, of another
foreign gentleman, whom, after long trial, I rejoice to call
my friend. He was not of France, but of a country which
is better in fky and foil, and in all other influences, perhaps,
but what is the life of all, the want of defpotifm being ex-
tirpated.

Life had opened on him with all the benefits of birth,
that is thought lucky. "His family were good people—he
had hereditary wealth—he was bred a fcholar---accident
had flung him into fair commerce---and nature's difpofi-
tions

tions had organifed him to be a gentleman. He was bleffed with a wife, of kindred merit; and he was, as early as he could be, a father. He underftood life too, and feemed formed to make it happy---and farther, his eftablifhments in town and country, in his hofpitalities, and in each act of neighbourhood, of order, &c. there was that fine tafte predominating throughout, which, as far as it goes, implies a blefling of radical perfection, in the firft vital principles of humanity, fenfibility of heart.

From all that was thus afcendant, he was caft down! and bereft of all! All of which, being extraneous and feparable from himfelf, he could be bereaved! On' an action in itfelf indifferent, he had a conteft with government—and not able to cope with unlimited guilt, inftigating unlimited power, on the alternative of menaced evils, exile, rather than imprifonment, was what he chofe to take. As he fled out of one door, the foldiery, 'fent to feize him, entered at the other. And thus was he torn at once from every thing precious in life! but a mind that had refources and an uncondemning heart!

In the firft delirious fpafms of anguifh and alarm, he threw himfelf about Europe, almoft from one end of it to the other! till checked by the fpent force of the little fortune he had left, he quieted, and came to himfelf. It was obvious he muft do fomething, and that it muft be done quickly.

Luckily, at the time, he happened to be near Geneva, where man afpires to deferve the free bleflings he enjoys —where ingenious labour is in every hand—where alone fcience and manners make the ftreets, prolong each good impreffion of the fchools.

There, in one of the unrivalled little towns, on the border of the lake oppofite Savoy, my friend, a wanderer no more, joined himfelf to an enlightened artizan—and, foon, with unceafing ftudy, he learnt to be a watch-maker.

With

With this acquirement, and with the French language, which he had maftered at the fame time, he thought himfelf able to ftruggle up after fortune, though the following her might lead him as far as London.

To London he came, and there I firft knew him. Subfifting by his labours in languages, certainly with oftenfible repute, but, no doubt, with latent melancholy, and arduous felf denial.

After a few months thus virtuoufly and ufefully employed, we were able to obtain for him a lefs irkfome eftablifhment at Paris. And there in his leifure from a literary purfuit, he bent the whole force of his mind to anatomy. And with fuch fingular zeal and fuccefs, that in lefs than three winters, he actually earned by it four thoufand livres a year! His labours in literature at the fame time continuing.

Led by one or other of thefe purfuits, he ran over a very wide range of the moft active life. And the politics of the revolution flaming on all fides, he kindled too, and became a politician!

Here, as elfewhere, he was equally prompt, intenfe, and indefatigable. He ftood forward well, on more than one occafion! And his talents, as ever happens through the thick and magnifying medium of party, were feen double.

The laft time I was at Paris, in the memorable July of 1792, he furprifed us at our hotel, in a drefs that had more parade than ufual—and a fingularity or two, like the petty devices of fome uniform. I afterwards found that it was fo. That he been that morning fent for by the laft wretched Louis! who wanting aid, that might give him capacity and truth, literally offered him a place of minifter! Decling that, Louis made another offer, which was pecuniary, of fome value, with no office attached, and with no refponfibility whatever! That too my friend had the magnanimity to refufe!

In

In the well known wonders, which happened after the following tenth of Auguſt, my friend was thus involved; and he moſt periloufly efcaped with his life! As he ſtood in one of the St. Honoré ſhops, with a broken pane of glaſs in the window, he heard his name mentioned with a menace! and from thence, providentially, he never went to his own houſe more! In the middle of that night, ſome perſons broke into his bed room, and not finding him there, they burnt the houſe.

They followed after him through all his uſual haunts; but again and again in vain. For he had the wit to avoid all theſe, and to betake himſelf to a houſe where, literally, he had never been but once before, and then upon a little commiſſion for me! and where the politics were directly in oppoſition to his own!

The gentleman of the houſe was a member of the Jacobin Club; and but rationally no further zealous for thoſe politics, than as they might begin in general good will, and end in general good!

That, and that alone, ſeemed the glorious perſonal impulſe of my democratic friend, when he was thus accoſted by my friend the ariſtocrat—without more ado his houſe, his heart, were open to receive him. He ſent his ſervants out of the way—and then ſecreted him in an apartment nearly joining to his own. And after nineteen days of never ending care of tenderneſs, the moſt inventive, and all attendance ſolely by himſelf, he contrived, by a ſtratagem not a little formidable, to get a paſſe-port, and to remove my diſtreſſed friend out of Paris! Nay, not ſtopping there, he drove him in his own cabriolet to Rouen, and there again he dextrouſly prevailed on the municipality to grant to his fellow traveller, as to an Engliſh gentleman, a paſſe-port for England.

At Rouen my two friends parted, both, as every body will conceive, with emotions of the higheſt order! one delivered

livered from death! the other with yet finer tranfport, exulting as the deliverer!

Where the laft of the two, the democrat, may be, I muft fay with forrow, I know not. I could have wifhed, as for an object moft exalting, to have met him here! It feems, not eafily poffible to wifh for more, than to meet him hereafter!

His name fhall not be loft, as was the kindred virtue of the Scottifh peafant, who faved Charles Stuart.

As for my other friend, he who fled to England, he arrived at my houfe, fine re & fine fpe, deftitute of every thing but his mental powers, and with looks that at once vouched for the trials he had paffed!

No longer in difmay and danger, a little time ferved to reftore his wafted health. His fpirits and powers rallied undiminifhed—he turned his back on politics, and commerce he determined fhould be his object again. On the mere unrefponfible word of another zealous gentleman and myfelf, two merchants in the city of London, with as much virtue as policy, generoufly advanced what money he wanted! And thus enabled, in lefs than two months, he embarked, freighted with no fmall capital, for ———.

There he fettled, and with fucceffes fo proportioned to his great fidelity and fkill, that he has already eftablifhed a mercantile character, and indeed a mercantile houfe, in a town, one of the moft opulent in Europe!

Such are the things to fhame, if any thing can fhame, the floth and ignorance of the fhabby beggars that have been fuffered to difgrace active life!—while emafculated vermin have been held forth as if they had been pattern men— and, apart from the plunder of almoft every one but them, who fhould have given the moft, the popular impofition has been aided by falfe pity—and the victims of fpeculation being held forth as the martyrs of faith! Such were the

Y fuggeftions

suggestions the low company, at the gaming table, excited in the rooms at Aix.

The profit from this mischief is computed at no less than 120,000 florins, per annum. Of which 15,000 florins, for a licence, are paid by the fellows who keep the bank! At Aix, this revenue, for permission to do evil, goes to the town; at Spa, the Bishop of Liege lays his hand upon it.

Aix, besides this, has a little other trade in woollen cloth, coals, steel works, particularly needles, thread lace. Their cloth is in good repute; they work it up well, and with a good deal of Spanish wool; some of the best has been sold for 3l. sterling the yard. A considerable manufacture is at Vervier, between Aix and Spa—M. M. Simony and Sauvage are the makers.

Of two and thirty canons and other dignitaries, the Pope and the Emperor are the makers. The patronage is six months to each, except when the University of Louvaine, in alternate years, collates during January and May. By the Concordat (Germanique) the Emperor names to the first prebend.

If the canon was a creature at all useful, there is one regulation, as to residence, which would be exemplary. His residence must be, through one entire uninterrupted year, before he can be permitted to receive any emolument from the sinecure—and if he should enter the choir once, after the church service be began, what is past of his probation is undone, and he must begin his residence again. This is good. But at an English chapel, Lincoln's Inn, there is a decorum better still—for there no interloper, irreverently past his time, can disturb the office. There, as soon as it begins, the aisles are closed, and beyond the outer area at the bottom, there is no entrance for any body.

Each existing Emperor has one of these canonries, and swears allegiance to the establishment to defend the rights and

and perfons of the place. In general the Emperor, as a canon, is reprefented by two chaplains, in each hard labour of the office, receiving the revenue and chaunting the maffes. Charles the Fifth, however, was there himfelf, affifting at the cannonient and humming them himfelf.

Aix-la-Chapelle is a town of high antiquity, the Aquægrani of Tacitus and Cæfar. The prefent French name is from Charlemagne's chapel. The town hall is faid to have been his palace. They will fhew you too, if you have nothing better to think of, the marble chair of Charles V. when the emperor ufed to be crowned at Aix by the Archbifhop of Cologne, as he is now at Frankfort by the Archbifhop of Mayence. And they would fhew you Charlemagne's fine library, if they could.—But though better than his own collection at Worms, the books at Aix, were according to his death-bed order, immediately fold, and the money given to the poor. It is further made hiftorically interefting by our two treaties, 1668 and 1748; and by men labouring with more capacity and ufe, when Luther and Calvin, near a hundred years before, (1574) chaced away popery, fubftituting fomething better in its place.

The magiftracy of Aix are two Bourg-mafters—one named by the bourgeois, the other by the nobles. Thefe, with a Mayor, a Senate of eighteen, a Council of 126, with other officers, an Ecclefiaftical Court of twenty, and I know not how many more, receivers, to the tune of two and thirty, twenty-two convents for men and women, may feem to make up a mafs of government, in all confcience enough for a little allotment of 20,000 acres—where, in eighteen villages, and at the extravagant calculation of eight perfons and a half to a houfe, the population has never been carried to more than 25,000! There are in all above fifty lawyers of every fort—and when they have contrived to get all they can out of a client, they difpatch him to Wetzlaer. There is the laft refuge of the unfortunate in the fhape of a final appeal.

Moreover in all caufes ecclefiaftical as well as civil, fupreme, the people are pleafed to have the Elector Palatine, as Duke of Juliers, to take care of the one, and the Bifhop of Liege to take care of the other! So what can Saint Barnard mean, when he takes the liberty to fay of Aix-la-Chapelle, " That it is a town which may be good for the " body, but it muft be bad for the mind!" The penal laws are imprifonment for debt—labour for fmall offences— and for great offences, death by decapitation.—The debtor is fuftained at two-pence Englifh a day by the creditor.— Torture upon fufpicion, is ftill perpetrated, and, yet more wonderful, the people bear it.

As far as the good or evil of the body may be influenced by phyficians at Aix and Spa—the account ftands thus— they have ten pound for the feafon, or for a fingle vifit two or three efcalins. One of them, Hanfter, fpeaks tolerable Englifh—another, called Limbourg, can fpeak what he pleafes, French, Englifh, or whatever he will. At leaft, if he do not, it is the fault of his induftry, and not his parts— for he is a very lively, knowing fellow.

This is the only infcription to be found—at St. Mary's.

Sub hoc conditorio
Situm eft corpus
Caroli,
Magni & orthodoxi imperatoris,
Qui
Regnum francorum notabiliter ampleficavit
Et
Per annos 46,
Feliciter
Rexit.

The felicity of a reign cannot be too often mentioned as the teft of its truth!

FROM

FROM AIX TO JULIERS.

AFTER paſſing the town guard, of 40 or 50 marvellous proper men, and inſerting here another omitted memorandum, that the little territory of Aix is an intereſting ſcene, as an Italian poet ſays of one of his country women, at once ſparkling, neglected, and gay.—The road to Cologne is ſuch, as a clever engineer, like thoſe towards Bath and York, would delight to mend.—For nothing can want mending much more.

And this too upon principle. For, at Aix now, as at ſome of our watering places in times paſt, the ways about them, have been purpoſely kept bad, for fear of too much reſort—who, not like the puppets of Ariſtophanes, immaculate and unconſuming, might lower the manners of the place, and raiſe the price of meat.

After this the ample plains of Aldenhoven gave forth an intereſt of another nature. Fit for ſuch ſuperior beings, as Charles the ninth, or the late moſt chriſtian king's great grand-father—the Macedonian madman, and the Sweed!

At Aldenhoven, blood was ſhed like water upon every ſide! And the whole region, ſtill ſtood aghaſt at the ſcattered bones! and at entire ſkeletons of men!

At Aldenhoven, the people of the French republic, under Lanoue, and Valence, were ſold to the Germans—and not for nought!—The Germans were made to pay pretty dear for them!—The diſcreet, exalted gentleman, who commanded, eſcaping unhurt!

Had diſcretion been imperſoniſied, and with an eſtimate of character, according to the rule of Horace, what words could poſſibly be equal to its deſerts?—what words, but thoſe which came from him, like a colliquative Diarrhœa,—when he tried to make, a teſt of action, from the prince's raiſe!

As

As if virtue could ſtand by and bow !—And manhood—moody manhood, had nought to ſay, lofty as he may look !—Tho' truth and ſpirit bid him on !—Tho' wit and liberty would make him venture !—Though heaven has bleſt him with a form erect !—and placed before him, palms pluck'd from Paradiſe——if he is, but ever upright, and ready to reach them !

Horace, however, tho' "himſelf had been a ſoldier," never ſaw any thing like Aldenhoven,—nor any other horror in battle !

His ſhield left behind, he went upon court ! Where, diſcreetly, turning his back upon death and ruin, he could know nothing of war, but the fortune of thoſe who baſk upon the parade of it—patronage and promotions, contracts and commiſſions !——Where, beſides theſe and other winning adjuncts, in the court-dreſſes of the object, he could ſee no more of that, than of nature !——Where Bellona, in the laviſh graces, in the prodigality of pleaſing, peculiar to himſelf ; contrived, ſomehow or other : to find favours for almoſt all !

> Rain'd influence—— to judge the price
> Of wit and arms ; while both contend
> To win her ſmiles——whom all commend !

So much for Horace and Aldenhoven, the fame of the court of Rome, and the bleſſings of war, as there and then by law eſtabliſhed !

Juliers, the town ſo called, ſucceeds immediately to Aldenhoven.—To the river Roer is a ſort of ſelvage, or ſalvage (as Skinner's etymology would certainly have it here) —For all the town knows it was the river only, that happened to ſave it ! And with it the only ſtrong, fortified hold, through the whole electorate of Cologne and Treves, between Juliers and Coblentz !—The French under Lanoue had a piquet of horſe and foot at the bridge over the Roer, on the ſouth-weſt ſide of it.

Juliers

Juliers, in its walls and works, looks well-conditioned and impofing, and feems throughout, like the Venus at Duffeldorff, to be in perfect good keeping.—The works are modern. But the place as a pofition is very ancient; as a Roman pofition, it appears in the itinerary of Antonine.

It appears alfo in the records of a yet better progrefs;—in that bright, afcending path of liberty and truth, when the people of the Netherlands difcharged and difcomfited their abominable prince.—Then, after the twelve years truce, following the laft fhabby failures of the tyrant, even in his own bay at Gibraltar.—The petty fortrefs of Juliers was a pretence for hoftilities!—The Archduke Leopold was fent by the Emperor to feize it, and fo to fecure fucceffion to the Dutchy.

He was, however, diflodged by the Dutch—And thus the forces of the Emperor, as well as Spain, forced to yield, to the good commanding genius of the people.—A people, fmall before, and of no reputation, yet proved to be invincible, when, according to heavens inftincts daring, they broke the yoke, and made themfelves free from the oppreffor!

By the treaty of Munfter, (Art. 88.) Juliers, (ftating both town and citadel) was ceded to Bavaria, whofe family had it from the tenth century; and the Elector's troops, 300 of them, held the place, when we faw it.

Such have been the viciffitudes, and fuch is the political exiftence of Juliers.—The Civil controul of the place is in a Bourg-mafter and eight Echevins, (inferior but co-operating magiftrates) chofen by the people. On ecclefiaftical jurifdiction, the Elector divides the patronage of all livings with the King of Pruffia, and the Elector of Cologne.—The value of church livings in the dutchy, is at the higheft 3000, at the loweft 300 florins.

The town of Juliers is, very properly, not a prey to finecure ecclefiaftics—We heard of no fuch impofitions as mul-

tiplied

tiplied Chapters and Abbays. As the population is not quite 2300, they support no more than one parish. And what refers to good conduct in a point higher still, the communicants at the sacrament, have been more than 1200!

This, a fact obviously interesting, was told to us, by one of the clergymen in the place. --The young people, I believe, are on this article, better ordered than with us. They begin to frequent the altar at an earlier age than we do; and continue, less interruptedly, the practice so well began.---

The Dutchy of Juliers, forms with Cleves and Gueldre, the states in the electorate of Cologne.---In the circle of the dutchy are seven baillages, besides the town of Juliers, the Abbaye St. Cornelle, two baronies, and two contès, one of which is Metternich. Aix la Chapelle is locally in it too, but politically it is out---as being what is called an Imperial and free city.---The population of the dutchy is called 296,500.------And the measurement of the territory is 75 square miles.

FROM

FROM JULIERS TO COLOGNE.

THE road for some considerable distance, is through flourishing aged woods, which belong, half and half, to the Dutchy of Juliers, and to the Electorate of Cologne.--- These are followed by two or three miserable villages, where there is nothing to be seen but hay and straw, and nothing to be heard of, but another memorial of mischief---in a battle near Berghen. It was on the plain, the south east side of the village---A bloody business---for which M. Turenne has to answer.

At Kulick's-dorff (Anglicè King-street) a village and convent, two leagues from Cologne, there is a hill in the road, where the eye wanders, not undelighted, over a vast quantity of ground. Far below Duffeldorff on one side, and on the other the seven mountains beyond Bonne, to the round hills over Mayence.---In the intervening grounds, large undivided lawns, corn fields, potatoes and hops---with many trees, particularly good road-side vistos, and among them the spires, towers, and pinnacles of Cologne.---For extent, variety, and charming animation, it is among first-rate views!

And so on roads, through the whole distance, not paved, which in summer therefore are good, but in winter evil,--- with well grown vistos, but no hedges, and of course no cattle also---with few farm-houses, and consequently where the farms must be large---So, your chaise, if you have it, pay what you will to the postillion, slowly will enter Cologne.

COLOGNE.

Maxima Cognati Regina Colonia Rheni,
Hoc te etiam titulo mufa fuperba canet.
Romani ftatuunt ---habitat Germania---terra eft
Belgia, ter Felix!——nil tibi diva deaft.
Scaliger.

Cologne is not a little interefting.

In the firft place, you may have Rhine wine and Weft-phalia ham, at not more money than elfewhere you muft give for pale town-made bacon, and dead fmall beer,—with no bad bonus into the bargain, of fifh from the river, and gibier from the woods!

2dly---It was the birth place of Nero's mother, fo the reader, when he has dined, may, if he can, write about Agrippina, as well as in the fine fragment of Mr. Gray!

3d---Which would have come firft, if the dinner, at a moft excellent table d'hote had not come in before it.— The people are worth talking about---For, true to themfelves, they are full of popular politics. Their conftitution, once Republican, and in fact, ftill pretends to be fo in form. That conftitution they are labouring to reftore! To reform what is living; to regenerate what is dead!

4, 5, 6, &c.—There is an univerfity—Infcriptions—A new theatre, dedicated to the decent graces, Mufis Gratiifq; Decentibus, with never ending farces out of doors, almoft rivals to the fhew, tricks, and the mummery of Rome— And which as times go, is new and comfortable alfo, and worth all the tricks in the world—There are few if any taxes.

So

So that if the immortal flatterer of Auguſtus had been, like the wife of Claudius, born here, he muſt have eſcaped what is perpetuated by Dryden, as an aſperſion on him of hereditary taint. There being no taxes, his father could not have ſuſpiciouſly traded by a place in them, nor could the proſtitutions of genius, been imputed, to the meanneſs of birth.

The people of Cologne, are diſtinguiſhed by political preferences by allegiance to the duties of citizens, by ambition for their rights. They are equally active in both.

Their government, fundamentally like the admirable Republic of Rome, ſhould be Republican alſo. There are manifeſtly the baſe and plan of the ſame happy ſplendors; but, further, thoſe ſplendors are made to fade away. The plan is abandoned, and without order or effect, peſtilent rubbiſh is, clumſily, piled upon the baſe.

The people of Cologne are, conſtitutionally as the phraſe is, acknowledged to be free.—With legitimacy, equality, moral, civil, and political. The laws, with each privilege of them, and each penalty, are ordained to be adminiſtered to every individual alike, each franchiſe is properly the appointed appurtenance of all—Offices are elective—Every citizen is an elector, and is alſo eligible—and when elected, is bound to bear each faculty of his office, in popular conſideration, equally to all!

Moreover the town is ſo far undergraced by the corporation ſpirit!—All occupations are open---And every occupier is a citizen!

Theſe principles of political aſſociation, univerſally wiſe, becauſe juſt and beneficent to all, ſeem to have been, however, offenſive to the few at Colognne, who, by indirect aſcendancy, would uſurp over the many! And undue influence has appeared at work, to taint and wither, the repreſentative ſyſtem—to ſtifle the beſt organ expreſſive of the

popular

popular will; and thro' by a senate packed by means, equally perverse and venal with their end. Self-elected, sordid, and uncontroulable, gradually to betray each much valued privilege, each dear bought right! To restore vassalage—and with each assumption of ill-got power to replunge the people back into the fifteenth century---in every thing but the ignorance of political intrigue, and the refined slavery of those doomed, sottishly, to bear it!

The ecclesiastics too, proportionably almost as multitudinous as at Rome, are active abettors of all such abuses; and call in superstition to connive at the impositions of fraud; while the retainers of the elector have gone a shorter way to work, and with a stronger arm—Attempting to invade rights incontestible by nature, policy, and time.

But the people of Cologne have hitherto successfully been able to cope with all. Tam marte, quam mercurio, force repelled by force; detection counteracted intrigue; ridicule routed folly. When unbiassed suffrages and purchased immunities were litigiously called in question, they were ready with a sufficient answer, though they went with it to Wetzlaer, where, in the historians maxim upon the summum jus, there is consummate injury in consummate law! When lately the ministers of the Prince called out his troops to enforce an arbitrary toll, upon the Rhine, the people also immediately beat to arms—and mounting their cannon on the walls, each man stood literally with the match in his hand—ready, if the Prince's people had crossed the river from Dreutz, thus to have encountered him with the salute they thought due!

In the public objects before men's mind, what can give more just animating rapture than the contemplation of a people, free and enlightened, and pure—temperate while they enjoy blessings—strenuous to defend them!

So

So much for the bourgeoisie of Cologne—as for the rest of the people, the clergy and the elector, they are as follow:

The Clergy are:

11 Chapters	40 in each,	440
19 Parishes	10 ditto,	190
In 19 Convents for men	30 ditto,	570
In 39 Ditto, for women	20 ditto,	780
	Total	1980

There are 49 chapels besides these! with nearly double the number of ecclesiastics!

These, with all other ecclesiastics, without any public or fixed functions, who live by masses, the orders attendant on the sick, the quæ solæ or initiating devout, &c. must be numbered at 2500!

For the chief chapters, a pedigree (four descents, two on each side) must be produced, as in the chapter at Liege—of course with the same allowances as in the memorable case there specified of the Cardinal Granville. The number of the canons is 60—of them, 24 have the right to chuse the arch-bishop, and to be chosen.

The value of church preferments is thus—

The Grand Doyen—600l. sterling—by beneficial accidents, like a lapse or fine in England---encreased a fourth more.

The Canonries—from 200 and 300l. down to 30l. sterling.

More than one canonry has been held by one ecclesiastic ---but that obvious abuse---plurality in church livings, with cure of souls, is not known.

The livings—are from 500 florins to 300.

Of the aristocracy the larger part are in the church. Those who are officially ennobled (with such frippery as the gold key at the coat pocket, from being chamberlain to some of the petty princes in Germany), are contemptible absurdities, known here less than in most other towns. The more wealthy capitalifts now are ranked with the nobleffe. For the heralds, like drill ferjeants in diftrefs for recruits, are content to take pedigrees, like men, under the ftandard!

The Arch-bifhop of Cologne, receives an oath of fidelity from the towns people, as protector, not fovereign, of the city. He is elected by the chapter, and to be elegible he muft exhibit admitted proofs of birth and pedigree in the firft order of nobility. The prefent gentleman is of the houfe of Auftria, the Arch-duke Maximilian.

As elector, he has fovereign power through the electorate, to enact laws and to execute them—to raife taxes—to make alliances, peace, and war---to coin---to have a military eftablifhment---to grant difpenfations, licences, pardons, immunities, and all church livings—life and death are in his hands —and, with the ordinances of religion, which he regulates at will, the inhabitants of the diftrict may feel his opinion beyond the grave!

The Dutchy of Weftphalia, the Domain of Comte Necklinghaufen, and the Bifhopric of Munfter, are held under a complex commendams by the arch-bifhop. The revenues of the Cologne Electorate, more than half of which come from Munfter, are 206,000 fterling pounds. They are the produce of toll duties on all freight paffing up or down the Rhine---and in certain local impofitions chiefly, ftated as amounting to 30,000 a year. Thofe impofitions are in Munfter chiefly!—The taille on land is varying as the agriculture may be vineyard or tillage. In the great difproportion of two to the laft, and nine to the former. A variety in part not wholly improper, to give a virtual premium to the plough, and to mark, what Rouffeau and Hume well obferve, the final preference corn muft have over wine, the neceffary over the luxury, in each of thofe trying emergencies, which fooner or later may happen to all.

The application of the revenue is, as might be expected, chiefly into the pocket of the prince---to pay the intereft

of

of the debt, and for other objects of ufe, as in literary and fcientific eftablifhments—of parade, another name for influence, as in the court at Bonne, and in fome petty eftablifhments and adminiftration in Weftphalia.

The government of the town is in bourg-mafters and a fenate. The bourg-mafters are fix. Two of them are in the regency for two years, and then are fucceeded by another two.

They are chofen by the people, and, to fay the truth, have been generally fuch as juftify the choice, faithful to their truft, honeftly adminiftering to the wants and wifhes of the people who employ them. We could not hear any inftance of intrigue and perfidy---nor, in the records of that town, is there any memorial of mean adventurers ftealing into the office, and then with more mifchievous corruption felling what they had ftolen. It was not in Cologne that the bourg-mafter, redeemed from bankruptcy by a bribe, therefore betrayed the town, and yoked it to the then minifter, to help him through his dirty work.

The bourg-mafter, when in his functions, is preceded by the fafces, as in old Rome, and wears a grave robe of purple and black.

A fenate, as it is called, fit with the bourg-mafters, and form a criminal tribunal and a court of police. They hear and determine in all cafes which they try: but the fentence is referved to a fuperior council, where it is fubmitted to the elector.

The fenate are 49. Of them 42 are chofen by the people. But feven, effacing each veftige of what is right, truth, freedom, common decency, and common fenfe, feven come in felf elected! And what is more wonderfully difgufting, the people fuffer them to take their feats!

Over thefe the people ftill retain, moft properly, a power inquifitorial and controuling. They form into twenty-two tribes or wards, in which the drapers are the firft; mem-

bers

bers delegated from each conſtitute a convention or council, who ſit every three months to audit accounts, to review the proceedings of the ſenate, to approve or to condemn them. Theſe deputies from the tribes or wards are choſen every year, ſo that their independence and purity are not at all endangered by time. This, a republican form, the people of Cologne cheriſh as the beſt part of their conſtitution; it is the moſt ancient alſo. As the beſt critic pronounces on the popular part of the Engliſh ſyſtem, "Vetuſtiſſima, ſi "antiquitatem ſpectes—ſi juriſdictionem, capaciſſima—Si " dignitatem, honoratiſſima eſt."

Eccleſiaſtical cauſes of the town are cognizable by a tribunal which the elector names, with the fiſcal and official are the prevot and ten eſchevins, who form the court; they muſt be natives of the town, and well circumſtanced in life, as we ſhould ſay, eſquires. Over ſeven baillages, beſides the town, they exerciſe in the elector's name a juriſdiction both civil and criminal.

The puniſhment of death is, with the ſound policy of humanity, rare. The warrant for any execution muſt be ſigned by the elector. Where labour is the puniſhment of the guilty, they beat ſtone (tarras) to powder for the builders. The carcan, or pillory, is often uſed. At Bonne it is near the gallows, a piece of maſonry forty feet ſquare, up ſix ſtone ſteps. At the will of the judge a debtor may be arreſted; but not, if he is inſolvent. This optional power in the judge ſeems dangerous, as opening a wide door for abuſes, but we did not hear of any abuſes entering---nor, what is better, were there any priſoners entering either.

The appellant juriſdiction is in the Council of Reviſion at Bonne. The proceſs coſts the appellant four or five thouſand livres. Thus Cologne eſcapes the delays and coſts of the Court at Wetzlaer. It appears wonderful proſtrations that every other town in Germany ſhould not ſimilarly aſſert itſelf, and chuſe their proper judges.

The

The police of the town, the town should be instructed to amend. It is defective both to the living and the dead. The first are starved by whole multitudes into beggars, through the ecclesiastical abuses---by the multitude of priests and the errors of their church, in regard to sloth, and a life they inculcate, at the best, speculative over-much.--- And as to the latter, when apparently dead from drowning, a mischance common on the Rhine, there is a neglect of all the means, in stimulants and warmth, to revive suspended animation. They bury also too soon, viz. on the first and second day. So that the fabulous resurrections of pretended saints, a pious fraud not uncommon in the annals of Cologne, are, though false traditions, not absolutely without use---If they ever have, as it is said they have, checked too hasty burial of persons not dead, but in a trance.

They have no laws to regulate buildings, so as to make them less liable to fire---nor when the dreadful evil comes, are there any mitigations by insurance. The nearest establishment of that kind is at Amsterdam and Antwerp--- of course our own fire offices are as fit for the business, and by a little activity they might have it---by any of our bankers, like Lockhart's, &c. who are known, and indeed respected through Europe.

The population of Cologne may give a timely lesson to any sapient state, more active for the prosperity of the new world than the old, and astonishingly labouring, by forced emigrations to multiply the inhabitants of America!

By similar ingenuity some intolerant and fanatic administrations have thinned Cologne; so that the houses mouldering, have shrunk on all sides from the town walls, and the inhabitants are not now a quarter the number that they have been! So long ago as the tenth century the houses were 10,000---and two centuries after the town furnished 30,000 men fit to bear arms! At present the whole population of the place are not many more. They have been computed

computed at 40,000. But on a late alarm when a strict numbering was made, the bourgeois were but 6000!—Reckoning renters, merchants, tradesmen, artizans, and some of the clergy.---Those living by masses and literary labours, unincluded in any convent or college!

Nor can decay, in any degree be wondered at, under the brutal impolicy which was with base submission suffered to stigmatize the tyranny of madness! Individuals and whole orders of men, whose skill and industry were the most actively useful, were thus, by the persecution of fanaticism and folly, forced to fly from the place. The Jews in the fifteenth century, and the Protestants in the seventeeth, no less than 1400 families at once were all banished—and so far manufactures and commerce were lost at Cologne, as in France after the edict of Nantes!

For the decay of trade was more than equal to the decrease of population! And though the respite of persecution has again permitted the Protestants and Jews to re-enter the town, yet they have not been able to recover the time or restore the markets which were lost. Indeed the toleration to them is very mean and bare---without the right of citizenship, without the public exercise of religion being allowed!

What business there may be, is chiefly done in Protestant houses—and of the following articles they carry outwards, the four or five first, are the least inconsiderable—hemp, salt provisions, wood, tobacco, wine, trass tufo-stone, tobacco-pipe clay, gins, millet, dried fruits, pot-ash, iron, copper, ribbands, a few stockings, and a little lace---the lace is 2 and ½ inch wide, very cheap. The manufacture employs 11,000 children.

The iron comes from the forges of Nassau—the hemp and salted provisions come from Westphalia—the wood from the Upper Rhine and the Neckar.

What foreign goods they want, they buy principally of
the

the Dutch, viz. groceries, spices, drugs for medicine and dying, paper, oil, cottons, and English lead and tin.----The sight of these upon the quay, with the names of our countrymen stamped upon each particular mass, made memory return to its first best bias, and cower over neighbourhood and home.

Cum sociis, natoque penatibus ac magnis diis.

When Capt. Cooke was surprised with the Wedgewood plate floating unbroken off Kamschatka, the excitement was more whimsically fortuitous; but the emotion was the same.

Such are the small remains of trade at Cologne. The seats in the Senate there are not, yet, ever sold.

The carriage of their trade, upon the Rhine, is circumstanced as follows---

22½ kreitzer to 45 the quintal, or 100lb.—sugar pays 45—coffee and spice 30—wine to Cologne from Mentz 12 or 14 rix-dollars, including the customs on the river.

Mentz is thirty-six leagues from Cologne. The Rhine runs powerfully from three to five miles the hour. For pulling up against stream, the horse towing costs 9 to 12 rix-dollars, and in harvest, or when forage as well as horses may be scarce, 16 to 18 crowns. There is a man to every three horses. The time in going up is from nine to eighteen days; in coming down three days, with delays at the customhouses, &c. The river is at times so swelled and rough, that trade cannot pass for twelve or fourteen days together. The swell, though but rarely, has been 20 to 30 feet. The boats carry from 1000 to 2500lb. weight.

These were the prices of some provisions, &c.

Bread	6 sols	7lb.	Brace of partridges	6 to 8 sols
Brown bread, half price.			Honey	6.
Meat	2 and 2¼ lb.		Sugar	20 to 32
Butter	6		Best tea	6 livres.
A hare	6		Coffee	22 sols.

A man servant, and to feed himself—twelve livres a month.

The keep of a house—60 to 70 florins this year. But this year is, by the war, one third dearer than usual.

A coat of silk and cotton stuff, including the taylor, thirteen florins.

English boots, a louis---half-boots, ten livres.

Taxes, ten per cent. on foreign goods.

Thirty sols on every connean of wine. There is a drawback of fifteen sols on exportation.

Labour, eight to twelve sols a day.

The interest of money 4 per cent.---Every mortgage, to be valid, must be negociated before a judge, and enregistered.

Land---to rent---two to four little crowns the arpent, near double our acre---to buy, 300 ecus to 300 livres the arpent.

Rents are paid in the produce.

Coals (from the neighbourhood of Dusseldorff) thirty sols for 136lb. weight.

Westphalia hams, ten sols.

Masters of languages, music, &c. two crowns (but whether great or little, fails to be remembered) for eighteen lessons of an hour.

House rent (also of that the memorandum is obliterated) but it is extremely moderate.

On the whole---we were told, and in such a manner that we could not disbelieve, that 100l. to 150l. sterling was ample for a moderate good family of five or six persons!

The revenue of the town of Cologne, as there is no territory out of the walls, cannot be considerable---the wine duties have been mentioned---the corn duty is 27 sols on each load of wheat and rye. These are all the taxes. For **the debt of Cologne**, uninflamed by any abomination like war,

war, is a trifle;---not more than a million of livres. In countries lightly vexed with impositions, intelligence like this, is not always with cafe to be obtained. And a very fenfible obferver, Baron L———, rather fmartly touched upon the obvious reafon, why.---" Among our neighbours " the Dutch, &c." faid he, " fuch queftions can be an-
" fwered as foon as afked; becaufe every man can fpeak,
" upon what every man muft feel fo woefully in every arti-
" cle and effort of life, in the forrieft food and raiment, in
" the ground the labourer is doomed to toil over, in the
" very window where he draws the common light and
" common air!"

The town, very properly, waftes no part of their revenue on military force; it is little more than fo many conftables in red. The town's-people are divided into quarters, officered, &c. as reputably as our train-bands. They keep the town-gates—and if they do not alfo keep themfelves, it is not their fault. For they certainly make pretty free with travellers, as they pafs into the town.

The Electorate is loaded with 6,000 men. Part of them are fupported by the chapter---part by the Dutch---to be forth-coming upon demand. In the prefent war, moft of them are demanded.---Their pay is two fols a day, and two pounds of bread!---They are cloathed every two years! Red and white are the colours of their trade.---Such are the materials, cheap as dirt all over the world, by which they metamorphofe and manufacture them into the hired heroes at Cologne!

The arts in Cologne do not particularly flourifh nor abound; Reubens was born here. The regifter of his baptifm is in St. Peter's church: and there, on taking a copy of the regifter, he gave, with his ufual magnificence, a very grand picture! the Crucifixion of Peter—painted, I believe at Antwerp, 1642.---The picture has a great deal of truth and

and fire, the carnations are exquifite, and fome of the anatomy, particularly in a contraction or two, correct and forcible. The value of the performance was, however, for a time mifunderftood; and Reubens piqued at it, is faid to have offered for it a monftrous deal of money, about 3,000l. fterling. A fum impoffible at that time; for if the painter could have been weak enough to have given the money, the parifh officers would probably have had the wit to have taken it.

In a family-houfe called Juback, Reubens is faid to have been born---and there is faid to be a fine family picture by Le Brun.—Architecture, with any pretenfion, except at the cathedral, there is none. The cathedral, as a vaft unfinifhed gothic mafs, has no competitor, but the Duomo at Milan. Conrad, the bifhop, in the thirteenth century, was wife enough to begin it---and as nobody has been fo wife as to finifh it, there is a proof, ftrong as all the intervening ages can make it, for Horace and his Nos nequiores---that men, like their houfes, grow worfe as their pedigrees grow old. A marble portal of the Maifon de Ville, was the only bit of Grecian architecture to be feen in the town---which, with all its antiquity, has found no prince in the fame humour with the emperor, who fo elegantly wifhed to leave the town ftone, which he had found brick.

Brick, plaiftered, or wood, with three to fix ftories, and a roof of tiles or flates—cornices and architraves to the doors, &c. of bafaltes---with iron bars to the windows, tin fpouts down the front, to within twelve feet from the ground---and gabel-ends to the ftreets, as Queen Caroline faid, made Old Brentford look like Germany---this is the fafhion of building the common houfes---in removing floors and propping the walls, the workmen feem as bold and fure as in London.

The collection of Baron de Hupfch (the antiquities are

the

the beſt of it) is rather better than moſt private cabinets in Europe—Comte d'Oëttingen and M. de Merle, alſo have ſome things worth ſeeing.—The Duke d'Aremberg reſides at Cologne often, and his eſtabliſhment is the beſt. Prince Charles too, has paſſed ſome time there; but he has no houſe of his own. Our countryman—Viſcount B. has been long fixed here; and with a hunting eſtabliſhment, the beſt in Weſtphalia.

THE

THE UNIVERSITY OF COLOGNE.

THIS is the moſt ancient univerſity in Germany—the daughter of Paris—the mother of Louvaine—and

Matre pulchra filia pulchrior,

ſaid Pope Urban VI. when comparing it with the parent ſtock—though what he ſaid had more eulogy than truth.

However, this Urban might ſay what he would, when he did ſo much for the place—for he granted, at a time when when popes could grant the rights, immunities, and ſome endowments there.——The eſtabliſhment was founded by the magiſtrates—or, in other words, by the people—1380 was the date.

The government of the univerſity is adminiſtered by the four moſt ancient bourg-maſters, with the grand provoſt of the cathedral and the chancellor—and the following, which is a literal copy from the college regulations of the preſent year, will ſhew all that any body can want to ſee, of the whole eſtabliſhment, diſcipline, diſtribution of time, lectures, and profeſſors.

The correſpondence and converſation of the profeſſors are almoſt entirely in the French language—the lectures are in German or in Latin.

THEOLOGIE.

M. Le Doct. Nobis—Dogmatic Divinity—from ſeven to eight in the morning.

Le R. P. and Doct. Vaſen—the Sacraments, with practical inſtructions—eight to nine o'clock.

R. P. and Doct. Curten—Moral Action—nine to ten.

Doct.

Doct. and Regent Krofch—the Divine Virtues—ten to eleven.

Doct. and Doren Marx—the New Teftament and the Acts of the Apoftles—(Traitera des Principes de la Veritable Hermeneutique)—eleven to twelve.

And occafionally alfo, at the fame hour, the fame profeffor reads, and very well, on the Paftoral Character and Office—and treats fummarily on the Application of the Church Laws at Cologne—laws, derived in part from the archbifhop, in part from the fynod.

The Regent Carrick—on the German church.

The fcope of thefe lectures is, from the 12th century to the Council of Trent, inclufively—one to two.

Doct. Schmitz—on Moral Virtue—two to three.

Licentiate Frangenheim—Moral Divinity—three to four.

L A W.

Doct. Biermann—Sur le Droit du Change—in fummer from three to four.

Doct. and Trefoncier Hillefheim—the Ecclefiaftical and Civil Hiftory of Cologne—Monday and Saturday—ten to eleven.

This profeffor having been noticed for the freedom of fome political opinions, infeparable from any fpirited good man, and inalienable from all—he now, in his introduction, is fpecific—that the liberty he enforces is literally conformable to the fpirit of law, and thofe clear definite principles which, from time to time, have even been (mirabile dictu) licenced to appear!

Doct. and Trefoucur Gyer—Inftitutions of Canon Law—eleven to twelve.

Doct. Zaaren (he is the chancellor)—practice of Canon Law—Monday and Wednefday—one to two.

Profeffor Wilmes—Criminal Law—theory and practice—in winter, four to five.

His text book is from Profeffor Bohmer.

Dean Dumont—Ecclefiaftical Law—Monday, Thurfday, and Saturday—eleven to twelve.

Thefe lectures follow Schenkl (Syntagma Juris Canonica).

Profeffor Cardauns—the Statute Law—in fummer, feven to eight.

Thefe lectures are among the moft agreeable to a mifcellaneous hearer, for they refer not only to the town and electorate of Cologne—but alfo to the contiguous interefts of Cleves and Berg, and the electorate of Treves and Mayence.

Licentiate Claffen—the Practice of Law—in Cologne—twice a week.

This too, now and then, is interefting; from hiftorical ftatements and local facts.

Profeffor Brener—on the Procefs of Law, through the German empire—Monday, Wednefday, and Friday—three to four.

This lecturer takes for his chief authorities, the printed works of Knor and Putter.

Licentiate Wunfch—the Practice of the Ecclefiaftical Court—with all their Recorded Cafes in the Confiftory—Tuefday, Thurfday, and Saturday—four to five.

Licentiate Duhmen—on the Decrees of the Council of Trent, and the Concordats of the German Nation—Tuefday, Thurfday, Friday, Saturday, in fummer—eleven.

Profeffor Nuckel—on the Feudal Law—Monday, Wednefday, Friday, in fummer—four to five.

Thefe lectures are grounded upon Bohmer—the laft edition is ufed.

Licenciate Dollefchal—Jus Germanicum Privatum—four to five.

This profeffor teaches after the printed works of Selchow.

M. Blanch-

M. Blanchard—Law of Nature and Nations—four to five. Martini's work is the text-book here.

Licentiate Bolſhoven—Hiſtory of Germany—and German Law.

On both ſubjects, the great outlines and leading principles are collected from the hiſtorical works of Putter.—In ſummer, ten o'clock—winter, three.

On practical queſtions, the profeſſor follows Bohmer.

Licentiate Duſſel—the Eccleſiaſtical Conſtitution of Cologne—(Jus Eccles, Specialiſſimum Eccles, Colonienſis)— Saturday—two to three.

M. Hanum—on Canon Law (after Schenkl)—every day but Thurſday.

Prof. Nuckel—the Pandects (after Bohmer)—nine to ten.

M. Blanchard—the Inſtitutions (after Heineccius)—eight to nine.

Licentiate Bleiſſem—Private Rights of German Princes.

Theſe lectures are amplifications upon Putter's Primæ Lineæ, Principum Germaniæ.

In civil and eccleſiaſtical law, there are private courſes alſo, by five or ſix of the laſt-mentioned profeſſors.

MEDICINE.

Doct. Paſſera—De Formulis—ten to eleven.

Profeſſor Meyer (he is the prime profeſſor)—Therapeutics—and Clinical Lectures—nine to ten.

He follows Boerhaave—and his Aphoriſms de Cognoſcendis & Curandis Morbis, are before him.

Prof. Walbraf—on Botany—in ſummer, at ſeven.—Natural Hiſtory, ten.

In Mineralogy, he follows the ſyſtem of Cronſtadt. In Botany Reuſs is the guide.—Theſe are in Latin.

Profeſſor Beſt—Anatomy—three to four—through the winter.

——————-Phyſiology—eight to nine—after Eaſter.

The Anatomical Lectures are in German—thoſe on Phyſiology, in Latin.—Haller ſupplies the authorities, &c. for the laſt—Leber, for the firſt.

Profeſſor Haas—on Accouchemens.

Plenck is held of the firſt authority for theſe.

This Profeſſor alſo gives a few leſſons on that department in Anatomy, which reſpects anatomical judgment and opinion as evidence in law—the opening and examination of parts, &c. &c.—embalming.

Profeſſor Caſſel—Materia Medica—four to five, in ſummer.

Our Dr. Cullen's works are the authorities.—Theſe lectures are in Latin.

This Profeſſor, too, has a few lectures on what he calls Le Medicine Judiciaire in Germany—and he is attended by the ſtudents of law and divinity.

Prof. Rath—on Pathology—in Latin—after Gaubius—two to three, winter and ſummer.

M. Brach is the Profeſſor upon Surgery—five to ſix.

Theſe lectures are in German, after Plenk.—In winter, Practical Lectures are given, and the operations demonſtrated.

M. Simons—the Diſeaſes of Children—eleven to twelve.

M. Muller—Chymiſtry—after Jacquin—ten to eleven.

Theſe lectures are in Latin.

W. Hume and M. Manver, give a few lectures on general Therapeutics.

PHILOSOPHY.

Profeſſor Winter—Phyſics—ſix in ſummer—nine o'clock in winter.

Prof. Dolimen—Logic and Metaphyſic—ſame hours.

For

For all thefe, Beck is the author in the higheft authority ---and for Mathematics alfo.

Prof. Cremer—Ethics—after Schwan—one to two.

Prof. Nobis—Mathematics—one to two.

Prof. Schwadorff---Phyfics---after Brewer.

Prof. Beck—Logic---after Contzain.

M. Letiman---Practical Philofophy.

M. Knippfchild, alfo gives lectures on Phyfics and Ethics ---and

Profeffor Everts, on Logic and Metaphyfics, through the the year, at 7.

The firft follows Brewer---the fecond Horvath.

Prof. Heyden---Reads on Elementary Mathematics---and on Experimental Philofophy, in fummer.

This is the Aftronomical Profeffor---In teaching he ufes Erxlebenand the Supplement of Lichtenberg.

Prof. Wallraff---Delivers a fhort courfe of lectures, on the fine arts, tafte, &c.

M. Chateaux, has a courfe of Hiftory and Geography---And M. Brachor in the ufe of Philofophy, of Hiftory, after Steinecher.

There are other profeffors, and thofe not mean men, who hold private claffes, and with whom as with the Italian repetitions, the ftudents, after any lecture, may go over it again.

Such are the eftablifhments in the univerfity of Cologne ---Which, for their own purpofes in the two firft faculties, divinity and law, are confidered very fufficient---In experimental philofophy, and in natural hiftory too, particularly mineralogy, Cologne is not defective. As a fchool for elegant learning, belles lettres, and for medicine, it does not feem aufpicious. The chymiftry is the beft part, the anatomy is the worft. Anatomical preparations fail, and the fubjects to fupply them, are I believe, fewer ftill. An hofpital,

hofpital, on a good plan, is in contemplation.—But till it be executed, that part of the medical ftudy muft continue wanting in the extreme. There is as at Liege, two fmall wards, to receive ftrangers---but ill ordered, as to cleanlinefs and air.

At Liege and Aix, the poor ufed to fend their new-born children to Paris, to the Enfans Trouves.—The fame fad cuftom, we are told, difgraced Cologne before the war.

On the Anatomical Theatre there is this infcription:
Theat. Anatom.

Hic eft, quæ Medicis fervit, Palæftra Chirurgi;
Corporis hic mouftrant offa, quod ora, docent.
Hic privata, capet, capet hic, Res-Publica, fructum.
Architypon, Pictor, Sculptor, et Artis, habet.
Hic vitæ vitium, vitare, volentis, imago
Ipfamet hic habitat mors, fine morte, domo.
Deo
Et falutis publicæ gratia
Erigit Magiftratus.

Here, her firft well-form'd hope, may Painting place,
Where Art meets Nature—And where Truth joins Grace!
Here muft the Surgeon arm his ufeful hand
And learn to fave the wonders he has fcan'd!
Here, too, fhould Medicine ponder every pore;
Elfe, vain pretenfion, waftes each potent ftore.
  Thou who madeft nought in vain, fuch fpirit give
To die for others—when we ceafe to live,
Thus dear to God and man, fuch works muft ftand.
The people raifed this!—and their fervants plann'd!

As a ftudent of any clafs, rank, and in any line, the expences at Cologne are very moderate; the greater number of young men do not fpend more than forty or fifty pounds a year. And really there feems no reafon why they need fpend fo much.

What

What they can get for their money, may not be so much, nor so well made as at better places, where also the fashion to study is the same, viz. Edinburgh and Pavia, and perhaps Gottingen too. But what they may get, is by no means insufficient, for the more obvious purposes of speculation and practice, as applying to either life.—Par negotiis neque supra, like the thick coarser woollens, and sweet light brown bread, not ill adapted to the markets of Germany. The laws and operations of nature, experimental science, and languages, in which colloquial Latin is to be reckoned, as well as the leading living languages of Europe; all these may be very copiously, though not very elegantly, learnt at Cologne.

The fees on graduation are of course like every thing else, in a cheap country, cheap too. To the chance customer, however, who is a stranger, the degree of Doctorate is dear, viz. From two to three hundred half crowns—For they say, not improperly, that "if a fellow is foolish enough to pant "after such trumpery as a foreign rattle, he certainly should "be made to pay for it, pretty smartly!"

Yet to buyers of a certain class, the thing has bonus enough to make it pass for a bargain For, if the fees are heavy, the examinations are light. So that, like a classic done into the vulgar tongue, it is adapted to gentlemen of all capacities!

Though there is an observatory, with the necessary apparatus, and the present state of the university, excludes all idea of any deficiency, but that of the little necessary care, yet meteorological observations there are none. Periodical statements of that kind, form a gratification at once elegant and cheap. Therefore it is a wonder, to be blamed, where ever they are wanting.

The curiosities of early printing are known at Cologne— and not known altogether, like the ass between the bundles

of

of hay, by approximation only. Yet at firft, undoubtedly there was no competitor with Fauft, &c. of Mayence.

But Cologne in the mean while, as to all this merit and this praife, was not infenfible nor unpartaking. Zell (de Hauen) flourifhed there! And Arnold Therhoerner. Their Thomas Aquinas, though after the firft editions of Rome and Mentz, wasin 1470, and is much prized. And fo is the Cologne edition of St. Auguftin, in the fame year! And a bible, of great antiquity (though precifely how great, is inafcertainable, as it has no date) is attributed (See Meermaun) to Zell at Cologne.—Cologne alfo, as further interefting to Englifhmen, as there our own William Caxton began his career for the public good, and printed there in 1471, the work of Le Fevre (Le Receuil des Hiftoryes de Troyes— The book, three years after, was the firft printed in London. And the year before that, 1470---J. Koelholf, gave his edition De Proprietibus Reram and St. Auguften.

In a later period Cologne was lefs active. The Plantins with Moretus made Antwerp carry all before it. Then, Publicè Utiliflimi, Bonorum Elogio Boni, are applicable only to them. Nay, infenfible even to the fame of Elzever, nothing like his New Teftament and Juftinian, were attempted at Cologne, though with all the obvious advantages of the fchools there for divinity and law! The princes and printers there, like the poftilions, motionlefs and dull, neither produced, nor promoted, any one edition of a good work, for good reafons, rare. The memoires of the Rochefoucault and Pafcals letters (Provencales) are the only firft editions which occur. And the laft, abetting the rage againft the Jefuits, an emotion in its excefs wrong, thus feems to fhow no motive better than prejudice, intolerance, and fpleen. Wechel about 1530, was mentioned by our connoiffeur at Cologne, as the beft old printing there.

Of Infcriptions alfo, the place, though an univerfity, and fo, neceffarily with fome talents in it, is equally bare. St.
Bruno

Bruno, it might be expected, would have had something said for him by his fellow countrymen. A more useful man, Adam Schall, the mathematician, who died at Pekin, forming a calendar there, was also a man of Cologne. So was Reubens—and so Vondel, the Dutch Virgil. And when a female mind, like Maria Schurman, could accomplish itself in twelve languages, and write well in four, besides her native tongue, a town, without any elation at all extravagant, might also have commemorated her.

Yet the church walls and tomb-stones are silent over them all! But the last, favoured by Christina, of Sweden, by Vossius, Huygens, Gassendi and Balzac, is secured in fame, as long as the errors of Rome may last, by being among the writers, prohibited there.

She was a disciple of Calvin—And what may further secure her name, the esteem it deserves,—she wrote, in Latin and rather ably, on the powers of the female mind. De Aptitude Ingenii Muliebris ad Doctrinas, et Literas Meliores, is the title, and with modern instances, it might do, sketched into English.

Every reader will, no doubt, be ardent to cite for himself—The examples should be, nay, probably they will be, irresistable; in a line too as long, as it is from Streatham to Naples!—With the charm of each dramatic fiction realised in England, by our Tragic and Comic Muse!

The following two inscriptions were given to us, but it was not mentioned in which of the churches they are.—The second, has merit, rather extraordinary! Merit, arising from novelty and importance. The arragement is singular, and the expression often exquisite.—The best are the third and fourth lines, the parenthesis in the seventh, and the whole of the close.

I.

Jacobus Merlo---1644

Conditur hoc tumulo, Jacobus Merio, facerdos
Curio dum Templo, Maxima Cura, Greges.
Qui, Cæcis Oculus---Claudes Pes---Panis Egenis
Defeffis Requies---Exalibufq Domus!
Manfuetus, Suavifq Bonus; Cenforque Malorum
Caftus, et Innocuus, Juftitiæq Tenax.
Lux Vitæ, Morum Speculum, Pietatis Imago
Sal Populi---Cleri Regula---Forma Gregis!
Laudibus his, Tantis, tamen Unica Gloria, Major
Poft, Scriptis, Nituit Congrua Vita, Libris.

The epithet in the laft line is happy, and fo is the power of condenfation in the fecond and fourth, in the feventh and eighth---What Merlo wrote was on fpeculative and fpiritualized theology.

II.

Murmellius 1538

Non Murmellius, hic Jacet Sepultus!
Sed Tantum Cinis Aridus Poetæ
Sed Pulvis Gelidæ Levis Favillæ
Parvæ Reliquiæ Silentis Urnæ!
Ipfe, ad Sedereas Abivit Oras!
Felix!---Elyfias futurus inter
(Ærumnis pro cul omnibus) Catervas
Quare, nec Lacrymas, Viatur, Ullas
Nec Mæftas Gemitu cie Querelas
Virtutis Comes Interire Nefcit
Mortem Præterit ipfa, fola, Virtus!

This excellent perfon, whom all muft wifh to follow, in merit and final fuccefs, had fame in his time, as a philologift and divine. He had been a ftudent at Cologne. As a profeffor he gave celebrity to a Dutch univerfity.---Thefe beautiful lines on him were written by Pafiphilus.

Arnold

III.

Arnold. Mylius---A. D. 1604.

This tomb, gives a veſtige of art, as well as what is more important.

He was a printer. And he did ſingly, what the London printers, the late Mr. Strahan and Mr. Allen, contrived to do together. Like one, Mylius was a citizen and ſenator, at Cologne. And like the other, his epitaph adds, that from his delicate integrity and rational piety, he may hope to be admitted, where citizenſhip is better!---The manuſcripts of Scot, (the ſubtle doctor as he was called) are in the library of the Auguſtins, and his other remains alſo continued to moulder in the choir---The date on the ſtone over him is 1308, with the circumſtances which befel him, that he firſt drew breath in Scotland, and breeding from France---that he lived in England, and that he died in Cologne. This intelligence is in two letters of Latin not worth repeating.

The courſe of exchange at Cologne, is thus at par---

On France   80 rix dollars for 100 ecus 60 ſousTournois.
On Amſterdam 155 ditto — for 100 rix dollars banco.
On Brabant   140   — for 100 Arg. de change.
On Francfort   111   — for 100.
On Hambourg 153   — for 100 rix dollars banco.
On Vienna   130   — for 111.

A rix dollar is 4s. 6d. Engliſh.

In drawing on London, I believe, they regulate by one or other of the firſt four.

Of money at Cologne.

Of this that is modern money, the wary traveller will take as little as he can---for what pretends to be the beſt, will not go beyond Bonne; and of the beſt not a little, is very bad.

Not ſo of the ancient coinage in Cologne---which makes a figure in the collections of the medalſtis there, from the fixth century to the preſent. The tenth century, 200 years after

after the archbishopric had been formed is the date of the first archiepiscopal coin. Till then the little specie in circulation came from the interior of Germany, from the Francs, and from the Romans—Formasque nostre Pecuniæ Agnoscunt, atque Eligunt. Though the bulk of what little business they might have had, must then have been managed by barter.

FROM COLOGNE TO BONNE.

THIS short ride, of four or five leagues, is interesting. There are not the abrupt, romantic charms of the Rhine above. But the scenery is powerful—from the extent of the surrounding hills, whence the eye roves from Cleves to Mayence—from the gay spirit and varied plenty of a valley twelve or fourteeen miles wide—and from a river beyond all others in Europe, unless it be the Elbe, of a temper that is magnificent. As was well said of Dryden's genius, and in his own words,

" The long majestic march—the energy divine."

The road, too, is in itself sprightly and handsome—with many well-continued flourishing vistas of elms and limes.— The agriculture too, begins to impress the traveller with a little force of novelty.

In the electorate of Cologne are the vines first seen upon the Rhine. There are none higher north.

The culture of the vine, as of almost every thing else, has some difference or other in different regions. In the chief wine countries of France, about Bourdeaux, in Champagne, and Burgundy, the vines are kept down to two or three feet high.—There is a pretty specimen of this in three acres of vineyard at Painshill, near Cobham, in Surrey —where the skill and unconquerable toil of Mr. Hamilton (the uncle of Sir William) shewed the power of cultivation! over every difficulty predominant! forcing fruitfulness from the waste, and amænity from a moor-heath! While in foreign trees from all lands, and in the precipitated enlargement of them all, there is the chearing demonstration for genius, that climate and time must obey it!

Such are the vineyards there.

Thofe in Italy are hung in fine-formed feftoons from tree to tree — gracefully waving with the common wind. Of all Italy, about Modena, the beauty is at the beft. Horace has this well, but Milton paints the vifion, which in the country before-mentioned is bewitching — he paints it with more glory.

> They led the vine
> To wed her elm—fhe, fpoufed about him, twines
> Her marriageable arms!—and, with her, brings
> Her dower — the adopted clufters, to adorn
> Her barren leaves!

There is a little vineyard, after this fafhion, in the gardens of Germany, except that there is fome fruit-tree inftead of the elm. There are alfo fome vines reared about poles, like hops. But the greater portion of them grow, as in France, fupported upon ftout laths; and, in general, are about five feet high.

The Rhine wine moft efteemed is not here, but about Oppenheim and Mayence; at Hochheim, a village at the north-weft extremity of the Mayne, where it unites with the Severn. Yet there is fome wine about Cologne and Bonne, which is not bad. And that upon the black bafaltes hills is the beft. For black, as is well proved by the familar experiments of Dr. Franklin, is the moft powerful agent upon heat; to attract, and to retain it.—This wine, of which there is not a great deal, is reddifh; from the fruit fermenting entire; unftrained from the hufks and ftones.— It is fometimes called *claret*.

In the garden-grounds of Cologne, a full third of the whole fpace within the town-walls, there is fo much vineyard as to have yielded 16,000 and 18,000 aume of wine— the aume is a meafure of 42 Englifh gallons.

The agriculture in this part of Germany, yields hops and cyder, both but indifferent, particularly the laft. Their corn, of all forts, is clean, large, and heavy; but the oats, rye, and barley are better than the wheat Much of it was houfed before the end of July, and the farmers, who
were

were active, had given the land a ploughing.—The hemp and flax feemed uncommonly vigorous and abundant.—The grafs lands they cut twice.—Pafturage muft be little; for there are no hedges. And that evil leads to another; for the want of enclofures, enlarging the lots of land, encourages the takings to be proportionably large.—There are farmers, we were informed, who rent fo immoderately as four or five hundred acres!—and have ten horfes, fifty cows, and other ftock proportionably large.—Their forage, failing of hay, is in the artificial graffes, chopped ftraw and coarfe bread—which is, and probably ought to be, thought better for horfes than unbruifed corn.

The foil, for the moft part, is a light fand. Gravel rare.—The rents are generally paid, not in money, but in a ftipulated part of each crop. The leafes from three to nine years—a term too fhort for any improvement of much coft. —The mere price of land is cheap: commonly lefs than a rix-dollar (4s. 6d. Englifh) an acre. Labour too is cheap, eight to twelve fols a day. For his markets, &c. the farmer has the river-carriage as well as on the road.—Sua fi bona norint, the farmers are happy here! They are not labouring under ruinous impofitions, with which fome countries are lafhed by the dæmons of rapine and defpair!—and they muft foon be politically free. As furely as there is progrefs in light, and immutability in truth!—as furely, as under the providential fway of what is wife and good, the fame principles, like the fame planets, muft be the fit apparatus for all!

Whatever may be the efficient caufe, the barbarities of feudal ufurpation at length fall away! they are hurrying to the diffolution they deferve—to the darknefs from whence they came. Even in Italy and Germany, they will, in a few fhort years, be known only by memory or defcription. Yet, even then, they may raife offenfive fenfations, like the monfters who have devoured one another on the Ohio, at their

horrid

horrid quantity of mifchief-doing power, yet poffible to be conjectured from their remains—in the enormity of their phangs, in the havoc of their grafp!

As to the people, their fhort defcription by Tacitus may be taken as authentic ftill---in their perfon they are coarfe and bulky---their countenance is ftern---their eyes are often light---their hair reddifh. And what muft be true of every people, may be faid fafely of this: viz. that the capacity for fkill and labour muft be differing in different men. Tacitus thinks they are able to bear heat and thirft with lefs force of refiftance than they can cope with hunger and cold. I have travelled in Germany, in the middle both of winter and fummer;—I was fure he muft have been pleafed if he (Tacitus) had been with us in the chaife—he would have feen, as we did, that they are equally infenfible to both! *Cælo folove affueverunt.* In conftitutional habitude, happily or unhappily, inacceffible to each extreme of thermometrical heat or cold, they fit aloof and indifferent, and bid equal defiance to both!

Again alfo, in contradiction to Tacitus, and his *argentum quoque magis quam aurum fequuntur*, I muft aver that the love of bullion feems dead in them—a French half-crown, nay, once, (to fave the gates of Mayence) a rix-dollar, with its jolly flat furface forwards, we offered to a poftillion—and it was offered in vain! And once, on the other fide of Manheim, I have feen blows alfo tried—and likewife in vain!

> A frame of adamant, a foul of fire:—
> No dangers fright them—and no hardfhips tire!
> O'er hope—o'er fear—extends their wide domain—
> Unconquered lords—of pleafure and of pain!

The laft experiment was tried by a young foreigner of fome fafhion. I endeavoured to reftrain him, in the obvious probability of the poftillion not dying in his debt. For I was in his chaife.

When

When the coup de grace was given by the young gentleman, and the thing feemed, in all reafon, done enough, he replaced himfelf on the feat befide me—and then with great gravity explained, that there could be no apprehenfion at all. " That he travelled as a nobleman acknowledged!— " that he had the gold key at his pocket! as chamberlain " to the K— of P——!—and the M—— of A——! " And he then fhewed me with his paffport, another prince's " voucher of thefe pretenfions (the P. B. of T.) as a cir- " cular warrant, as he faid, for fuch rights!"

How unanfwerable all this was, it was impoffible to deny. —I did not attempt it. And at parting, I had his good word, " for being open to conviction, and prompt to the " admiffion of truth!—an enemy to all barbarous innovations—and fteady for the fettled order of things!"

" Who call it freedom—when themfelves are free!"

D d   BONNE

BONNE

IS the refidence of the Elector, and has been fo fince the thirteenth century. Then it was that the prince bifhop firft left Cologne---and for no bad reafon, becaufe Cologne had left him. Even fo long ago, the popular and republican politics, were potent and prevailing at Cologne. The town fired; and Engelbert, then bifhop, went off, like empty wadding, to Bonne! However, in one fenfe, the principle of combuftion feems not to have been wanting at Bonne. The palace has been burnt four times. The laft deftruction was in 1777. Then, upon a plan of Clement Auguftus, whofe memory is, very juftly, more dear to the people than his plan, the prefent palace was built. And, in part, there is the fame wild, ftraggling profufion---fimilar multiplication of fuperferviceable objects, with which Louis XIV. among other infections of bad tafte and cruel wafte, tainted Europe! The Elector Palatine, of that time, carried the Cacoethes to Manheim, where he built like a quarry above ground! and from him the evil, though with lefs virulence, was brought to Bonne. A palace was built, as much too big for the revenue, as, fome think, the revenue is for the ftate—and enormous departments reared, in all the foppery of awkward pride and falfe pretence, for the parade of tafte and fcience, rather than their ufe.

The prefent Elector, who has the reputation of being a man of fenfe, has, accordingly, introduced a better order of things. He has abolifhed fome eftablifhments—and reformed thofe which are fuffered to remain. He has diminifhed his houfehold. And like a man of humanity and honour, he has checked his expenditure, to keep pace with his income—" debt and mendication, faid he, " are equally " guilty; and till my nature forfakes me, I will fhun the
" fhabby

"shabby infamy, both of one, and the other!" What he said, he has done. Without any deficience towards thofe who truft him, without the leaft freſh burthen upon them, who pay for his fupport, he has proceeded with new dignity; becaufe with new wifdom, with new ufe!—He has made œconomy adminifter to public good: and what he has fpared from himfelf, he has well diftributed to the advantage of others!

As his objects were not influence and error, but independence and truth, he has difburfed on the public fervice what was faved on the reform of his houfehold, &c. He has formed and fupported, very fufficiently, a college at Bonne. With eftablifhments for general learning, divinity and law, he has bought and built (a very pretty building it is) a fchool for experimental fcience and anatomy. He has provided a botanical garden for the public. And, till time and chance may fupply another collection for the ftudents, he has opened his own library to all, with reading-rooms, defks, fires, &c. &c.—and every accommodation that can be wanted.

The theatre, in his palace, he has clofed. As bad, in itfelf—becaufe, low, dark, ill-aired—and worfe, as now a gaiety out of feafon, referring to the unexampled horrors of the time!—when one half of Europe are writhing at death's door, for nothing but the guilt and folly of the other half!—There certainly may be modes of letting money go, more ufefully, than upon experiments of idle mirth, and of doubtful pleafure.—" A theatre!" faid he, " like Racine " and Corneille, nay, fuch as our own Leffing has made it, I " think, with each man of tafte, a great object of rational " preference for every people—but what are fictitious woes, " when each heart is rent with woes that are real?—The " too real woes of all around us, call for every particle of " time and of fympathy we can fpare!"

The theatre, of courfe, has given way to better things.

The college, or univerſity I believe it is called, has, beſides pecuniary ſupport, the perſonal countenance of the Elector. With much delicacy, he propoſed himſelf to be the chancellor—probably, thinking it brilliant even for his ſtation, to preſide over thoſe purſuits, which, when accompliſhed, form the moſt uſeful ſucceſſes of human nature.

The next chief officer of the foundation, who is called curator, is M. Von Spiegel.—The profeſſors are theſe: M. Maderſladt, a clergyman, and M. Vanetti, give the botanical lectures—M. Rougemont, a Frenchman, anatomy and phyſiology—M. Worſer, in chemiſtry—M. Wagel, in medicine. —The other faculties are with M. M. Hidderic, Schneider, Thaddaus, and Ginetti. Mr. Kidgell, ſo well known in an affair with Mr. Wilkes, is the profeſſor of the Engliſh language. Not knowing Mr. Kidgell, we could not call upon him: as we might have been inclined to have ſeen the interior, upon ſuch a viciſſitude in ſuch a man. But he was ſhewn to us in the ſtreets. And then, the only time we heard him mentioned, they ſpoke of him without diſreſpect. He walked compoſed, and without any infirmity--- upon the whole, ſtrong and portly, beyond his years.— This little mention of ſuch a man, probably will, from ſome motive or other, be intereſting to many people—but to none more than to Mr. W——; for his good-humour, and forgiving nature, are, if I think rightly, equal to his wit.--- After the well-known perfidy of Lord ———, ſome years elapſed without their having any further intercourſe. It was in the Beef-ſteak club-room that they met—and being both before their time, were alone. Mr. W. then greeted Lord ———, and, with courteſy equally unexpected and commendable, held out his hand, and ſaid, with the moſt frank good fellowſhip, " Sir, I hope we are no longer other-
" wiſe than friends. This is the firſt time we have been
" together for many years. Let us employ it, if you pleaſe,

" in

" in the beſt way we can, and forget we have ever been
" aſunder."

What he will ſay upon this, I know not. I forgot to tell him of it, the only time I ſaw him ſince my return—as to ourſelves, it was a ſight that made us penſive;—with the melancholy and the pity of him, whoſe pilot yielding to an improper propenſity, fell from his ſtation, and was loſt!

> " O nimium cælo, ac pelago confiſe ſerene!
> " Nudus in ignotâ, Palinure, jucebis, arena!"

Mr. K. was ſaid to have had Roman Catholic orders given to him by the archbiſhop of Mechlin. But he wears a lay-habit—and indeed he ſtill keeps his benefice in England. So that the report is impoſſible to be true.

The ſtudents, at preſent, are about fourſcore. The expence of their reſidence is more than at Cologne. The ſeſſion begins at both on the day of St. Martin, in November, and ends about Midſummer. At Cologne, as has been ſpecified, there are ſome lectures which are continued through the year.

The botanical garden, though young, is advanced, and comprehenſive, though ſmall. The rock, and the apparatus for aquatic plants, are both too ſmall—the other departments are leſs objectionable—the plants are in good order—and the whole is well kept. There is nothing yet very rare; but of common things, there are ſome ſpecimens rather uncommon. As incertain human characters, that may occur to every one, though not be good ſort of men, they may be good men of a bad ſort. Of thoſe ſpecimens, we noted—a potentilla fructifera, a Lavatera triloba—an antheos Œthiopicum—cactus coccinellifera—and a nereum oleander—though a ſpecimen, finer ſtill of that, is in the garden of the Elector.

In the anatomical ſchool, not yet amounting to what can properly be called a collection, there is nothing remarkable,

but

but a curiosity of woe—a human calculus, tremendously as big as a human brain!

Medicine is well stated by Johnson, to be an admirable occupation, as it enables a man, with most reputable profit, to turn science to account!—he might have further enhanced it by a moral preference; by a thought, nothing less than consecrating, on the purifying effect upon the temper, from pain and sickness, apprehended and felt.— These are the masters of life, which at once teach all of us what we are; to think about others, and to know ourselves.—And if Chilon and Linneus be right, this is the characteristic distinction of man!—His completing attribute of complex excellence, both in duty and privilege, in merit and in reward!

Et e cœlo defendit Γνωθι σεαυτον.

The calculus had a string passed round it, in each direction—and it was one foot seven inches—by one foot five.—In the subdivision of German measurement, eleven inches make a foot.

The growth of a college should be a chearing object, as it implies the advance of science, active for human good. But it is not an unmixed emotion here. For it is impossible to overlook, that there has been a waste of time and money—that both had been better employed upon the old, and yet vigorous, establishments at Cologne, than in an attempt, very likely after all to fail, of building a new bottom at Bonne—that a small state like this, not more than sixty square miles, one university must be enough—and that, probably, there cannot be either wit or money enough for two.

We did hear, indeed, what we know not how to believe, that it was not meant to have two: that the new foundation was planned to rise upon the ruins of the old—and that in a pique at the popular politics, unanimous at
Cologne,

Cologne, some dull and narrow minister had advised a downright attack; a declaration of despotic exclusion; that no student in any faculty at Cologne should have any promotion, in the power of the Electorate to bestow.

As if, in any order but one, men of talents could be said to hold what they have at the will of the Lord—as if a minister, however unnatural, could always confound right and wrong, and vote laurels where they were not, or wither them where they were!—as if a lawyer and a physician must not go for what they are worth!—or as if dullness, with any stamps or titles, could have the currency of merit!—The avocats Du Roi used often, most deservedly, to be without a brief.—And in another country, " You are " my doctor!" said the King to a man so entitled by his minister, " you are King's physician! but if you make a " patient of any one man in my dominions, by the Lord, " we'll take your head off!"

So much for the proscriptions against Cologne—which, to be sure, are likely to do the mischief that might be meant—when Nature's laws may chance to be disorganised! —when matter may lose attraction, and heat forget to mount—when there may be no more spring in what is elastic, nor splendour in what is bright!

" Principes ex nobilitate, alios ex virtute sumunt!"

While men are men, and accident or violence assail them, they will look for aid and refuge where they may be found in men—with genius and experience, sensibility and skill— and not in pretenders, who have nothing to offer but gibberish upon waste paper, a patent for a nick-nack, a warrant for a name!

It is really too contemptibly absurd to think of a little court little this, being held up as a bug-bear to men! and that talents, and their excitements and rewards, could

shrink

shrink and shrivel into a petty span, like the confines of Bonne!

For Bonne, though inflated with all the foul air, which satyr, whether right or wrong, has imputed to courts and cities, and artificially big with all the flattering remnants of charters, privileges, and walls, yet has, after all, not more importance than a parish. There is many a parish more populous and more pursy. Bonne has but 1000 houses. Of course the people cannot be more, at the most, than 8 or 10,00. And of them, a large part, perhaps an entire eighth, are made up, but badly, of Jews, courtiers, convented ecclesiastics, and canons!

The Jews are about 250---they occupy twenty-five houses, all in one street---which is, as usual, a bye word for dirtiness and wealth; the wealth, too, got by brokerage. That equivocal being, spawned between idleness and pride, who through eighteen centuries of time, most marvellously unchanged, has never ceased to say, *I cannot dig, to beg I am ashamed!*

The canons also must prove their ancient stock.

> Nostri quoque sanguinis auctor
> Jupiter est---totidemque gradus distamus ab illo!

Nothing less than nobility will do! Aye---and through sixteen quarters.

> And some who boast their sixteen quarters,
> One may mistake---for chandlers daughters.

The canons are 36, with 21 vicaires, and a provost.— The provost is the arch-deacon of the whole arch-bishopric. And in virtue, as it is called, thereof, he holds not only an ecclesiastical court, but a civil court, which takes in some complainants, in the first instance. The chapter is as old as the fourth century. The present church was built in the twelfth. There is nothing about it worth attending to,

either

either within or without; the ground plan is low, and the tower is wood.

Besides the chapter, there are four parishes and eight convents for men and women. One of the latter it were unjust to condemn; for the establishment is well employed, in the education of young women.

The parochial clergy, as becomes an ecclesiastical state, cannot be supposed better fed than taught. Their annual income is but from 300 to 600 crowns.

The Elector is chosen, not by the Chapter of Bonne, but by the Chapter of Cologne. The present gentleman, lucky enough to be so well placed, is the Arch-duke Maximilian of Austria; he had it about ten years ago, at a time of life, when what little life can give is most worth having, viz. at thirty-six.

The revenues and rights, or at least the power of the elector, have been mentioned before. At Bonne, where he resides, we heard of his private life; and, it is a pleasure to say, we heard nothing but what is blameless.

War and the chace, barbarities so rife and monstrous in Germany, are not the disgrace of this prince. He has ever disdained that trade which is more offensive than a carcase butcher, and his amusements are something better than those of a blood-hound. So the flattery Augustus had equivocally from Ausonius, is happilly not applicable to him.

Mirantur casusque novos, subitasque ruinas.

His army, fortunately for the people, is no more than one regiment, the electoral contingent to the empire, with a small party of fifty men, like the marechaussées or gens-d'armes in France, for a horse patrole on the roads, and for himself, only, on occasions of parade. In war, as at the melancholy time when I last saw Bonne, 200 troops were there. The rest were in the disasters of Flanders. In peace,

peace, it is their practice to be employed by the Dutch. The pay of the private is 6 sols a day.

The chace is here no drain upon the country. During the former elector's time there was a very wasteful establishment of horses, 150 or more. Now there is no such idle ruin. There are but thirty—and these are found enough for all the purposes of use, amusement, and show. Though riding, and driving an open carriage, are among the exercises, are most and rather studiously affects.

> Primus erichthonius, currus et quatuor ausus
> Jungere equos.

Though antiquity thus records the charioteer, so illustrious as first to drive four in hand, they do not say of him, as may be said of the elector's stables at Bonne, that every day, from dawn to dark, his carriage horses are kept harnessed, and his roadsters ready saddled. And surely this is not unpleasant, except for the beasts; for if he was right who sighed to lose a day, he must be more magnificent, who tries not to lose a minute.

The elector rides an English horse. He mounts his secretary and a servant or two (his suite is no more) upon Hanoverians, whom we could not find remarkable for any thing but for a je ne sçai quoi about a thick impenetrable hide, and the amazing quantity they consumed!

The care of horses, as far as mere stabling is concerned, is no where generally understood but in England. The Duke of Orleans was the only man who had a stalled stable in France. At Bonne, as elsewhere in Germany, the best horses of the Prince are in nothing but standings of no more than five feet and a swing bar.

Music, another favourite amusement of the elector, is also cultivated very modestly. His band, singers and all, are but forty. They assist at the mass, every morning, in
the

the palace. And, twice or thrice a week, he gives a concert; in the winter at his palace, in the summer at the Fountain on the Hill, or the Redoute and Garden La Popiniere. Reifche is the name of his firft mufician.

That garden, not ill planted and turfed by the late elector, is not abfolutely without tafte. The fcenery is pretty within, and rather ftriking without. Over the Seven Mountains and the Round Tower, on the hill fouth of Bonne---it is called Gottefberg—tradition tells us it was a temple of Mercury; and any body may truly tell tradition, that it is one of the fineft ruins upon the Rhine—a region where fo many ruins are fine!

In the garden there is a mineral fpring, which has fixe air and iron, magnefia and falt—and therefore, analytically and fynthetic too, they would have it a rival to Spa. Accordingly they have built a theatre there, a faloon, and other rooms; where, befides dancing, which may do no harm, they have tried to introduce games of chance, diffeminated with other evils from the late Court of France, as trente-un, rouge & noir, and biribis. The poor French emigrants appeared to take this, like what moft revived their maladie du pais, and gave way to it naturally. Some few low nobility of Germany joined them, but it was, when we faw it, a miferable object of unfuccefsful vice.

The elector makes no ufe of the place, but what is good and amiable. He gives little galas there—there he paffes many a folitary ftudious hour—and there, in a very fmall cottage by the well, he fleeps, unattended, literally with no more than a couple of fervants in the houfe. A practice, in itfelf trifling, but worth mentioning, as it implies confidence and fimplicity—that he is not tired of himfelf, nor diftruftful of others. It had been well, for human nature, if, of every prince, in every period, truth could have faid the fame.

The

The water has been analyfed, and thefe were the component parts in a pound of it—

Of fixed air	16 cubic inches.
Mineral falt	7 grains.
Magnefia	3 grains.
Lime-ftone	2¼ grains.
Common falt	1⅓ grain.
Iron	¼ of a grain.

The tafte is not bad.

The elector in his palace, as well as in his occafional retirement, is accuftomed to live as becomes manhood—free, but not exceffive, though merry yet wife. His public gala days are three times a year; often enough to bring people together, and not too often, where, as in other courts, moft people have too much caufe to care that they may be kept enough afunder. The hofpitalities of his table are frequent, and never ftinted by penury nor pride; but, in his own indulgence, he feems ftrict—fimple at leaft, if not abftemious. Of courfe he is no dupe nor martyr to medicine—he literally has no phyfician. For fear of accidents, there is a furgeon upon the eftablifhment, and that is all. His name is Renfer.

The reft of the prince's private eftablifhment will be difmiffed in few words. He has twenty-four footmen in livery, and fix out of livery—forty fellows about his carriages and horfes—and eighteen in his garden, which are four more than the late French king had at Verfailles— and yet the ground, which is but a few acres, has nothing at all, but nine beds of ftocks, a few large geraniums, a little vineyard, no tree above a poplar, and but few even of them, and not a few puddles in the walks, above twenty feet fquare!

Some hot-houfes are building, and it is high time they fhould be—for when we faw the place, though it was the end of July, there was not a fingle cucumber in fixteen

frames

frames—nor indeed any thing like good fruit or a flower. A fault, local merely, for at the table d'hote and in the common market, at Cologne, we had found white cherries fingularly fine; finer than the fruit at Paris. The plan, when done, will have a fig houfe of 60 feet, a pinery of 100—four more building of 60 feet each, for peaches, and flowers, &c. and hot walls of 100 feet more—with cabbage gardens, and all forts of kitchen ground, clofe to the palace, under the very windows of it, and in the walk to the beft point of the whole, a terrace on the Rhine.

With a terrace, in part already embanked with mafonry immoveable—with a power of lengthening a water walk, upon fuch a river as the Rhine, for more than a league—with furrounding grounds all his own, in a circuit of many miles. In a valley four leagues wide, the hills bold and broken, clofe, covered with woods, and vines—with thirteen churches, and feven and eight villages we counted in the view—with feven mountains (the Seven Mountains), their ruins and their towers—why is it not, what it at once might be, one of the moft delicious and imprefling places in the world? what, but Mr. Repton, or any other good pupil of Mr. Browne, can be wanting?

There wants befides, too probably, the predifpofing power to feel fuch aid to be wanting—to underftand its value—to to relifh its effects! For in all the ftores of Lord Bacon, there is no truth more certainly experienced, than what he teaches upon the culture of ground—that its perfect adornment depends upon the perfection of tafte—and, that men may long build wifely, before they come to garden well!

Whether Bonne has got fo far in tafte, as may be called the building point—I know not; there is nothing in the palace but the dimenfions, which are impofing—there is a gallery 330 feet by 40—and a faloon 190 by 50. In the allegiance of univerfal good-will, we wifhed the elector, like the fage, to think of filling his palace with friends. The

deco-

decorations need not raife any fenfations that are uneafy—there are no pictures to mortify thofe who have lefs money than tafte. The glaffes are in little bits, joined together, from Franconia. A fpecimen of the gobelin, where the campaign, under Marfhal Villars and the Duke of Bavaria is, as moft people but the contractors, &c. muft have wifhed it, in little.—And fome woollen tapeftry, from the Weftphalian manufacture at Ham.—Among the portraits, which are thirty or forty, there is George II.—and the Dauphin, father of Louis XVI. where the likenefs to the fon is very ftriking.

The collection of Natural Hiftory, though better than Baron de Hupfch, is beginning to droop---for what is florid muft fade, and what is brittle will fall!- -The mathematical inftruments too, yield to time—and like their maker, the Paris Le Februe, give way to their betters.—But nothing of our Herfchel, of Mr. Ramfden, of Nairne or Adams, is to be found.

The Library, a handfome collection, is more handfomely ftill, open to the public every day, from four to feven. And every body may write who can write.—An expreffion I had from the librarian—though he on my enquiry had it not from Gray's epitaph, though Gray probably took his from Swift's Memoires of P. P.—O reader if thou canft read——

There are no very curious books which we could hear of. There are fome Englifh writers—Among whom Kippis is, and Sam Johnfon is not.

The librarian had not heard of our fplendid printing in Boydell's Shakefpeare, and Bowyer's bible.—But we gave him a fmall fpecimen of their extraordinary perfection; he compared it with Bafkerville's quarto Terence (one of his beft works)—And then, more fully admiring, he feemed to think the elector would be pleafed.

The

The States of the Electorate, claim certain special rights, and hitherto have asserted them —Besides precedence and local regulation, they very properly maintain their right to tax themselves, or what is much better, not to pay any taxes at all.—Their contributions, when they make any, are expressly termed spontaneous, and eleemosynary—" Sub-
" sidia Charitative" are the words—And to shew how likely men are apt to agree when their object is truth—they have a colloquail turn upon record, very like the famous reply of bishop Andrews to king James—when another bishop with less wit and honesty, had assented to a questioned right of arbitrary taxation—" You may certainly take that gentle-
" man's money, who is so polite as to say you may."

The States are four chambers, viz. 1. The chapter of Cologne, who represent all the clergy in the diocese.—2. The nobles (commonly counts) possessors of the chief fiefs. —3. The chevaliers—also holding fiefs.—4. The tiers etat, the seventeen deputies from as many towns—Of these Cologne is not one—Bonne is. The most southern of them is Andernach. The rest are the small towns between. Westphalia holds a meeting of states apart. So does the district of West Kecklinghausen.

The taxes of the Electorate have been mentioned, at Cologne, as 10 or 12 per cent. on foreign goods---Tolls on the Rhine, which between Bonne and Andernach are three —and form more than a moiety of the Elector's revenue. And a land tax, very sensibly bearing more heavily upon the vineyards, and sparing the corn.---The tax is two, not shillings, but sols, per acre on the corn lands—and nine sols where there are vines. This is therefore virtually a premium for the plow---and, as Mr. Hume, with his usual sagacity observes, that in a contest between a land of corn, and a land of wine, the land of corn must eventually have the best of it.

During

During the laſt century, the territory of the electorate was accurately admeaſured and enrolled, when to the wonder of every body, it was found that the elector and clergy were ſeiſed of nearer a half than a third of the whole! theſe were the ſtatements—

The whole territory—60 miles ſquare—347992, tourneaux of land.—This is an imaginary meaſure, liable therefore to much uncertainty and error---it means as much as a man, though with what aid of cattle is not defined, can work in a day.

1. Of theſe the Clergy have - 98,328¼
2. The Nobles and chevaliers - 92,391¼
3. The Elector - - 50,30¾
4. Land-owners living on their farms 131,119
5. Land-owners living in towns 21,122

The ſtatement, has a ſide light that is rather intereſting, for the fourth, the country gentlemen and yeomen, the moſt uſeful order of the whole, is a large proportion. Almoſt utterly unknown in Spain and Italy.—Since the Revolution, moſt happily multiplying in France. But for ages paſt, and let us hope, through ages to come, the ſtrength and glory of Britain.

The number of the nobles is, no where, that I know, to be found. The Elector's librarian, an intelligent gentleman, told us that about 100, he added rather above 100, were regiſtered at the laſt diet. But it muſt be a thing of much mutability, for certain offices are allowed to confer nobility, and as they are openly ſold, any body may openly buy them. The market is fed too and forced like the market for muſhrooms;—if the buyers are more than ſellers. The nobility thus ſold ready made, has been in the title of counſellors, eccleſiaſtical counſellors, civil counſellors, counſellors of the court of the public chamber, and of the privy.

The preſent Elector has not ſuffered theſe vermin to encreaſe.

The two chief minifters are the grand bailli, and the bailli de la cour.—The firft M. Le Baron de Walvenfels, is in great refpect for fpirit and independence. The chief nobles, as to appearance in their eftablifhment, are C. de Metternich, Heldenbufch, Gymhi and Weich.

The appellant jurifdiction, of the electorate, is in the fupreme court at Bonne. The recovery of this right of not appealing to Wetzlaer, a prerogative inherent to each electorate, had been fufpended to Cologne.—It was recovered by the good fenfe and zeal of the prefent elector. The other tribunals are the council of regency—a prefident and twenty four members—each noble, that is as far as hereditarytitle can make him fo; and generally alfo with a fief. In this court comes every queftion of feudal tenure—and the perfonal caufes of thofe fo holding.

The city court is formed of four bourg-mafters—two of them fit alternately.

The police of the town, has nothing in it, but what muft raife a wonder there, for what purpofe—magiftrates, of all orders, are kept—for the streets are narrow, the pavements are defpicable.—There are no aquæducts from the Rhine, no underground fewers to it—no fcavenger—no lights—no architecture to grace the town—no walks to ventilate the people!

It feems incomprehenfible, for what purpofes any magiftrate can think himfelf paid, if not for good and wholefome objects like thefe.—To infpect, compare, decide, execute, day by day, if not hour by hour, to leave things better than he finds them.

The only good changes we could hear of, were two.— 1. That all burials were out of the town.— 2. That there were no longer any mifchievous nonfenfe like town walls, which acted like a burial of the living! Thofe toys of grown children, fortifications, are abolifhed.—And the grafs, that now grows there in good crops, is let to the towns people, to feed animals, which, we cannot fay, are as good as officers of ordnance!

Both of thefe changes are, obvious improvements, and and both come from the prefent elector. They are the more likely to be popular, or at leaft deferve to be fo, as they came from his relation Jofeph the fecond.—A man, whofe merit is on no fide equalled by his praife.

For the poor, there is a collection, but how affeffed and levied we could not find, of 130 crowns a week. A late Elector left by will 24,000 crowns to build a houfe for the poor.—But as yet, they have not been able to find a place. —If Mandeville and Kaimes be right, it were better were they never to find it. Of Arts, befides what we have mentioned, there is little to be faid. They build with brick.—They burn coals, water-borne up the Rhine. Much animal food, for the market, comes from the country of Berg. Some bafaltes, from the neighbouring high-lands, appears on the pofts and pavements of the ftreets.

At Cologne, as at Liege, Bruxelles, Ghent, and Bruges, there is a new eftablifhment of a club, (called La Societè Literaire) where, for a louis d'or a year, from each fubfcriber, there are all the new pamphlets and foreign journals. Of courfe there may be warrantable hope of light fpreading through Europe. For the journal even of Mirabeau, though an irrecoverable proftitute, was one efficient caufe of French defpotifm coming to an end. So that there are but beacons, it matters little, upon what foil they may ftand.

In the Cologne club, there are about a hundred members, and the Elector, very prettily, has put his name down for one. They meet in the Hotel de Ville; and every ftranger, finds eafy welcome.

Antiquities there are none, that fell in our way, though we looked with all the eyes we had, to find the traces of thofe who had been there before us, of Drufus, and Julian

the

the apostate—Of Helen, who was called a saint, and Martin of Tours, who was one—And yet both have to answer for horrid evils! For, if Mosheim be right, the monks sprung from St. Martin, as from Helen issued Constantine, who was, whatever else Eusebius may say, a warrior!

<blockquote>
Whether the creature sinner-it, or saint-it,
If folly grows romantic, we must paint it.
</blockquote>

Of the cross, just out of the town on the road to Coblentz, this is the brief memorial——

L'An 1333
L'Empereur Wadham de Juliers,
Fit Elever
La Grande Croix
entre
Bonn et Goddesberg.

Other inscriptions, are not fit to be mentioned; we were shewn one on Burchordst, one of the council and chancellor of the chapter, which from the high-sounding beginning, Clarissimo Nominatissimoque Viro, broke all promise, and ended in nothing.

FROM THE RHINE

TO

COBLENTZ.

Salve Amnis--laudate Agris, laudate Colonis!
Dignata, Imperio, debent cui Menia Belgæ!
Amnis, Odorifero, Juga Vitea Confite Baccho!
Confite Gramineas, Amnis, Viridiffime, Ripas!
Naviger, ut Pelagus.

OF river fcenes, where the effect refults, without much offskip, merely from the ftream and from the banks, there are none in Europe with more grandeur than the Rhine.— For mere amænity the eye need not wander further, the heart cannot wifh for more, than the Thames pours forth, from Strawberry Hill to Ifleworth—unlefs perhaps there be a referve for a league on this fide Lyons.—For amænity with grandeur, and a vaft offskip from the highlands in the diftance, with multiplied villas making amænity again, there are no fcenes like the Soane, between Macon and Lyons—none at once fo magnificent and fo gay!—For amænity and romance, a man may be well content with the Taaff and the Dee, even though he may have never feen the narrows on the Rhine and the Rhone.—But for grandeur, from the ftream and the banks, the Rhine from Bonne to Coblentz, and to Meintz, carries all before it.

If there can be a rival, it is, I am told by a friend of much experience and tafte, the Elbe near Drefden.

In this grandeur of the Rhine fcenery, art too is grand, as well as nature. The power of cultivation is feen on every furface of the foil—on the top of the mountain, as well as at the bottom; on the rock, as in the vale! And man's

domeftic

domeſtic cares, ever equalled if not greatly overpaid by man's domeſtic joys, encreaſe and multiply at every turn! At every turn, the larger farms look like hamlets, and almoſt every village is a town. There is no ſpot of land without a crop! No man without a home! No beggar! No waſte!

Arts too, and cultivations, of other kinds, combine, glorrouſly, to aggrandize the ſcene. For all the ſalient points, all the objects moſt obtruſive on the ſenſe, all were of the dark and barbarous ages—all of a malignant character, thank God, are now happily malignant no more! Each has had juſtice done on it by time—and is ſeen doomed to riſe no more! all uniformly prone to the rubbiſh and ruins from whence they came—yet variouſly miſhaped, as the paſſions and chimeras of the monſters which produced them.

Hope, like vegetation, opens through each ruin! and beautifies it at every chink; no viſions appear but what are chearing, of brighter probability, of better days, from the ſplendor of truth, from the bounty of time. That the ſame power, which working by the advancing ſenſe and ſpirit of man, brought to nought the fortified uſurpations of the Romans and the Francs, the Pope's ſupremacy, and the Baron's feud, will continue to act with like beneficence, and break down each petty faſtneſs which remains of tyranny and ſuperſtition. The Legend and falſe Miracle, the Breviary and the Fief!—That the Path of Duty and Privilege, may be free and open to all!—And that no Structure of Man's Device ſhall have the Front to look upwards, but what Obeys the Attributes it ſhould adore, in Juſtice, in Mercy, and in Peace, a Defence for the oppreſſed, a Refuge from the Storm!

The beſt of theſe points, and where theſe emotions are moſt forcibly impreſſed, and moſt willingly received, are the following—

At Goddesberg, the tower, a short league out of Bonne; and so fine an object from it.

The Seven Mountains, another league on the opposite shore of the river, there the ruins which appear, as are some of those of antiquity, as high as the fourth century, the work of Valentinian.

The mountain of St. Apollinian, where the head of the imagined saint is still exhibited, as a cure for the epilepsy!— And one of the poor fellows of the house not seeing the drift of the equivoque, assured us " that it was still as much " a cure as ever." And, accordingly pilgrims, in the days of such popular folly, used to resort there!—In the dark ages, what little light there was in life, was the property of the ecclesiastics.—And hence in taste, as to the choice of situation, which is nothing but good sense applied to that object, they excelled. In every part of Europe, whatever might be the specific excellence of a spot, scenery, aspect, land or water, it seemed to have been perfectly understood by those ingenious gentlemen.—And of each set of habitations, what Mosheim calls a monkery, is pretty sure to be the best!

It was near the bottom of this mountain, at the angle of the great bend in the river, opposite Unkeel, and the mountain of basaltes above it, that one of the most remarkable, and the most interesting men in Europe, M. de Calonne, met with a tremendous accident in the year 1791! The road there is, by strange perverseness, yet suffered to remain so narrow that but one carriage can pass—The bank abruptly opening to the Rhine, is not, as in some places, protected by any fence, while on the other side there is a wall to mound up the little mould there may be, in a fine vineyard on a perpendicular hill. On that side, therefore, any little deviation in case of accident, is impossible.

It happened so then to M. de Calonne—one of the horses

was unruly, and flew, where alone he could fly, down the steep bank, and dragging the other horses with him, chaise and all, into the river.—As the carriage was closed, M. de C. in two or three minutes must have been suffocated, if in his good sense, accustomed to philosophical speculation, he had not instantly broke the windows. And when broken he would have been drowned, but for the activity of the most fortuitous aid!

So early as the second century, inscriptions shew, what due care the Romans had of this road—let the council of Cologne do likewise. And if Marcus Aurelius is too much for them, they may get an example nearer home, in what the Elector Palatine did when he enlarged and finished what antiquity, less spaciously, had began.

Viam
Sub M. Aurelio
Et L. Vero
J. M. P. P.
Anno Chr. 262
Munitam
Carol. Theod. Elector Pal.
Dux Bav. Jul. Cl. M.
Refecit et Ampliavit Ann. 1768.
Curante
J. L D. Goldstein pro Principe.

At Sinzey, on leaving the town, on the Coblentz side, which is a dependence on the dutchy of Juliers, is a scene of great beauty and force—with a single tree, a large lime tree, in itself very fine, for a fore-ground, with two villages one above another, washed by the Rhine!—The ruins of an old castle that had lorded it over them! A convent of St. Helen, on the soft descent of a hill, in the midst of gardens and vines, and the distance vast, of two mountains losing themselves in the clouds!

At

At Argenfelt, a worn-out refidence of the Comte de Legen, and at Breifeg Parfonage, with the caftle of Rheineck as the chief object, both are fcenes exquifitely picturefque. The refidence of an Englifh clergyman, be it on what fcale of expence, and in what character of country it may, from Mr. Whaley's cottage, to Stanmore, from Denbighfhire Rhaiada to Hadham, generally implies tafte in the treatment of the place, and all thofe cultivatious aids, whether little or great, which are the contributions of a cultivated mind. But this is not one of the matters they order better in France, nor even in Switzerland either. We received hofpitalities at the curès of Marcatell, on the lake of Sauffen. His houfe was on a knolle, with exquifite grafs land falling gently each fide; on one fide he had a little lake of three leagues long, backed by the fnowy heights of Andervall, Weil, and Sweitz.—On the other fide a boundlefs view, fublime and beautiful, of mountains, moftly cultivated to the top!—The arrangement of windows and fences were fuch that, though not in darknefs, we fat in deprivation of the fcene. And here at Breifeg, the clergyman has contrived with two walls, to fhut out the Rhine on one fide, and the caftle Rheineck on the other! Rheineck too, has a little of that hiftorical enhancement, which, whether good or bad, moft minds feel as in a fcene magic! for here it was, that Comte Zinzendorff, a name quite well enough known for a revival of the religious errors of the Turlapins of the 13th century, bought the property, which gave him the rank and vote of an immediate fief of the empire. The rank and title he had without buying, has been told already by Warburton.

The point after Breifeg, and ftill with encreafing captivation, is the great hyte, (called I believe Wefterhold)—and here, though the river is fine, the road has the fcenery finer ftill.—The road runs gently, but not inconfiderably rifing, through woods above, and woods below it, --they flourifh

to

to the rivers edge. The river runs at the bottom of them with fpeed, quickened by the obftruction and narrowing by the ifle.—The ifle has fine meadows and aged trees.—Before Neuwied, with its handfome modern buildings and poplars are on one fide, and the antiquities of Andernach, the caftle and the tower are on the other---framed as it were, in the Hammerfteim rocks, and the four mountains are the villages of Broght, Fornick, &c. &c. with a main ftation for the trade of the Rhine—while all the highlands and pinnacles that are paffed from Rheineck to the Seven Mountains, form the back-ground maffes, and clofe the fcene!—The trade of the Rhine in this part is peculiarly interefting—For befide the wine from the two rivers, and the bafaltes, for the buildings and pavements in all the towns thereabouts—the Dutch from thence get the foffil tarras, fo neceffary in the formation of thefe dykes.—It coft 31 rix dollars for 200 the cubic feet.—Of which price feven rix dollars are given for the tarras—and the reft for carriage and tolls.

Andernach is a fine fituation, not only for fcenery, but for which moft people may think weightier---for commercial effects. It is one of the beft pofitions on the river, yet little is made of it. The chief tradefmen of the town feem thofe who make their market in the fhops of fuperftition! For though the population of the place is but 4000, there are no lefs than five convents, befides the parifh church---which again, is like a French privateer, manned treble; for the curè told me his church had fix vicaires! " Tria Fata," added he, with unexpected vivacity, " we are more than " twice the number of them!"—When a fine boy in company, whofe good manners are equal to his other powers, made a quotation, eulogiftic upon the number fix.

   Ter Tribus ad Palmam Juffæ certere Camænis,
   Ore, Manu, Flatu—Buxu, Fide, Voce, Canentes.

The ruins of Andernach, rather impreffing at the end towards Coblentz, are of great antiquity. The memorial of Valentinian is in the parifh church.—Drufus, the general of Auguftus, fortified and built there.—And if Julius Cæfar did not crofs the Rhine there, as moft probably he did not, but a little higher up, on the bridge fo well preferved by Palladio—the philofophical traveller will find it well worth his while to crofs here to have a few minutes peep into the condition of the petty principality of Neuweid.

NEUWEID.

NEUWEID.

THE pretty white stone town, in the midst of poplars, on the opposite bank of the Rhine.

This prince is, very happily for his fellow citizens, his neighbours and friends, one of the few gentlemen of that order, who seem to understand themselves and their condition,—that they, like every body else, are ordained to live under the universal and equal laws of responsibility.—That with so much privilege and enjoyment, there should be so much duty and merit.—That pre-eminent rank ought to arise proportionably with pre-eminent use!

Accordingly his life, embodying these ideas, has been adorned unceasignly with a series of exertions, manifestly tending to the public good!—None of the German trade in war—no shuffling into corrupt influence—no pilfering of a private treasure!—All was the policy of virtue, pure, disinterested, humane!—He began with the moral glory of self government, to shew that he was fit to govern others. He discharged the debts of his predecessors, though their superstitious sacrifices, wasting their lands, had diminished his means of doing it.—He reformed and retrenched in every department. Religious toleration was unbounded. The game laws and all other feudal oppressions he abolished. There are no longer any droits d'Aubaine, no arbitrary fines, no impositions upon property, whether bequeathed or sold—no taxes upon ingenuity and labour—no personal constraint.

The place is free to all; and every tradesman or artificer, who has any thing to do, may do as he pleases. Each new comer has at once the rights of citizenship—and nothing to pay for them, but, after four or five years, like the other citizens, a contribution of two half crowns.—And even that, he do not pay if he builds—if he builds with ftone he has fifty years exemption—if in wood, he has ten years. The ground, for a houfe, is given by the prince to every fettler, without any quit-rent whatever!

Thefe and other privileges were ratified by a public guarantee, in a placard written, figned and publifhed by the prince himfelf; dated March 12, 1762. And from that time to this, they have never been known to fail. With the moft liberal conftruction, with the moft beneficent obfervance, every iota of each declaration has been fulfilled to all!

The fequel of the ftory gratifies as much as the beginning. Thefe virtuous plans, in each part, have been executed with fuccefs, equal to their merit. The town and territory, already vaunt a new afpect, one of the beft upon the Rhine! The population is doubled! and ingenious arts and economic induftry, and manufactures referring with the beft, becaufe the moft neceffary applications to life, all have encreafed ten-fold! Iron works, cotton weaving, paper making, printing, watches, cabinet making, flourifh daily, more and more!—The iron made there, has already made a great impreflion on the market of Holland—The forges and founderies, already give plenty, to above a thoufand men, and cheap as life is, and all that keeps it well together, in Germany, there are feveral men who are carriers about the works, earning with only a fingle horfe, above 30 crowns a month!—The fteel trade, alfo looks to be very thriving.

The cotton manufacture is already important; and not a month paffes without its being more fo. This was the firft eftablifhment of cotton work in Germany. It is not much above 20 years old, and yet, there are now near 3000 men at work, and their circulation at a fair, has been forty or fifty thoufand florins. Their chief articles are nankeens, handkerchiefs, and figured goods, either for furniture or drefs. Like the Swifs, their colours are very fhewy; they dye well.

Their

Their paper trade, includes furniture paper.—And their defigns and colours are of the beft fchool, Reveillons at Paris.

In education too, as well as watch-making, they feem refolved to follow the Genevefe and the Swifs.---And there is a plan of ftudy, in an eftablifhment faid to be very thriving, for the living languages, as well as the dead---for mathematical learning and mechanics.

Their printing, like the trade in Flanders and Holland, goes to other books rather than German—Chiefly French literature and the moft popular Latin claffics.—And there are already two Journals, one in French, and one in German, printed at Nieuweid.—For it is not found neceffary to have any impofitions on the prefs there. In public conduct, as well as private life, what is wife and virtuous, cannot have any thing to fear!

The prince in the mean while, has advanced in the advancing welfare of all around him. And without the fmalleft fcandal, like begging or extorting a fingle rix-dollar from his people, but merely from his own money funds, he has built two new palaces, from which the eye of morality, as well-landfcape, may revel with fair fatisfaction, over the ruins of the old.—The caftle of Frederickftein upon a rock, is another fine object to him.

But his beft objects, though he has an horizon of thirty leagues, are thofe which have been raifed by himfelf. Each fubftantive good work, for the profperity of the common weal, to foothe the lot, and to fatisfy the neceffities of our common nature.---To aid the advances of civilization--- and on his appointed ground, to leave life better than he found it.

Such is the praife of the prince of Neuwied. The rare and enviable praife. He began life with the treaty of Vienna, and he ends as glorioufly as he began it. He was employed, in making peace, once—but in making war, never.

And yet, as times go, he might have pleaded poverty in apology for any affection he might have had to the obvious

profits

profits of war—for there are but feven and twenty villages, and three towns, in the whole of his little territory—and his revenues at the firft, were not much more than an hundred thoufand florins'!

 Blufh, grandeur, blufh—Proud courts withdraw your blaze
 Ye little ftars—hide your diminifhed rays.

COBLENTZ.

COBLENTZ.

THE time for seeing Coblentz was in the winter of 1791-2—then the French princes were there; with all their followers—a council, an administration, ambassadors, and an army.—It was then a hard matter to get into the town, and still harder to get any thing when you were in. Lord S ‑ ‑, then going down the Rhine, from his friend Mr. Gibbon, at Lausanne, was, I believe, forced to stay and sleep, if he could, on board his bark.

The princes then lived in the hotel of the Comte Vander Leyen, Rue St. Castors—the street going down towards the Pont Volant.—A large old house, built on all sides of a quadrangle; where there was nothing good, but the space of the building, the court-yard, and the garden.—They held a kind of court five times a week—and for those occasions, two rooms were laid into one—that they were not the same as to symmetry nor size—and that the furniture, curtains, girandoles, &c. were totally different. The court was at night, about seven o'clock to ten. And open, I believe, very generally to all comers. Almost every man there seemed a soldier—and whether in uniform or not, all, with no exception that I saw, were in boots.—Comte d'Artois himself was so dressed, and all his people—in short, every body but Monsieur and the Elector. Four or five hundred people might be present. The room was as full as it could hold.

At one end of the room, the right on entering, there were four or five card-tables, where the French princes were at play, the Elector and his sister, some other ladies, a German nobleman or two, two or three French officers, and Prince Nassau (that Prince Nassau who is now in the service

service of Pruffia). They play d very low—and at small games, as Loo and Cafino.

There were fifteen ladies prefent, of whom twelve or thirteen were French. Their names, for obvious reafons, it yet might be improper to mention. Mad. C. afterwards openly in Champagne, was not in the room. Nor another beautiful lady of great elegance and merit. And there were nearly, if not quite, all the French women of much fafhion then at Coblentz.

The card-playing ceafed about nine o'clock—and then the princes mixed in the crowd, who made openings for them as they paffed. They, both, were very unaffuming: nodding and talking, familiarly, with all around them.

When the Elector and his fifter left the room, the princes immediately followed. They went down ftairs together, with fome fmall ceremony, but with much more kindnefs. And at the coach-door, when they took leave of each other, there was a fhew of fincere and unaffected feeling in it, on both fides, equally very ftrong. It was a parting, that would have done for an uncle and his nephews on a longer feparation than theirs was likely to be. In any other place, and time, it might have feemed too much, perhaps, for a mere good-night (and it was no more). But, under their circumftances, it was not fo.

I was with a young man of ftrong mind, Mr. B———, the nephew of Lord K.—and he thought and felt as I did. It was an interview fingularly impreffing.

When the Elector drove away, the princes returned up ftairs, where the crowd continued as before.—About ten they left the room. Neither the Elector's minifter, Baron Dumenick—nor M. de Calonne, were prefent.

Thus it was five times in a week—on the intervening evenings, Sundays and Thurfday, the fame fort of affembly were at the Elector's palace.—Where the room, and all the furniture, luftres, &c. were very magnificent – but all the

gentlemen,

gentlemen in boots, as before—the crowd was very great; as I should think, above fix hundred people - when the Elector and his minifter, the princes and their fuite, entered, and paffed to the upper end of the room—where there were a few card-tables, as before. The princes had externally no inconfiderable ftate. For, befides the parade of councils, audiences, and reviews, they ftill endured the fame guard as they had at Paris. The four hundred who ufed to attend Monfieur and Comte d'Artois, all had come over. Of the King's troop, the garde du corps, two-thirds (twelve hundred), were alfo with the princes.

The French troops then at Coblentz, and near it, were chiefly cavalry—and the temporary apparatus, ftabling, magazines of forage, &c. were rather curious. Reckoning draft-horfes and all, we were told there were at one time more than eight thoufand horfes; but we faw nothing to make us believe it. And in all, they reckoned upon having twenty thoufand. But they were not the only unfortunate people who have reckoned without their hoft.

The infantry, as the Mirabeau (the Vifcount) corps, Mr. Sinclair's—the Scotch—part of the Irifh brigade—the Anvergne, d'Allemagne Royale, &c. &c. were cantoned in the neighbouring towns. Party, the whole time, ran high, and fo unabated by any exigence, that old M. de Condè was the whole time at Worms. And M. de Breteuil, another man of fmall parts, but a candidate for adminiftration, was with him.

The councils, which were often enough, were held at the prince's lodgings. The princes were accuftomed to attend. M. de Calonne, the main-fpring of every movement, was of courfe there—fo was M. Le Baron Duminich, the minifter of the Elector. The foreign minifters alfo, fometimes were fummoned—and any man of figure in the fervice, as the Prince Naffau, &c. The councils fometimes were long continued. The day on which the Czarina fent her fecond

H h   difpatch

dispatch (the first had the pecuniary supply) with the address to the French army there, the council which met soon after ten, continued till six in the evening.

There were some few ecclesiastics who had joined the forces at Coblentz---and among them, two bishops---St. Omer and Arras. The ambassadors to the French princes, there at that time, were from Sweden and Russia. A Spanish ambassador was then said to be on his route. There was also said to be an humble agent or two from courts of *less character*, but they were held, as I understood, very properly, in the dark.

The residence of M. de Calonne was in the new square (Clementstadt, as it is called, after the electors name) at the corner opposite the palace, next the river and the Chartreuse---there he held a regular office of half a dozen commis, with his brother the abbé; and himself also working with his untiring spirit and capacity, from morning to night. Promptitude and perseverance, generally to be found but in two different and constructed minds, are in his mind united. When Mr. W—— wrote his celebrated answer to Lord H———, ex improviso, in a rapid moment, amidst the distractions of a public meeting in Guildhall, there was sufficient praise upon the merit of speed. Odd exertions of the same sort M. de C. did daily, in the undelayed furthering of dispatches. And too probably, sometimes, not without the faults of genius; rashly yielding to the allurement of the first idea.

Before the supply came from Russia, there had been less considerable contributions from different quarters. On any emergence, M. de C. made a sacrifice from his own resources. The Elector too, was unceasingly generous and kind.

Though the corps of emigrants at Coblentz were, for the most part, officers, yet some of them were in want of petty sums, and daily supplies. An establishment was therefore

fore formed, and pay diftributed, juft equivalent to a daily diftribution of the mereft neceffaries---the cavalry officers had at the rate of fixty livres a month; the infantry, forty livres. But it was officially announced as an army notice, that in compliance with the obvious exigencies of the time, thofe gentlemen who could, fhould, do without the money---leaving their arrears to be paid at a more convenient feafon. And accordingly moft of them did leave it. For, to do them juftice, whatever may be the opinion on their caufe, cæluim non animum, the pecuniary failing was in their circumftancesonly, and not in their fpirit!--- We dined with fome officers of the garde du corps; and one of them faved us from a trifling impofition. We could get no fmall money in change, and fo, what was wanting, one of them difburfed for us. When we went to pay him, he was on guard at the prince's. No importunity could pofitively make him take the money; and no alternative occurred, but to tofs it into his fword-hilt.

In the gentlemen with whom we were fo lucky to affociate, what was gay and difinterefted, was not the only good part of their mind. We faw, in more than one inftance, a trying proof that they had candor at heart---that they felt correctly, and that, even when obvioufly againft themfelves, they had fortitude to avow their feeling. Thus at our dinner, two officers about the princes joined heartily in praifing the admirable talents of our chief parliamentary fpeakers in oppofition; and, rather ably, quoted, through the French tranflation, from Mr. Sheridan's fpeeches and Mr. Fox, as well as Mr. Burke. At another table, an Englifh gentleman, with at leaft as much of man as wit about him, produced, with his ufual independence, a panegyric on Condorcet---when, to the aftonifhment of all, he was joined by another perfon, in talents and pofition, of all the Frenchmen at Coblentz, the firft! He praifed Condorcet too---for the extent and vigor of his powers---but did not think his

accomplifhaccomplishments precisely fit for the unceasing rapidity of the work he had then undertaken, his daily journal!—The Elector's minister, a very capable gentleman, was there, and so were other men of parts, the nephew and brother of M. de Calonne—and it cannot but gratify them to be reminded of a trait in their excellent friend, so admirable for many fine endowments, but for none more especially, than the most delicate candor, the most liberal confideration!

As to the political plans of the French cabinet then at Coblentz, it is much easier and more sure, to speak but negatively, to say what they were not, rather than what they were. They were not, I have reason to believe, so guilty nor so mad, as to think of attempting a restoration of despotism. They talked with due sensibility and ambition of a free constitution—but with what modifications they might mean, I know not :—I do not think they knew themselves. Montesquieu's traditionary fame of the English system passed there as elsewhere, more read than understood—for it is, essentially in the books, a popular system—and to be popular seems an universal instinct, felt alike by the vicious and the good; with the one, it is an appetite and a pleasure; with the other, a duty and a reward.

The effect of so many strangers in the town, was very visible, not merely in the markets, by the increased stir and prices there—but in the diminution of stir elsewhere!—The towns-people and the peasants seemed over-awed out of all national character—nay, in some instances, to have lost the most ordinary powers of loco-motion and spontaneity—like what some naturalists represent, when a sparrow happens to have hatched a cuckoo.

However, with a sensation, perhaps, and an expression, like tingling after numbness, the burghers began, rather awkwardly, to fling about, and oppose the continuance of the French.—Even the magistrates made remonstrance!—like the left-handed lunatic in Beotia, wishing even com_
merce

merce to fail rather than bate a jot of a political prejudice or perfonal picque!

They were anfwered as perverfe folly ought to be. The French were fuffered to ftay at Coblentz till the appointed time for their march—a march that led them to be facrificed, by combined perfidy, in Champagne. In the mean while, there could be one effect from their ftay, and that for the place, muft have been good—the circulation of money among the moft ufeful trades. So that the French at Coblentz, like the Englifh in Flanders, muft have enriched their neighbours, however they might happen to have beggared themfelves!

COBLENTZ.

COBLENTZ.

Fraternis cumlandus aquis, vos pergite juncti.

COBLENTZ has many local recommendations—good buildings, fine scenery, concurring rivers, (and hence its name) wines too that never fail, pit coal, lime, and wood.— It is, except it be Meintz, the best residence on the Rhine.

The Moselle too, which here joins the Rhine, should also be worth talking of, or else Ausonius must have talked much in vain. For he has given it almost five hundred verses; which, in their turn, appropriate every thing which could come within his reach from art, from accident, or nature. And to crown the whole, as he thinks, he calls on Homer to give up his Simois, and Virgil the Tyber; as if, apart from poetical convenience, there had been any local preference or elementary charm either in one or the other.

> *Fraternis cumulandus aquis—vos pergite juncti*
> *Et mare purpureum gemino propellite tractu.*

This too, though good as precept, prophecy will not hold— for after all the tributary streams from the Necker, the Mein, and the Moselle, &c. this accumulation of waters, magnificent as it is, ends in a mode unworthy its swelling temper, and full command of circumstance, without an æstuary and without a name, errorem fortuna tuum, in a dirty and ruinous alliance with the frogs and the fens, the lakes and the logs of Dutchmen!

Yet as to the poetry of Italy and Greece, if it cannot hold water, it need not to be beat from its wine—at least not by any thing to be got on the Moselle. The Moselle is a small and bad edition of what you have upon the Rhine. The Rhine wine becomes, under propitious afpects and foftering fkies, thriving, venerable, and mild. The Mofelle is ever auftre, cheerlefs, and weak—and feemingly incorrigible, never gets thofe rich, gay, companionable qualities which the fun gives to the growth of Burgundy, the Falernian vineyard, and the Alicati (which is Greek)—and which, but very feldom, Hockheim and Oppenheim, are found gathering from time. Bad Mofelle, and worfe beer, are the ordinary beverage; but at all proper tables there is French wine, and what the Englifh call Old Hock, (there Rhine wine).

On the vineyards, as on every other ufeful object in art or nature, the Prince Bifhop, like a virtuous and philofophic man, as he is, has given correfponding care. But care, even like his, cannot reverfe the laws of foil and fky, of heat and cold.

What can be done, he has tried, and will I hope long continue trying to do. He has revifed every department of the ftate, and fearlefs of what folly and corruption canted about innovation, he has co-operated with the people for every poffible reform. The impofitions are leffened—the magiftracy are purified—the police, in all its parts, importantly improved—commerce quickened and extended—fcience cultivated—and life, in every detail, made better, wifer, and happier!

In fome regions, God knows with how much reafon, the name of ruler is never mentioned without inconceivable abhorrence of what is guilty, and contempt at what is bafe. But it is not fo at Coblentz. There the people, apparently to us unanimous, were lavifh of none but the kindlieft opinions towards the prince, and expreffions of the beft earned praife. They fpoke of him as happily exalted above the mean amufements of a court, or the dark defigns of it! Of a large expanded mind, and a free matured fpirit, ambitious,

bitious, through rectitude, of the public favour, and capable of no small venture and all sacrifices too for the public good!

They told us, and I would repeat it, as we heard it, with the rapture due to truth recording good deeds, that in the time which the present Clement had been their chief magistrate, the whole state had put on mended looks! and was not in fact like the same! So much was their whole constitution, in powers, in principles, in pursuits, in opinions, and in manners, all substantially and vitally, so much altered for the better!

In spite of his profession, not less likely to be free minded, but more liable to seem tender at any slavish prejudice that might brutally assail him, he struck at error, though perhaps, in some sort, convenient to his own circumstances, and certainly pretending to some sanction from time!— And he aimed, effectually we trust, in the proper place. The root he pointed at! as the skillful woodman might, who sees heights that he cannot reach, and width that he cannot grasp, in the rank spreading of some sycophant weed, flourishing as it fades the glory of the forest!

The schools were the object of the bishop. There he saw and has ably striven to check, the radical principle of error, ramifying into all its fantastic forms, from excessive indulgence, excessive mortification, excessive sloth!

And while he checked—he was ready to rectify too. He forwarded the useful growth, while he lopped the luxuriance, and while he weeded the soil! Instead of the empty noise and barren verbiage of the schools, he has instituted the living languages and useful knowledge! mathematical learning, classical taste, natural history, and experimental science, are the chief accomplishments in the compass of man—and these, it is endeavoured, shall flourish now on the ground before defiled, with polemic divinity, monastic superstition, unconditional subjection, and all those mockeries

of

of barbarism, which, as far as such jargon can be explicable, tend to nothing but general stupefaction! not to make our frame invulnerable, but dim, to the vilest evils which can assail us—the pestilence which walketh in darkness—and the horrors of a dungeon with a chain!

Besides abolishing these abominable evils, he has otherwise need to rectify action in its source. He has founded an establishment for widows and orphans—he has began and continued it from his own funds, and thus, irresistably called on others to complete it.

He has prohibited extravagant funerals. "They are," said he "a vain, an idle offering to the dead, often to the "distress, and sometimes to the ruin of the living!"

He has established public libraries, with all the adjuncts of instruments, charts, and globes.

He has suggested and formed an insurance against fire! That the Roman empire, in its best days, did not think of. —He has added to it, like them, an aquæduct; and that necessary element is now continually supplied!

The roads in the electorate of Treves, now rival the turnpike trusts near London—they, near London, are done by the collective powers of the people. Through Treves, the prince, with all the merit, is to have all the praise. He has with the magnificence of real use, shaming all pretenders to the heroic, expended on this object 350,000 crowns! And through the whole territory the people accordingly bless him! The roads are excellent—and they have foot paths, posts, and mile stones!

All this good, and much more, he has done—and with no sensible departure, as to expence, from the established rule! " I have not, it is true," says the prince " accumulated " a private treasure—but, neither have I taken from the " treasure of any other! I have not begged nor borrowed " from the people a single kreutzer!" a low coin not equal to a halfpenny.

The elector, with his arch-bishopric of Treves, holds the bishopric of Augsbourg, and the provostship of Ellwangen. Both of which furnish revenue and an honorary title, if honour there can be in profit without equivalent labour to deserve it—for the chapter and magistrates of Augsbourg and Ellwangen, discharge all the functions of government, civil and ecclesiastical, without any aid from the elector.

The archbishop to which the electoral dignity connects, is elected by the Chapter of Treves—and all the forty canons must be of uninterrupted nobility through sixteen descents, both paternal and maternal. "Every body sees," said Duke ———— "how much this must preserve the "unerring sagacity, the incorruptible purity of every mea- "sure!" When chosen, the elector is invested by the emperor and confirmed by the pope. To this as to all bishoprics, the elegible age should be thirty. But with this, as with more momentous qualifications, his Holiness can dispense.

The territory of the electorate is about 135 square miles, not reckoning Augsbourg and Ellwangen, which are about forty miles more. This territory is subdivided into thirty-seven bailliages, with a population in all above two hundred and eighty thousand.

The revenues are about 73,000l. sterling—of which the Bishopric of Augsbourg supplies a hundred thousand florins, and Ellwangen eighty thousand. The expenditure, with all the elector's economy, which is both virtuous and wise, cannot be made much less than the income.

The government has so far a popular cast, that no pecuniary imposition can burthen the country but with the participation of the people, testified by their deputies, called states. And they are not only the nominal, but the real representatives of the people. There is no such outrage on their constitution, on the constitution of common sense and decency, as any of the deputies being nominated by the aristocracy.

ariftocracy, though the nobility and clergy are very numerous and powerful, having two thirds of all the landed property between them!

The chief adminiftration of juftice and civil government are in the Privy Council, the Aulic Council; the Court of Regency, and Revifion. The appellant jurifdiction, in all caufes for above 1000 florins, is to Wetzlaer. The right de non appellando, otherwife inherent to the electorate, having once lapfed for want of claim.

In the councils the members are but few. For the elector's object being not private peculation, but the public good, he has in no department encreafed the number of placemen—in fome departments he has diminifhed them. In the chief council, where the elector acts as prefident, the numbers are reduced to four.

The minifter of ftate (now M. Dumenick), an ecclefiaftical minifter, a prime lawyer, called Councellor of Regency, and a marfhall, are the chief officers of bufinefs.— For parade there is a chamberlain, a cup bearer, and a treafurer.

The elector exercifes all the functions of fovereignty—coinage, laws, foreign treaties, punifhments—which may include excommunication, banifhment, and death! But which, to do him juftice, are rarely, if ever, included by him! The ecclefiaftical jurifdiction of Treves ufed to ftretch over Lorraine; and among the fuffragans of the archbifhopric, were Metz, Verdun, Toul; Nanci, and St. Drez. When the French revolution, as the Englifh reformation had done before, abrogated all fuch extraneous fupremacy, pecuniary compenfation was offered for every tenure fo abolifhed. This offer, obvioufly wife and juft, was by too many of the feoffees injurioufly refufed. Some of them, more fage, were willing to accede. The Cardinal D. I know, was among the number of the latter. And, from the general character of the councils at Coblentz, a provident acquiefcence was, I have heard, at firft in contemplation there.

The military eftablifhment is worthy a fyftem of fenfe and feeling becomingly moderate—one regiment of infantry and about thirty, or forty horfe.

The ecclefiaftical order are more extravagant! in Coblentz alone there are five churches, two of them with numerous and wealthy chapters, and feventeen convents. At Treves, with as many churches and chapters, the monafteries are thirty-five. As to the value of thefe appointments, the canons are 2000 florins—the livings generally one to three or four thoufand livres. The clergy, particularly abbayes and other grofs finecures, have been lately taxed, moft properly for the fupport of the new ufeful fchools. Above 6000 florins a year have been fo levied. An operation this, by which the demon of fuperftition may be gradually wrought to defeat itfelf. Of the nobility, who are alfo numerous, thefe families are the moft leading, Metternich, Vander Leyen, Kempeufch, Baffenheim, Burrefheim, Boos, and Kerpen.

About Coblentz, as through the reft of Germany, the nobility are not, like many of the noble families in England, employed in ufeful arts and extenfive commerce. The elector has done much for their encouragement—and nature has done more. But referring to the manifeft opportunities of the place, the two arms of Coblentz, as an old claffical writer calls the Mofelle and Rhine, yet are fuffered to continue idle. For commerce, Coblentz feems the beft pofition on the Rhine. And two or three active able Englifhmen might without difficulty prove it fo. Grain, wine, hemp, are the beft productions to be fold; thofe to be brought from England, the manufactures of Manchefter, Birmingham, and Wolverhampton, and Sheffield.

The taxes are chiefly duties on objects of confumption, wood, wine, falt, &c. The duties are levied at the different

toll-

toll houses on the roads and rivers, and being charged ad valorem, muft be reciprocally liable to fail of equity and effect for thofe who pay the tolls and them who receive it.— There is a fort of poll tax of a florin a year on each family —half of which is mitigated on the widow. And a land tax nearly as light as in the electorate of Cologne, and more equal on all rents, tithes, and any income whatever.

On the whole, life, for economic advantages, is not low. Money goes as far as at Cologne. For the general fyftem of government the ecclefiaftical are better than the lay electorates—for there can be no fuch peftilent mifchief as a minority—and the age required, thirty inftead of eighteen years, implies a better hope, that he who is employed in the arduous office of government, will be lefs unable to govern himfelf. The celibacy of their perfuafion rids the people from any burthen for a family; no young Julus, &c. And through the ecclefiaftical character they efcape further ills, in not meddling with wars either as a diverfion or a trade. No prince is to be fold and no peafant to be bought. Public debt, confequently, there can be none.

In the arts which are moft neceffary, agriculture and building, the country is not backward. The foil aids them in the one, and materials in the other. The farms have no peculiarity at all noticeable. The new fquare, Clemenftadt, is among the prettieft places upon the Rhine. They build with rough ftone and ftucco.

The elector's palace is one of the beft buildings in Germany; though the roof of black flate, with the number of chimneys and windows in the attics, fpoil the effect of the facade, where the lower parts are in a good ftyle, with an Ionic portico, and dependant colonades along an extent of 180 yards. The offices are in two femicircular wings.

The internal difpofition is fufficiently fplendid and gay. The rooms of ceremony are nine in fuite—the one in the centre is the largeft, 56 by 36. There is contiguous a

gallery

gallery of 120 by 48. This gallery has five windows to the Rhine—and oppofite to them five looking-glafs doors, which occafionally remove, leaving very cleverly fo many openings between pillars, and fo uniting with another hall of the fame fize. Here it was the evening affemblies of the elector met, when the French Princes were at Coblentz.

The French, with their gobelin work, have long had a monopoly of all Europe, but England. In England, tafte and cleanlinefs have changed it for fomething better. At Coblentz the gobelin, the chief rooms, except the throne, &c. which according to cuftom are crimfon—as the blind man faid, " like the trumpet in battle!"

The imitative arts offer nothing very curious. There are forty or fifty portraits by Germans, about as far from Lawrence and Beechy, as they are from Raffaelle's, Pope Urban, and Leonardo of himfelf. Menagcot, the Frenchman, has given four large pictures of Antony, Scipio, Belifarius, and Paul—and there is a model of Mad. Langham, with her child, at the refurrection, awaking from their tomb. It is with models, as with fketches, they are almoft always more impreffing than finifhed works. For finifhing weakens, as it were by dilation, the fpirited effence of original ideas. And the emotions which all men may feel, very few have ability to exprefs. It is fo with the exquifite fketches of the prefident in our popular academy. It is fo in this model of the monument, in fuch juft repute, at Hindlebank near Berne. The model too has the confecrating line from Haller, and which he, like Boerhaave and Linneus, illuftrious for the piety as well as philofophy of his opinions, derives from the fource the moft high and the moft holy, the fpirit of God in the language of his fon—" Lord, here I " am, and the child which thou has given me—of thofe " which thou haft given me, have I loft none."

The palace though new, and on the whole elegant, has not yet any ground made into pretty landfcape about it.

Hard

Hard as it may be to get land, it feems yet harder to adorn it. That is to come, when the fulnefs of time will let it, and the maturity of tafte. Could we difpofe it, that point fhould not linger. The genius of cultivation fhould have powers equal to the genius of the place. For the Rhine winds round it with objects of fingular magnificence.— The Chartreufe on one hill, and Ehrenbreitftien on the other —a fortrefs on a mountain, which for impofing romantic effect may be fecond to Gibraltar.

We cannot therefore wifh with more good will to the place—and well remembering the unexpected kindnefs and advantages we had there, we fhould not teftify lefs. I owe to Coblentz fome hours and views of life, among the moft extraordinary which can be compaffed in the furprifes of talents and of chance, and in the wonders of contraft, in temper ftruggling with deftiny! whofe extremes, like thofe of elementary heat and cold, are extraneous merely, and leave the unconquerable fpirit with will to rectify, with power to redrefs itfelf of all.—What Fontenelle therefore, with his *Ideès du Beau*, would have referred to the beautiful of action, and Euripides would have feized as a fit theme for the fublime.

Των γαρ μεγαλων αξιοπευθης
Φημαι μαλλον κατεχυσιν.

FRANCFORT

FRANKFORT.

THE road to Frankfort is one of the best in the world—for any body on whom you may have a *post obit!* If you are in luck, it may do for him in limine, in the first passes up the steep, stoney, mountain of Ehrenbreitstien!—He may break his neck—or if only a collar-bone, it may suffice! as in the case of King William, in Bushy-Park!

Secondly—if he looks at the fortress of Ehrenbreitstien, where there is a view over twenty or thirty villages from Mentz to Luxembourg—from Luxembourg to Cleves—he may chance to see some of the good citizens of Mentz, here taken care of since the siege!—and with humanities too, like the prison, worthy of the twelfth century!—All that may make a tug at his heart! and then, like Lord Falkland, drooping under the woes of patriotism, he may never laugh more!—or if he has the heart of a Roman emperor in his bosom, he may die laughing, at what all others would grieve!

Third—should he survive so far, there are, after all, twenty German standen or leagues, with the other trials of German roads, German post-horses, and more feræ, German postillions to boot—of course, the odds are so many against him, that he may depart like ——————, in a passion*.

There are, however, trees enough, if every man could that way get rid of his care—oak, elm, ash, and often in large masses, like forests—all particularly fine, and most ineffably so the Elector—for to him they belong. When they cut any trees, they leave two or three feet of the stem, which soon having shoots and foliage on all sides, forms a singular hedge, neither ugly nor weak

* The Reader is requested to fill up the blank above, as Sterne did several from Lord Bacon and Montaigne.

This mode of leaving fo much ftem in every fall of wood, was rather wondered at by a traveller who came from a country rather remarkable for talents as to taxation—when the prince faid, with much dexterity and fineffe—" What " you expect our woodmen to be as nimble-fingered as the " financiers are with you; and that our bills, like your " taxes, fhould cut up every thing by the roots!"

The new plantations too, are prodigious—chiefly of poplars and firs. The foils are, where not rocky—fand and clay.—There is a little gravel.—Some of the clay is red, as in Devonfhire, of the fame hue, but not the fame depth in the vein. Nor is there any thing like the fame abundance or force in the crops.—On the weft-fide of the Rhine, on the laft week of July (27th) the corn was houfed, and the land ploughed—on the oppofite fide, in Limbourg, a week after, no corn was cut, and moft of it was as green as in a cold wet fummer of Scotland—the fummer had been immoderately hot. The hufbandry feems penurious; with more rye and barley than wheat—there is but little natural grafs. And fome Turkey corn, efpecially nearer Frankfort.

The effect of this country is fatiguing to the eye, from the vaft dimenfions of each diftribution. The fhapes and furfaces of lands in Yorkfhire and Cornwall are very huge. But here, informe, ingens, the magnitude is monftrous, almoft to deformity. It was Auguft when we paffed—but in fpite of fun-fhine and warmth, it was dull and dreary, wherever the woods failed. The farms too, like the afpect of the country, are enormous—the houfes are very few; hedges there are none!—and except in the mile-ftones, the country feems to have obeyed a like raving with Dido, and every trace of humanity is deftroyed.

    Abolere nefandi
   Cuncta virum monumenta.

At Frankfort, however, and all immediately around it, they live and move again—naturally fhowy, and rationally gay—in the bleffings of a Republic, formed on independence, toleration, and peace.

Hence, trade at Frankfort is very flourifhing. And tradefmen there, difplay a fplendor of wealth and elegance, not out-done even in all the ufeful magnificence of merchants in London. The houfe of Mr. Schweitz, the banker, which we faw, is a fpecimen, really not a little curious, both for expence and tafte. He has fix rooms in fuite—the two beft 40 and 36 by 24, lofty in proportion, with painted cielings, Scaglionla columns, inlaid floors, double chimneys, double doors, and what-not—ftairs with ftatues in the niches, baths, court-yard, &c. &c. &c. The defigns were given, for we thought it worth while to enquire by whom, by Maredi, an Italian, and Prenge, of Manheim.—The whole coft, five-eighths of a million (florins)! where materials, untaxed and contiguous, are fifty per cent. cheaper than in London; and labour, of the beft workmen, but 33 kreutzers a day!

There are many commercial houfes; not lefs than two hundred and fifty to three hundred, completely firft-rate; And I believe verily, with a character too no lefs abfolute and adorning. Altogether free from any of that political latitude, which, we once heard, had been the misfortune of another town. Where more than one tradefman, of ten thoufand a year, and with manners and endowments, as they faid, yet more alluring, had been, literally, at the back of fome minifter—technically fufpicious, and morally low! and yet even fuch men, capital as they were, on fuch inftigation, manifeftly bafe, had confented, aftonifhingly, to mix with the humbleft accomplices in plans of political impofition and falfe alarm! Some of them, no doubt, unconfcious of mifchief, and above it—like the mob only, and not like the pickpockets at a fire. Indeed, energy of character, both intellectual and moral, is the recorded renown of the town. And prior to any other, it had what the Proteftant

teftant reader muft deem an honour, the vigor to attack fuccefsfully the impofitions of Rome ! to refift the fupremacy fo fantaftically ufurped by the Popes ---and, in fpite of the Nicene council, to have the idolatry of image-worfhip, abandoned and abolifhed.

The fame free fpirit has been well fuftained ; it is the prefent glory of the people, and their reward, in the complex bleffings, fo derivatively enjoyed !

Opinions are free. And thus, like the primary vital elements, have efcaped all forced, artificial, tendency, by ftagnation to putrefcence. And with their purity, they have kept their variety too. Perhaps a grateful offering in his fight, who has made manifold works---but in wifdom all !--- All nations, and languages to do him fervice !---who has gracioufly vouchfafed the fame lights unto all---but with different interventions, with different pofitions, with different powers, to fpeculate upon each. Who has uniformly written his law in each heart, but has organifed with diverfity, to us, darkly as we fee, admirable, each tongue which may tell indeed, each nerve which can feel it !—O Lord, how manifeft are they works ; in wifdom haft thou made them all. "*Impulfore Chrifti*," fays Suetonius, and perhaps blafphemoufly, on the perfecutions of Claudius, but every mind, fofter and more enlightened, will apply it to more human objects, and to better times. To the code of Carolina, where univerfal toleration, even through each moft minute conceivable demand for it, was fo providently diftributed by Mr. Locke—and to the treaty of Weftphalia, where it pleafed them to allow what God has given, liberty of confcience to all !

Thus Frankfort, too, foothes and ftrengthens the mind, with objects like and emotions of candour and benevolence ! with the venerable fight of a peopled and bufy town, elaborate to embody and adorn, what may feparately feem religious truth ! In opinions different: but in practice the fame—each refpecting and protecting each ; but in the defenfible, if innocent variety, of that beft worfhip, a well-ordered life, bent, before the God of univerſal good, humbly, but zealouſly, to work together with him, and ſpeed, undelayed by any human perverſion, his bleſſings, peace, freedom, neighbourhood, fraternity, to all!

In this manner, to the mind's eye, indeed to the outward ſenſe, the public worſhip of Frankfort is its moſt attractive feature. For it is not only all voluntary, but far beyond the magnitude of the place, magnificent! With new-built chapels for each perſuaſion; ſome of them ſplendid, with ſcaglioula columns and other ornaments, but all of them, a model for Rome and London, in the neceſſary attractions of perfect cleanlineſs, good arrangement, light, warmth, and ventilation.

Not, that, church architecture, almoſt every where defective, is here complete. The fronts, undiſtinguiſhed from common dwelling-houſes, want the portico and colonades, of ſuch appropriate decorum, for the congregation to iſſue. The light too, through common faſhes, is an apparatus not removed enough from common life. And pews and galleries, though not pent up with ſuch penury of ſpace as where chapel-dealing is a trade, yet needleſsly offend the eye; with a diſtribution, which nothing but uſe, and the more becomingly predominant ideas of the ſolemn ſervice, can prevent all, from pronouncing barbarous, and as ſuch, fit for nothing but to be diſmiſſed!—*Natura tua vi*, the light ſhould derive from above, and the form ſhould be a round. Michael Angelo (if he is any authority in architecture) Bramanti, and whoever elſe might work at St. Peter's, have proved even there, how ſide-lights muſt fail. Or if they ever can be admiſſible, that the only bearable form of them muſt be the window of Palladio!

This is made manifeſt by Mr. Wyatt, in his deſigns for the chapel at Kentiſh-Town. A work, though ſmall and frugal, yet of ſuch taſte, contrivance, and knowledge of effect—as are not unworthy of his genius. A genius, which in his firſt grand effort diſplayed powers more tranſcendant

than

than any since the other admired wonder of the same name, the Pantheon at Rome! In a generous solicitude for the noblest art, in the service of the noblest object, it were to be wished that there was a parish-church built by him—for he would certainly improve the whole interior—and probably restore, with some new perfection, if it could be, the form so justly praised in the popular buildings of antiquity, where the people met together, connexi gradibus had their sittings, in rows, by gradation rising from the ground!

Small as the population of Frankfort is, not more than 36,000, and rather more than a sixth part of them are Jews. The people have contrived to allow themselves, what they consider as a privilege, a multiplicity in their places of worship. The Lutherans have seven. The Catholics as many. The Jews have a synagogue. The Calvinists two chapels. One of the last is French—and that, with the Eglise Reformè, should be seen. And there is another, which will be a remarkable building, for a Lutheran congregation.—It is without angles, but not quite a circle—127 by 102 are the measurements, and 86 feet high—having two tiers of gallery.—M. Hesse is the architect. The red stone of which it is constructed, comes from Franconia—and very cheap, as the carriage is water—and yet the estimates are above half a millions of florins!—and that without any per centage for the architect; which, in Germany, indeed throughout the continent, is a mode properly reprobated, as a premium for extravagance and waste. M. Hesse does this as town-architect—an office with a salary of a thousand crowns a year. They who can be anxious about the place where the Electors of the empire have their chamber, and where the Emperor is crowned, will find it here; in the old Gothic equilateral cathedral. He enters at the north door, and his exit is at the west.

The trade of the town is a speculation rather more interesting. For through Frankfort, as through a central point of circulation, the asperities of Germany, are softened

by

the productions of better regions—by the manufactures of England, the wine and oil of France, and the multiplied articles of luxury and ufe from the Eaft Indies and the Weft.—Woollen cloth, Manchefter goods, hardware, buttons, &c. are our manufactures that have the moft favour. And it was an honeft gratification to hear, the reputed well-won fuperiority of our tradefmen—that bills on London were above par two and three per cent.—while, of fome other nations, as in the north of Europe, Ruffia particularly, their paper credit was not current—unlefs indorfed and vouched by fome Dutch or Englifh houfe, known capable of the guarantee. The louis d'or alfo is generally faleable at fome fous (10 to 16) above par.

The Italians fell fome manufactured filk—and the Swifs and Geneva people, watch-work and the tools for it. Of the two fairs, one at Eafter, the other in the autumn, the circulations, in favourable times, have amounted to two or three millions fterling. The laft year's commerce fell, like other needlefs facrifices, butchered by the war!

The nominal duration of each fair is three weeks, but really lafting almoft as long again. The trade of moft moment is difpatched fome days before the fair—till the fourth day of the fair all merchandize paffes free. Except Leipfic, there is no German fair with fo much refort.— Frankfort once was a prime market for printed books—but the magiftrates demanding a gratuitous copy of every new work, the trade at once fled to Leipfic. A warning this, from mutual detriment, againft arbitrary claims, and their rafh agitation, either on one fide or the other.

The commercial regulations on bills of exchange at Frankfort, are different in the fair, and out of it,—In the fair, the bills, unlefs with a fpecific mention of another date, are payable in the fecond week. On failure of payment, they muft be protefted on the Saturday in the fecond week, between two o'clock and fun-fet. At any other time, the

ufance

usance is fifteen days, reckoning as one the day of acceptance—with four days grace, Sundays and festivals not included. At four days sight, there is no grace. The course at par with London is 14½ batze a 4 kreutzers for a pound sterling.

Frankfort, as a residence, is not expensive. Being a republic, the government is a cheap thing. And being pacific, there is no pretence for any very burthensome taxes. There is no imposition on real property, in the shape of land or house tax, no tax on windows, hearths, &c.—There is no poor-rate—no burthen for street-police, lights, and scavangers. What little money is requisite, arises from customs, droits d'entrée, on consumption, and from a capitation also well proportioned, and bearing very lightly.

The capitation is this, a fortune of 10,000 florins a year pays 52 florins—that is little more than one-half per cent.—like the land-tax in Mary-le-bone and some other places, not a penny and half a farthing in the pound! Those who have 5000 florins, pay 26. And they who have no more than 500 florins, pay but five kreutzers (not quite an English halfpenny)—in this rate and exhibition of circumstances, there is no schedule made officially, as at Nuremberg, &c. but each individual rates and reports himself.

The droits d'entrée must vary as the quantity of commodities must be variable. But the revenue from all, including the capitations, at the maximum, but 600,000 guilders, or 30,000l.

The magistrates of this respectable and free republic, are of course elective. The electors are the bourgeois, about 14,000. They chuse a senate of fifty-one, and two bourgmasters. There are three judges, also elective; and all of the Lutheran persuasion. None of these places are jobs. Their remuneration, less in profit than honor, is held in this popular preference of their fellow citizens. The judges have 300l. a year. Such is their simple and unexpensive

apparatus

apparatus for the little law-making they find wanting at Frankfort.

For the execution of the law, in civil and criminal caufes, the fenator and judges fit in rotation. The proceedings, as elfewhere through Germany, are in writing. And the appellant jurifdiction at Wetzlaer, in actions for debt, a ftranger may be arrefted for the fmalleft fums—but a bourgeois of Frankfort muft have a hearing before a judge, prior to any arreft attaching legally upon him.—When imprifoned, the creditor muft maintain them at an expence of about fourpence Englifh the day. There were no debtors nor criminals when we were there. The criminals are punifhed by labour—which is by beating the *tarras* (before defcribed) to powder, for ftucco—capital punifhments are very rare. The laft we heard of was nine years fince, a woman for the murder of a child. And the criminal fuffered, we were told, not by the gibbet, as men are punifhed, but by having the throat cut!—a punifhment more offenfive and abhorrent than the guillotine, as it imbrues a human hand (if an executioner can be called human) in the needlefs abominations of blood.

The guillotine, by-the-bye, is faid, not truly, to have originated with the penal law of Scotland. It is of more antiquity, for a fac-fimile of the inftrument may be feen in the well-known work of Bochius, of Antwerp, the 18th plate, with fixteen or eighteen Latin verfes, hexameter and pentameter, not worth repeating, on the oppofite page – and according to a report, eafier given than received, the drawing was aided by Caracci!

On Baron Reifbeck's authority, the money fpent in lawfuits was faid to be 50,000 rix dollars a year—whatever they might be in his time, they are not fo now; for the game-laws, one chief fource of the mifchief, are every where relaxed—and the other caufe of quarrel, contefts in

the

the burgefs court, and for the magiftracy, oppofition, we found, gradually abating.

Reifbeck, whom, by-the-bye, I never met with till March laft, was praifed and tranflated by Mr Matty, a gentleman whom it is impoffible to mention without fond and ftrong emotions of regret, regard, and praife—" *femper acerbum*, " *femper honoratum!*"—It was the book, which ftumbling in his way, urged him to learn German. But the book was over-rated by him, whether referred to amufement or to ufe —it is not ample nor correct enough for what is to be didactic—and it wants elegance and vivacity for what would be gay.

The amufements of the town, though not inelegant, are lefs commanding than the ferious objects of it. There is a theatre, new within thefe twelve years, a rounded oblong, with three floors of boxes, not ill-accommodated. As we fauntered about in the ufual fearch after the fine arts, we could hear of none but a Mr. Phorr, a painter of horfes— from whom there is nothing to fear by Stubbs, by Gilpin, or by Gerrard.

The military eftablifhment is no annoyance to the place. For though they have a few foldiers, they very properly keep them, fparingly, on fix kreutzers a day. A peafant whofe mind may be in fuch a ftate of exaltation as to go for a gentleman foldier, may think himfelf well off with the cheap celebrity of a hero—it feems to be fuperfluous that he fhould be infulted with pay!

Yet, as Mr. Cuftine had thought proper, againft all orders, to play booty, and marching a detachment to Frankfort, had levied 1,500,000 florins, and demanded 500,000 more, that, had been a pretence for foreign troops; and a corps of Heffians and Pruffians were in poffeffion of the town! The hofpital was held by 2000 Pruffians fick!

More formidable than thefe, were fome freebooters we faw at the inn. Where, after fupper, in the great public rooms

rooms, a gaming bank was opened, with rouge and noir !—but with the good policy and virtuous induſtry of Frankfort, it is impoſſible ſuch an evil, ſo deadly, can be ſuffered to remain.

Such is the free city of Frankfort, which has the praiſe of Scaliger, and what is more, which deſerves it.

> Multa laboratis debet Francfordia fulcis
> Multa racemiferis vinea culta jugis.
> Nec tamen in Brutus ſola hæc commercia rebus,
> Hic, animi, æternæ ſed cumulentur opes!
> Quod ſi res, paucas, operoſa eſt dicere merci,
> Non mages eſt, cunctas res operoſa dare.

If the traveller does not go to Mentz, he may ſee at Frankfort ſome of the great curioſities in early printing, of Fuſt and Schoeffer.—As the Pſalter and Breviary of Mentz—the Agenda Moguntina—and Boccatius de Certaldo—Fabula de Segiſmundæ Filiæ Tancreda Principis Salernitani, Amora in Guiſcardum a Leandio Aritino, in Latinum tranſlate—12 pag. 8vo.

Without the year, but with the marks at the end of Fauſt and Schoeffer.

There are three citations alſo remarkable, of Charles V.—two of Pope Paul III. to the Archbiſhop of Cologne—three of Nuncio to the Dean and Canons of Cologne—this is in eleven pages by Schoeffer. And the Bible of 1462—with a variation in the printing of the date, viz. in Vigilia Aſſumptiones *Gloria* Virginis Mariæ.—The epithet is not in the other copies.

THE RIVER MAINE TO MENTZ.

To Switzerland from Frankfort, the direct road is through Heffe Darmftadt; and fo croffing the river Necker, to purfue the palatinate. But recoiling from the black and barren mountains athwart the way, and yet more difgufted with the name and the notion of Heffe, we took a boat at Frankfort, and went down in five hours to Mentz.

Rivers, wherever practicable, are fo delightful as to turn a journey into a jaunt. It is fo on the Thames, the Severn and the Wye. It is much more fo in Germany, where what you enjoy is enhanced by what you efcape.—Where the rivers rid you of the roads, and all thofe multiplied abominations, of a certain Prince of Tours and Taxis, being ftill fuffered to monopolize the whole market, in the fhape of poftillion in chief!

Another bias to this courfe was given, by curiofity with an object lefs humane; to fee the laurels, as the craft call it, which the Pruffians had purchafed at Mentz!

" Of Victories, for which
" The conqueror mourn'd—fo many fell!"

The fiege was juft finifhed. On July 15 the laboratory fired, and the citadel was burnt! On July 22 the town furrendered. On July 25 the Pruffians had poffeffion of the leading forts, Charles, Philip, Welch, Elizabeth, the Double Fencibles, and the Two Gates of Caffel.—On July 29 the capitulation was figned.—On that day and the following, the French evacuated, the convalefcent fick going to Metz and Thionville, &c.—And on July 2d we entered it, but being ftopped at the gate, we profited, like Fabius, of delay; and fairly wrote out, the Memorabilia of the Maine.

THE MAINE,

Says the dictionary*, " is a river! which ariseth on the
" east-side of the circle of Franconia, and running from
" east to west, dischargeth itself into the Rhine at Mentz,"
—Washing, at Frankfort, if it could, not the Augean stable,
but the electorate chamber, in the way.

At Frankfort we first became acquainted with the Maine.
And though he was moving flow, when we wanted to be
going quick, yet difference of opinion did not keep us apart.
In the manner of one of the finest passages in the finest
biography we honored him; and he endured us.

He had to endure much more; for he had to witness,
with us, the monstrous preparations of the war.

At the first village we saw, where the magnificence of the
house would not let us rest on the outside, we were doomed
to find nothing but varied wretchedness within!

The master of the house, M. Volungarro had not long
since died. And his widow seemed to have had enough to
kill her too! For she had been most inhumanly bandied
about, with all the aggravations of cruelty and sport.—Her
house had been pillaged, alternately, by the ruffians on
all sides.

The family of M. Volungarro were of prime note in the
trade of Frankfort.—And this mass of building, is far more
vast and shewy, than any thing we have among our merchants
in London. The facade, with the wings, was above 500
feet, as we measured each part by our steps. It had served
at once the three purposes of a villa, a manufacture, and a
tobacco warehouse. When we were there, all was gone!
It was forced to be an hospital for the Prussians! Above two
thousand of them were in it! They were wounded and

* Vide the Dict. of Arts, &c. &c.—grand thick octavo edition! Owen
Loud. 1764—p. 2001—Art. M. A. I- Et Vide—M. S. Penas Me.

drooping

drooping more grievously than even the rest of their miserable remains at Frankfort.

We were not of those, to refuse pity to Prussians. So after a short struggle, we checked the thought that they were such warriors; and fairly yielded, solely to their woes!

After this great building, there is no other on the river at all a conspicuous mass. And even that, expensive and shewy as it was, was destitute, like a town-house, of every recommendation beyond the walls.- -A few rails on a piece of dwarf brickwork was the separation from the common dirty towing path, with but little garden upon one side, and no land on either. The river also there is uncommonly dull, narrowed by a bad ayte, which is made worse by shabby willows.---The choice of situation and the surrounding culture of landscape ground, both seem to be very easy, yet both are to be found in frequent instances only through Great Britain. I had added Ireland too. But I know too little to speak about it. And if I recollect right, the Marino, beautiful building of Low C. has very indifferent ground, though the position is so very exquisite. And as to the scenes of Switzerland, to instance from the most capable men, M. Necker has a high wall between him and the lake of Geneva, and Voltaire from whom, as from Mr. Pope, better things were probable, and the origin of a fine taste, Voltaire, in the midst of scenes fit for his astonishing mind, has, more astonishingly, a barn at one window, and a horse-pond at another!—Such is Ferney!

The river, though it continues without any artificial objects which are remarkable, has many natural charms; and sometimes there are such swelling hills, woods so flourishing upon the steeps, and so many dwellings among them, with such bold, mountainous, lines in the back ground, that the country brings to mind some of the scenes the most enchanting, upon the borders of the river Soane. And for a mile or two, before the two rivers join, the Maine uniting with the Rhine, used to be the force of cultivation superlative

tive in all its charms! trees, gardens, vineyards, villages and villas, while the points and pinnacles of Mayence clofed the fcene with the objects and ideas of fcience and commerce, of neighbourhood, order, and blifs—multiplying and progreffive, from man to man, from the individual to the community, from Mayence to the full country! through all the region anterior to it.

> Friend, parent, neighbour, firſt it will embrace,
> His country next, and then all human race—
> Wide and more wide the o'erflowings of his mind,
> Take every creature in, of every kind—
> Earth fmiles around, in boundlefs bounty bleſt,
> And heaven beholds his image in his breaſt!

Such ufed to be the honeſt fplendor, the virtuous gaiety of this delightful fcene.

But they were all no more!

All had fled, and yielded up the field to rapine, havoc, and difmay, the foe of mankind and the dæmon of defpair!

Gravafque.

> Principum Amicitias! Et Arma!
> Bellique Caufas! et Vitia! et Modos—
> Nondum Expiatis uncta Cruoribus!

At one contiguous village, Cofteim, before flourishing with all things ordained to make nature gay, the retirements of virtue and the dwellings of health, every thing was one unrelieved mafs of cturelefs defolation! Every bit of building, with the exception of but two fmall ruins, was razed to the ground!

One of thofe exceptions was the altar end of the church—as to the other, was a petty band-box of a dwelling! Of thefe little walls, five-eighths were remaining; with two cafements of a cottage, and in one of the two windows a toilet ftood, feemingly untouched! A Venice glafs, fays Sir William Temple, may laſt as long as an earthen pitcher.

At another diſtrict, Hockheim, fo renowned for the excellent

cellent wine, hence called Old Hock, the whole vineyard was laid waste! By that assassin, fortification, the spawn of quackery and fear, the whole glory of it was cut up! into the hideous forms of angles, traverses, ditches and projections. The trees were filled, for abbatis and pallisadoes, for fascines and for fuel!---The only wood to be seen! La Favorite, the palace of the prince, was burnt, and literally not one stone left upon another! all carted off towards the same sort of hellish sacrifice! to make fronts to bastions, and pillars and roses to arches, sally ports to covered ways! In Cassel, in the Fauxbourg to the southward, and in the little town of Weisenau, scarcely any house had escaped! All were more or less, demolished! and the higher points of the town, the citadel to the churches, shewed, as we approached, much of the devastation by the flames!

The spectacle was shocking!---

It excited all the varieties of horror, indignation, and scorn!

There were above two hundred people on the water, approaching Mentz, from all the country around. We were obliged to pass among them, and we heard them all. It was astonishing to find, with what unanimity they spoke, with what force, on what they deemed the cause of the enormities raging through Europe. To our great surprise, no one there referred them primarily to the French!

Upon entering the town, the crowds, in each street, from distress and from curiosity, were so great, that it was difficult to pass. Yet, there was something much more extraordinary in the general demeanor of the crowd! they moved slow! they looked pensive! they were silent! as if overpowered at the dismal calamities before them, and so suspended from all customary action!---Since Dresden in the last German " war," said a thoughtful observer, who had much experience and more feeling, " Since Dresden, I never " saw any thing so dreadful!"

With

With a guide given us at the inn, we went over the whole town. The firſt impreſſion from the miſchief was its multiplicity. All parts of the town had ſuffered; every ſtreet, and almoſt every houſe, the marks of the cannon ſhot, diſtinctly round in the different dwelling-houſes which they had pierced we tried to count; but we ſoon deſiſted; they were ſo numerous!

In ſome diſtricts the whole neighbourhood had been demoliſhed. The whole commercial eſtabliſhment, and all wreck of ſubſtance gone! And the loſt owners, no where to be found!

One gentleman to whom we had letters remained --But remained only, as it ſhould ſeem to a ſad deſtiny of a hard ſtruggle with diſaſter! his houſe and all its property had been burnt, by a German bomb! And, after long ſearch we found him fled for refuge to the ſteady courteſies of an humble friend. He received us, very manfully, and forcing his eyelid to preſs down the tears, which as he looked over our letters had began to guſh—he apologiſed, and told the ſad reaſon why he could no longer ſhow to ſtrangers the hoſpitality which had been his cuſtom---which he had ever wiſhed! "But," added he, "you may finally depend upon " having no inconvenience for the night," (for we had told him the inns were full) "And the worſt, if you fail of every " other lodging, you ſhall have mine!"

O no, ſir, ſaid a fine boy with proper ſit eagerneſs of ſelf-denial at ſuch a ſacrifice.---" we can ſleep any where!"

"Can you ſo, young gentleman," replied the venerable merchant, "I wiſh I could! But you muſt let it be as I ſay. " It matters not where a man may paſs the night, who is no " longer apt, God knows, to paſs it in ſleep."

He immediately went out with us. And his character, unlike his property, not being in the reach of accident, overcome all difficulties; and immediately got us what we wanted.

In

In this abominable defolation, the total of the buildings was as follows—

Of Private Dwelling Houfes—one hundred and three.
Of Churches, Seven.
The Citadel.
Part of the Convent in the citadel, with many curious books.
The palace of the Provoft.
And one palace (la Favorite) of the prince.
The other palace, the old building, at the north end of the town was, in great part, ufed as an hofpital. And therefore, to the honour of both fides, was refpected and fpared. It had, I believe, no hurt whatever.

Next to innocence is repentance. Next to not warring, is the unerring mitigation of war. Humanity, till very lately, ufed to be the cheap and moft glorious pride of nations. It was fo when the French, exempted Capt. Cook and his expedition from the American war. It was fo when at Gibraltar, the fine conduct of Sir R. Curtis called forth the more arduous virtues of the Englifh!

This was the firft effort of the fame fort in the prefent war. And, it cannot be the laft. Till all men lapfe again into barbarians; the credit of this return to humanity, each fide properly labours to claim:—of courfe there is fome return of hope alfo, that humanity may again be followed by both.

The palace of the Provoft had been the prettieft building in thofe parts of Germany we paffed. A fine Corinthian portico, a double ftair cafe, and magnificent rooms, are yet to be made out. The detail, were all in ruins, ftill fmoaking when we faw them. The plans, of the architect Manzin, are yet extant.

All thefe, fuffered by the German artillery, during the fiege.

The prince's palace, la Favorite, alone fell by the French; and as it was pretended by them, and according to their logic,

M m not

not without provocation. For this was the place, where the conſtitution received the firſt provocations.---Here the fugitive French, certainly much better in their own country, were, with needleſs oſtentation, received. And when M. d'Artois and his brother fled; this was the place, which ſaluted the raſh experiment as a triumph, and made the whole region redden, with what are called demonſtrations of joy. The illuminations are ſtill mentioned, notwithſtanding what has happened ſince; and the monſtrous intervention of folly, ſo much more fatal, ſo much more flagitious.

The palace was much vaunted by idle people; how juſtly it is not now eaſy, or neceſſary to ſay; for the French uſed ſome of the materials in their new raiſed works, and let the reſt go to the poor, from whom, like moſt buildings of this ſort, they had originally come. Nothing remains but ſome marble frames, of ill ſhaped angular little ponds, and bits of the parapet which parted it from the paſſengers. For the houſe was cloſe to the road, without any landſcape ground, with no good trees, no graſs in itſelf, and on the oppoſite grounds too, with no decoration whatever! It is an error leſs retrievable, that the people do not remember it, by any virtue whatever.

The havoc in human nature, made by the ſiege, muſt have been enormous. The French when they entered Mentz had 22,000 men! when they ſurrendered, but 8,800 could be found! and of them 3,000 were ſick! Cuſtine had drafted off 4,500 to the north, but all the reſt of the deficience, is to be imputed to the war; to its accidents, and ſtill worſe to its diſeaſes.

The loſs of the Germans was induſtriouſly concealed. But it muſt have been no leſs deplorable. Five thouſand ſick and wounded were in the hoſpitals about Frankfort. As many more had been carried further, and their mortality was ſo vaſt at one time, that the people on the Lower Rhine had, not quite unreaſonably, ſome apprehenſions that the dead bodies

bodies, in such numbers, might for a time poison the river! As such, it was incidentally a year of jubilee to the fish in the Rhine below Mentz.—At Bonne and Cologne no body would eat them.

Of the townspeople in Mentz, during the whole siege, but five people were killed! This may seem almost incredible; but it is precisely true. And one of them, a rash young man, risked his person needlessly—more than once neglecting the common care, by which, to all appearance, he might have been saved—a fact communicated to me by his brother! two of the five were women.

What number perished, indirectly, from the war, but with no other efficient cause of death, pining under cureless woes, cannot be detected till the period when all things shall be known, till the final allotment must ordain a catalogue of punishments, equiponderant to each catalogue of guilt! At present, in darkness more than natural, they seem to have been almost ever industriously hid! While inanity, has let them on unchecked even by reproof; and monstrous! not a word been heard, either of reparation or of remorse! not even of common sympathy!

> Dii qui' us im erium est animarum, umbræv silentes
> Sit mihi fas, audita loqui! Sit, Numine vestro,
> Pande e res alta terra, et Caligine Mersas!

The sufferings from dearth and deprivation during the siege, fell most heavily on those who had least deserved them! The French army had abundantly most of the chief articles held necessary to life. But the townspeople not having magazines, were forced to buy, and to pay enormously for what they bought!

Mutton sold for 60 sols a pound of 16 ounces—beef 100 sols.—The price before the war was three sols, and when I passed on my return before Christmas, it was nine sols.— Bread and salt, now but two and three sols the pound, were, in the siege, nearly as much raised as mutton and beef.— Woollen and linen cloth was trebled and quadrupled in price, and shoes were at almost any price, ten to twenty florins! Eleven florins make a louis d'or. After the capitulation the price was fixed at five florins—and before the war the people had them for a florin and a half, or two florins—for the use of draft oxen, and the quantity of oak bark, make the materials, like the manufacture of them, very cheap.

The army of the French Republic had stores which were prodigious. Bread corn, woollen cloth, wine, and gunpowder, all for many months. The artillery which were taken were said to be 400—150 of which had belonged to the elector. The wine, which had also been gathered by the prince, the convents and chapters, was the perfection of Rhine wine, the first growth and the greatest age. The woollen cloth, of which there was enough to clothe the army for two or three years, was not like the flimsy worthless linsey-wolsey rags which are the living shrouds of hired heroes, but was cloth of prime coarse quality, stout, thick, soft, and elastic. It was as good as Yorkshire —far better than any thing at Abbeville. We asked a French prisoner whence his coat came, but he could not tell us.

When the French general chose to surrender, the only thing he pretended to want was medicines. As if they could be wanting where there was bread and water, vinegar and wine. One Prussian officer, a partisan of this hypothesis, which was convenient, told us that he had been a prisoner in the town, and was slightly wounded—that, with the usual decency of present war, the French had allowed him to send for his own, a Prussian surgeon, but when he came to dress him, no medicines were to be found. But another gentleman, with as much intelligence and less restraint, scouted that idea as untenable; and declared the want to

have

have been of something very different from medicine—and that if there had been no other weapons used than iron and brass, and lead and steel, the town might have defied the attack, and repelled it for ever.

The pecuniary losses of the town resist all estimate. For where is the financier, however hackneyed in his trade of calculating on the calamities he has caused, who can work precisely, without any given proportion, on a series almost infinite?—on interrupted trade, maimed intercourse, blighted population, artificial dearth, multiplied dangers, and precipitated death?

The debts of the French were very inconsiderable; adverting to the long time they were at Mentz, and to other circumstances, not inseparable from armies as most nations know to their cost, viz. their negligent economy, and their unbridled power of doing harm!

On the first rough calculation, the ostensible debts were computed at no more than five or six thousand pounds sterling. And even some months afterwards, when a number of collateral articles were brought into the account, as the expences of prisoners, money, as usual advanced to officers, &c. &c. the total was less than a million of French livres.

For the payment of this sum, the French general, D'Oyrè, and the French commissary were kept as hostages. So at least it was said, on one side—while the popular party, by far the most prevailing in the citizens of Mentz, give another reason for their stay.

The French, during the greater part of their stay at Mentz, made all payments, very fairly, in the gold and silver coin of their country. When the town was invested by the Prussians, and of course the supply of the precious metals failing, they then had recourse (as in Sweden and other countries, where there is constantly the same sort of want) to certain arbitrary signs, stamped upon paper and bell metal, which had no value but what was agreed to be given to them.

Both thefe were on the capitulation, when the accompts were clofed, very properly called in and deftroyed—the French commiffary, the recognifed agent for the French Republic, giving in lieu of them, a formal acknowledgment, payable to the bearer at Paris.

Like an Englifh victualling bill? faid a gentleman interrogatively.

" O yes, very like—the victualling of a camelion," faid another.

In one point, thefe acknowledgments are rather better than our navy bills, as they are for much fmaller fums!—The largeft bill, as the brokers would call it, being for no more than 200 French livres. One of thefe was fhewn to me by a very refpectable tradefman (the brother to one of the five perfons who were killed)—and he, among others, really certified to me the general good conduct of the French during their ftay at Mentz, that they were unoppreffive, civil, and juft.

The bell metal and the paper money are both already curiofities! for both are exceedingly rare. This is the fuperfcription on the paper money,

The paper money—

Monnoye de fiege,

10 fols,

a changer contre billon,

ou monoye du metal fe fiege,

(Signed)   Reubell.

Houchar.

Siege de Mayence,
Mar. 1793.
2de de la Rep. Franc.

The difference in the fpelling of the word monnoye
(thus

(thus according to all good authority), is noted in my memorandum to have subsisted in the paper money which I saw.

But whether the words and date marked within the inclosing line belong (as I think they do) to the assignat or to the bell metal money, I forgot to mark; and at this distance, I cannot remember.

The bell metal money I saw, though I tried in vain at my bankers and elsewhere to get it.—It was a very small and very base coin. If I recollect right, with the Roman fasces on one side, with Le Rep. Franc. round it, and Siege de Mayence on the other. But, again, I must own it is not in any note, and therefore I cannot speak positively.

The new coin, both gold and silver, of the French Republic were found to be not only unexceptionable, but unusually good—and as such, as soon as circulated, they were engrossed by the Jews—who sold them to the Dutch for a few sols (six or eight on each crown and piece of gold) more than their price current! This is very extraordinary —but it was undeniably true.

The King of Prussia also circulated new French money, during the siege, viz. crowns, loui d'ors, and double louis. They were dated 1788—and of course with the king's head, and the usual superscription. The gold is more red than in the louis d'or of the French—and the value, both of the gold and silver, differs so little from the real French coin, that we received both indiscriminately, at Mentz and Manheim. What difference exists, is however below the par value of the French money, as the bankers there told us, two or three sols in the crown, and four to eight in the louis.

Till the King of Prussia fell upon this expedient, his payments to tradesmen, troops, &c. used to be in the money of the petty German states contiguous, particularly Hesse.—

But

But the money was so very vile that it would not pass but with a discount of ten or twelve per cent.

The French prisoners made a very interesting part of this singular scene. It is but justice towards the King of Prussia to say, that they were treated well. And it is equally due to the fortitude of the French to say, that they deserved it.

We saw them under the first heavy pressure of their captivity, and we visited their hospitals. We talked with many of them; and all were uncommonly well tempered—unextravagant and calm, but determined and sanguine. They spoke with animosity only of the perfidy which had betrayed them. A large party of them, above two hundred, were marched each day, at noon, to receive their bread—and the manner of giving and receiving, quite unembarrassed and free, was equally reputable both to the Prussians and the French.

In a shock of accident so very violent as in the attacks and defences of a siege, it was not improbable to expect, that the emotions and practice of men might be found flung up into some rare extremes of good and evil. We hearkened after both, and in both armies; but we could hear of neither.

The character of either army, as to mere intrepidity, we tried to collect, as well as it could be collected from reciprocal report. The French praised the Hessians, as decidedly the best troops. While the Hessians, the Prussians, the Bavarians, and the Austrians were, without any exceptions, in our hearing unanimous to acknowledge the never-ceasing vigor of the French.

At the table d'hote we mixed with sixty or seventy officers of the Germans, and there we heard them speak upon the existing tactics of the French. Their praise was unqualified, and of the highest order. They told us, to see their

new

new works at Caffel! (the village fronting Mentz on the confluence of the Maine with the Rhine) they protested
" they were all aftonifhed when they faw them. That
" they were unique—for the fpeed of their performance;
" and their fkill, yet more admirable when performed!—
" That in the whole complex confideration and conduct of
" the place, in underftanding and taking all the advantages
" of the ground—and combining with new fcience," (if fuch an object can be called fo) " all the oppofite excellencies
" of the old mafters, of Blondel and Pagan, as well as
" Scheiter and Vauban. It was a work to wonder at! a
" work of fuch genius and fuch labour, as they never heard
" of before, and did not imagine they fhould ever hear of
" again!"

We had neither inclination nor power to difpute the point with him, and we were inclined to admire the excellence of that temper which could be fo generous in an enemy's praife,

A Swifs gentleman, however, referred it all to circumftances, and the power, which occafions ever have to make men. " On a given quantity of impofition and oppreffion," faid he " a nation muft arm—and what an armed nation
" may do, in any direction, cannot but be ftupendous!

" Look at our cantons of Switzerland!—little as they are
" —yet what have they not done! What will they not
" ever do, as long as men are men, while there are any
" fuch nerves as William Tell, and the rough hand of a
" tyrant to brace them!"

The flame of truth, like material flame, will fpread by contact and approximation. It caught even a Hungarian volunteer, who ferved on horfeback! He faid—" what will
" not a man do in defence of a Free Conftitution?—For
" our country, Hungary, has a conftitution, and we are not
" to be thought like the Croatians and Sclavonians, the

" Hulans,

"Hulans, and the Coffacks—animals, little lefs inhuman than the favages of America!"

As the Heffians knew America to their coft—the converfation finifhed there. Paffing from the Drave and the Don to the Delawar and the Schuilkill, from free-booters to free men --from the State of Hungary, which the fecond Jofeph did make a little lefs flavifh, to the Republic of America, which Mr. Wafhington, &c. happily made—a little more free!

MEINTZ.

MEINTZ.

OLD PRINTING.

" Thou haft caufed printing to be ufed! and contrary to the king!
" His crown! and dignity!—has built a paper-mill!"

SHAKSPEAR.

THE moment humanity could efcape, and we could fairly turn our back upon the heart-rending horrors, the diabolical barbarity of a fiege, we betook ourfelves after that art, which may yield counteraction and reftoration to the mind, when perverted and degraded by the craft, of all others the moft mifchievous contemptible.

The art of printing at Meintz, is, philofophically, the feature the moft prominent, and the moft attractive!

For at Meintz, the art, fo magnificently bountiful, began! though no fmall preparation for it might be atchieved, by the luckly labours of Lawrence Cofter at Harlem. And therefore, the people there, do well to affert what little honor they can claim, and confecrate the name, and wooden moulds of Cofter; on which alone that claim can be attempted.—The Mirror of our Salvation *(Den Spiegal Van Onze Zaligheyd)* is the title of the book, which he thus worked off. And the book and moulds are depofited in a coffer of filver and filk, with other treafure, at the townhoufe; each magiftrate being entrufted with a key.

All this is done not without fome fhow and folemn ceremony! and it were well if parade could always juftify itfelf upon fo decent a plea.

There is a ftatue too of Cofter—and his houfe, in the market-place, is ftill diftinguifhed by an infcription:

Memoriæ facrum

Typographia, ars artium omnium confervatrix, hic, primum Inventa, circa annum 1440!

The perfon who pointed this infcription to us, though a Dutchman, was aftonifhed when, in anfwer to his demand for fome infcriptions in England, we told him there were none; on the houfes of Shakfpear, of Bacon, of Newton, and of Locke.

Another gentleman prefent faid conclufively, there were no infcriptions in England upon any houfe whatever.—It never was the fafhion.

The Dutchman, however, who had a guide and dull defcription of London, faid that there were infcriptions on fome of the tax-offices—as " femper eadem" upon one, and " dieu et mon droit" upon another. There was no anfwering a reafoner like that.

This work of Cofter has no date. The firft work printed with a date at Harlem, is 1485—" De proprietatibus rerum."

Still, however, for the work of Cofter being of a date prior to this, there is a lurking probability, not eafily to be got over, at the bottom.—A probability from the comparative inferiority of his performance—that Cofter, like every other man, would do the beft for himfelf—that if two modes had been before him, he would not have taken the worft---he would not have ftamped the paper as he did, only upon one fide, with moulds made of wood, and immoveable, if he had known, what his fucceffors at Meintz certainly did, the mode of printing on both fides the paper, with types moveable, and of metal. The Bible, the Latin Vulgate of Meintz, printed with moveable metal types, was finifhed in the year 1450---if not in the year 1450---from thence to 1455.

Of this the copy is loft, which was in the Benedictines convent at Meintz! Another copy (and now the only one known) remains in the Mazarine College at Paris. At leaft it did remain there, when I was laft at Paris, Auguft 1792. And there I doubt not it is ftill---and will be, as originally

originally meant, among the other numberlefs curiofities, fplendid and ufeful, in the new Gallery Mufeum and Public Library, forming by the Republic---a collection, which in various excellence, will rival Florence and Naples, the Bodleian and the Vatican.

Such is the fure evidence, better than what Cicero can produce to fix the birth-place of Homer, to prove the birth-place of printing to be Meintz. A printed book anterior to this Bible is not known.

The honor of producing this Bible has been again a contefted point, fome attributing it to John Gutenberg (or Guttenberg, for his name is fpelt different ways) and to him folely; before his partnerfhip with John Fuft.

> Clarus Joannus en Guttenbergius hic eft
> A quo feu, vivo flumine, manat, opus!
> Stemmate præftabat, vicit virtute, fed illud—
> Dicitur hinc, veræ nobilitatis eques!

But legal inftruments, ftill extant at Meintz, prove a partnerfhip then to have fubfifted between them.

Guttenberg, who had, as thefe lines of Arnoldus Bergellanus fpecify, fome luftre of genealogy, which he by his merit made more, is generally admitted to have been the inventor of the moveable types, and to have began them. And that Fuft, alfo a citizen of Meintz, joined him, both with money and ideas, when Guttenberg, if not nearly exhaufted, had laboured under a confiderable drain of both— that metal types, the matrixes and punches, &c. if not invented by Fuft, were by him effentially improved. His types were firft of brafs---then of lead. Types at prefent have 3-25 of iron, and as much antimony with the lead.

Peter Schœffer was not concerned with them in the Bible. It was not till feven years after that he was admitted—marrying Fuft's daughter, making further advances in the
foundery,

foundery, and finally, when Guttenberg and Fuft were no more, continuing the eftablifhment by himfelf. As Lipfius faid afterwards of Moretus, the fon-in-law and fucceffor of Plantin, the typographical wonder of Antwerp, he was the heir of his fkill and conftancy, his merit and his fame!

The firft idea of the types is faid to have ftarted upon Guttenberg from the fortuitous impreffion of his feal-ring,

"Annulus in digitis erat illi, occafio prima."

And from thence he advanced to the fimple experiment of marking his name

"Redderet ut nomen litera fculpta fuum."

Thence by an eafy tranfition, and by multiplying only, he advanced to printing books. Making his wine-prefs a printing-prefs. As the art of dying black, and making ink, had before come from the wine lees—

"Robora profpexit dehina torealaria bacchi
"Et dixit, preli forma fit ifte novi!"

Such is the operation, when talents go to work kindly upon accident! and fuch the real tranfmutations, the ufeful wonders, matter is made to fhew, under the fubliming chymiftry of the mind. And thus a tranfcendant glory in Newton and in Harvey, arofe from the glimpfe of a moment, and the frolic of a child.

The expence of printing the Bible is not exactly known —of the firft money advanced by Fuft upon his partnerfhip, no fpecific voucher remains; but the fecond depofit is proved (viz. December 6, 1452) and that incidentally eftablifhes the firft—for it ftates Fuft to be fupplying another fum of 800 florins. And if tradition is uniform, that Guttenberg had expended 2,200 florins more. (They are gold florins) in all, therefore, 4,000 florins.

Though the prime copy of the Bible be loft, there remains another at Meintz, evidently printed by Fuft---but as certainly after he was joined with Schœffer!

This

This Bible is without name or date: but it is to be referred, with almoſt a moral certainty, to 1465 or 1462.—Theſe are the chief obſervable peculiarities in it—there is no title—no initial capitals but what the illumminator has painted in red or in blue—no letters to mark each ſheet—no numerical mark of pages—no catch-words—no punctuation—no diphthongs.

There are other more minute, and leſs conſtant, particularities. As the letter c for t in ſanctificacio—juſticia—and in Jeſaiæ, chap. 27.—This error—ponam circulum in avibus tuis.

Inſtead of " naribus tuis"—as in our tranſlation, ſo well fortified by the beſt commentator, Biſhop Lowth, citing Hieron. The Talmud—and Jonathan's interpretation of the Hebrew םיג.

There were errors of the preſs, though not ſuſpicious as that of Nic Janſon, in his date of 1461—for 1471—(in his edit. of Decor Puellarum.) And ſcarcely conceivable, as in the appendicular title-page of the Pſalms—which, though the firſt book printed by Fuſt and Schœffer, and with an oſtentation of care is printed Spalmorum Codex, inſtead of Pſalmorum. In this book, for the firſt time, appeared the name of the printers, and of the publication—the year and day are both mentioned, viz. " 1457, in Vigilia Aſſumptionis !"—The name there, by-the-bye, is printed Schœffer.

A perfect copy of this is ſaid to remain at Meintz. It is extremely rare, and for a long time, but only two more perfect copies was thought exiſting—viz. at Vienna. The copy in the library at Freyberg is very incomplete; but lately the librarian at Leipſic found a perfect copy—and another paſſing through the hands of M. de Goze and the Preſident de Cotte, was ſold, in the collection of M. de Gaignel, for 1340 livres. Lord Spencer alſo, I am told, has a copy in his fine collection at Althorpe—and if ſo, that is the only

copy

copy in this country. The Duke of Marlborough has it not—nor the King.

This was the firſt book produced after the junction of Schœffer with Fuſt. Fuſt's department was the compoſitor's—Schœffer that of the preſſman.

Between this and another edition of the Pſalms, alſo in folio, there was no publication with any date. In this ſecond folio, of 1459, Schoiffer (for ſo he is ſpelt) is ſtyled " Clericus"—a term expreſſive not only of the ſacerdotal functions (which Schœffer did not exerciſe) but of any man who had a character for literature and ſkill.

This book is ſaid, by the French critics, to be as rare as the firſt folio—but it is not ſo. Of the copies remaining at Meintz, one only, they told us was burnt—three are preſerved. This is in the King's library at Buckingham-Houſe.

The Pſalms being ſo very rare, the different ſubſcriptions to each edition may be very acceptable here:

SUBSCRIPTION TO THE EDITION OF 1457.

Præſens SpalmorumC odex, Venuſtate Capitalium decoratus, Rubucationibuſque Sufficienter Diſtinctus, adinvencione artificioſa imprimendi, & caracterizandi, abſque calami ulla Exaracione ſic Effigiatus, et ad Euſebiam, Dei, induſtria eſt Conſummatum, per Johannem Fuſt, Civem Moguntinum et Petrum Schœffer de Geruſheim, Anno Domini Milleſimo 1457, in Vigilia Aſſumptionis.

SUBSCRIPTION TO THE EDITION OF 1459.

Preſens Pſalmorum Codex: Venuſtate Capitalium Decoratus, Rubucationibuſque Sufficienter Diſtinctus adiventione Artificioſa Imprimendi ac caracterizandi, abſque ulla Calami exaracione ſic Effigiatus, et ad Laudem Dei ac Honorem Sancte Vacobi eſt Conſummatum, per Johannam Fuſt

Fuſt Civem Moguntinum, & Petrum Schœfher de Geru-
ſheym Clericum.---Anno Dei Milleſimo. 1459, 29 Die
Menſis Auguſti.

On the junction of Schœffer with Fuſt, Gu·tenberg eſtabliſhed a printing-office apart at Straſbourg; and in the
year 1458, one year after their firſt Pſalter, and one year
before the ſecond, the Dialogues of Pope Gregory were
publiſhed by Guttenberg alone.

It may be curious to know the other works, publiſhed by
Fuſt and Schœffer; and as they are few, they may be ſtated
---viz.---

Anno 1459---Durandi Rationale Divinorum Officiorum
---folio. Still to be found at Meintz---though it is believed
two copies were deſtroyed in the ſiege. It is not very rare.
There are copies in Lord Spencer's, Duke of Marlborough's,
the King's, and Mr. Cracherode's libraries.

Anno. 1450---Catholicon---a grammatical work. By Jo.
de Janua---Folio.

John of Genoa (not Geneva---(though each was called
Janua, or the Roman entrance into Italy)-- was a Domini-
can, who ſo early as the end of the thirteenth century had
Greek literature; and, like that fine writer of our own
country, with ſo much Greek literature now, diſtinguiſhed
by manly virtue, and rational piety. Such a name, therefore is an honor to any church; and as ſuch his is conſe-
crated at Pavie.

This Catholicon is extant at Meintz.

1460- -Conſtitutiones Clementis V.

That year they had a ſecond preſs at Meintz.

1461---Decor Puellarum.

1462---The Bible --in 2 vol. bound in one. 481 pages---
242 in vol. 1. --239 in vol. 2. Each page has double columns.

The placing is thus different from our Bible. After the
ſecond

second book of Chronicles—the other there follows thus:

 Manasseh,   Esther,
 Esdras, in 4 books, Job,
 Tobit,   Psalms,
 Judith,   End of vol. 1.

Second vol.—Proverbs, and so on to Malachi inclusive; except that they place Baruch between the Lamentations and Ezekial.

The Maccabees follow Malachi.

The small part of the Apocrypha, not before mentioned, are omitted.

The volume continues with the four Evangelists—all the Epistles of St. Paul follow, as in our order.

The Acts follow at the end of the Hebrews; Then resumes with James till it finishes, as with us.

Of this, commonly called the Meintz Bible, more than one copy is at Meintz—and several, eight or nine, at Paris. A copy on vellum sold for 4086 livres at Paris in 1784.— This also is in our four great collections.

1462—The German Bible (the first) abovementioned.

No copy now to be found at Meintz.—But one, in the Consistorial Library of the Duke of Wirtemberg.

There is also a copy at Buckingham-House.

1466—Two copies of Decretal's—and two of Tully's Offices—" Non atramento plumali, canna neque. Aurea, " sed arte quadam perpulchra, manu & Petri de Geru- " sheim pueri mei (Schœffer) feliciter effeci!"

The improvement, that great object in printing-ink, has been of late years, chiefly with the Spaniards. By the activity of the President of the Royal Society, the Spanish ambassador, and the King's librarian, some of the ink was brought to England, and by the subtle experiments of such chymists as Dr. Fordyce and Dr. Pearson, London now has ink yet more perfect than even that of Madrid. What

              Tust

Fuſt did cannot be judged. For who ſhall gueſs at any thing like proportions in decay, from the evaneſcence of colours, and the attritions of time?—From Fuſt all is gone but his Gothic forms, and the merit of founding them. And in the fourth century from hence, where will be the ſplendid captivations of Bodoni and Bulmer? Their profeſſional ſkill and taſte entitle them to be thus mentioned with Guttenberg and Fuſt!

On the books choſen to be publiſhed by the firſt printers at Meintz, a different judgement muſt be formed. Their bible, both in Latin and in German, manifeſtly conſecrates their labours towards the beſt everlaſting praiſe!—But apart from that ſacred work, and their edition of the pſalms, moſt of their ſelections muſt be diſmiſſed with indifference, if not with neglect.

Guttenberg, it is true, died in 1468—and Fuſt in 1466, withdrew, and went to Paris. But Schoeffer continued for five and thirty years longer, publiſhing always one book, and ſometimes two or three works in a year.

Yet among them all how little is there beyond the dark ages, or, at moſt, the chill twilight beyond them, except another bible and the pſalms. The only works with any reference to elegance and uſe, were a Valerius Maximus, and Fuſt's Morſel of Cicero, above-mentioned—with Juſtinian, ſome of Auguſtin, and of Thomas Aquinas, the Epiſtles of Hieronymus, the Homilies of Cryſoſtom, a Herbarium with figures, and a Hortus Sanitatis. The Valerius 1471—and the Cicero's Offices 1465—are the only firſt editions. There was a German Livy too, in 1500—by the younger Schoeffer.

And this was all!

At at a time too, when moſt of the chief Roman Claſſics, and ſome of the Greek, were elſewhere paſſing through one or two editions! Rome, early, had given Virgil.— Milan,

Milan, the year after, Horace and Quintilian. Paris, at the fame time, Lucretius, Juvenal, and Perfius. Naples, Seneca. Florence, Homer. And Venice, Ariftotle, Theocritus, and Ariftophanes.

London, Meminiffe Horret, London was, I fear, the fole analogy to be found of practice equally bad! of courfe implying a correfponding defect on one fide or the other, either in the demand or the fupply, in the public patronage, or in the printer's fkill.

Till the year ninety-feven (1497) there was no Latin Claffic in England! then Pinfon printed Terence, fome, perhaps twenty, years before Boethius had appeared; but it was with the verfion of Chaucer. They had printed alfo, Lord Worcefter's tranflation of Cicero de Senectate, and Cato's Diftich, by Burgh the Arch-deacon of Colchefter —a profe narrative of the Æneid, the Metamorphofes, and the Fables of Æfop—and above all, Lydgate and Chaucer.

All the reft of the books printed in England, till the opening of the fifteenth century, were little more than the publication of difgrace, both as to power and will! that the country was dark, and wifhed to continue fo, and that there were no organs for any founds but thofe of childhood and inanity, cant and horfe-play, chivalry and fuperftition!— Such barren abfurdities as the Siege of Rhodes and the Golden Legend, St. Catherine and St. Elizabeth—the Hiftoryes of Troy, King Blanchardyne and Queen Eglantyne his wife, the Ladder of Perfection, Coat Armour, and the Golden Fleece!

In the ignorance and vulgarity of the people who directed fuch objects for the prefs, the Dutchefs of Burgundy and the Princefs Margaret, &c. there might perhaps feem fome apology at the time; but how will our firft printers, Caxton, Penfon, and De Worde, anfwer to their cotemporaries and

to

to themselves, for such cruel inculcation of ill, such a wreck of consequences from opportunity and art?

It was monstrous to look back over such a dreary waste, without any thing like a living principle in all around; the principle to look upward with common instinct, and to open for the dew of Heaven!

For the religious sense, as in literature and science, the country, and they whom the people trusted with the government of it, seem to have been equally unashamed of sterility and neglect, while every other nation rationally gloried in having their bible before them again and again. In England, the ten commandments and the paternoster were the only parts of it to be seen. Even they were not vouchsafed to be thought necessary till the year 1484.—And as for any thing like useful learning, there was no attempt to divulge it, till forty years after, when some of Erasmus came forth, as it were, in spite of us, and the Greek physicians began to be given by Linacre and his friends!

Such was the bright and benignant object, which arose with such happy splendor upon Meintz! such too were the first curious appearances which followed, like meteors in the dawn. .Proceeding, as its progress were more or less free and open, to mark, with more or less felicity, all the workings of man—creative of each spot it lighted on—in its privation, characteristic of darkness and decay.

> Quid tantum oceano properent se tingere soles,
> Hyberni, vel quæ tardis mora noctibus obstet.

The liberty of the press, which Blackstone, in common with all mankind, maintains, essential to a free state, was not annoyed in the first outset of printing. Guttenberg, Fust, and Schoeffer, all departed in peace, without having their press groan under any such slavish imposition as a licence!

That

That flate device, of a licence (for it is nothing more than a bungling copy of that vile original, the ftatuary under the paw of the beaft), was firft enacted in the year nineteen (1519) upon the fecond Schoeffer. The book was Ulrichi de Hutten Eq.

De Guaiaci Medicina & Morbi, &c. liber unus. At the end after his name and date—

" Cum privilegio Cæfario Sexennii."

The Livy of the year before this (and by the bye the aforefaid Mr. Hutten was the editor of it), has been mentioned as thus ill diftinguifhed; but erroneoufly, for that decretal of the Emperor Maximilian is for a very different purpofe—for inhibition to other bookfellers, the better to fecure a *monopoly* to John Schoeffer. The words exprefsly are,

Omnibus Chalcographis inhibemus, &c. Volentes tibi, tum omni vel ob hoc divinum inventum, favore et commendatione dignum fuccurrere.

The intercourfe, if the confequences had ended with Schoeffer, would have been no more than right, of one pretender impofing upon another. For, though Maximilian might not know it, there had been feven editions of Livy before his appeared; and he could not help it, that in fpite of his inhibition there were more than feven editions after it. But what was a more material point to him, the power of a licencer was thus acknowledged and familiarifed —of courfe was eafily to be exercifed ever after. Schoeffer had at the fame time another reafon for his getting the monopoly—for he had local power worth transferring, being, befides an extenfive tradefman and artifan, a leading municipal officer in the town. In the fubfcription to the Mercurius Trifmagiftus, 1503, he is fpecified with this addition—" Primarius Civis Metropolitanæ urbis moguntinæ."
—At Bath and Caftle Rifing, they have ftill old ftories of

burgeffes

burgesses that were imperative, and must have had whatever they would aſk.

In regard to the Livy, Schoeffer ſhould have diſdained any meretricious aid from humbler acceſſaries, as he was lucky enough to have a prefatory puff from Erafmus himſelf—who compares John Fauſt (for ſo he ſpells the name) to Ptolomæus Philadelphus! and as Fauſt's ſon-in-law claims for this publiſher of Livy, all that he deſerved, hereditary praiſe.

In the ſubſcription, or appendicular title page, to the Pſalter and the other books printed by Fuſt and Schoeffer, the words expreſſive of their pious humility cannot be overlooked—Ad Euſebiam Dei, or Dei Clementia, are in them all. Like Mr. Boyle himſelf referring every work to the ſupreme being, whom he never dared to mention without a pauſe, and a ſenſible alteration in the tone of his voice.

The younger Schoeffer at firſt did the ſame, and Deo Favente, and Gloria Deo, are in his early works, till he got the monopoly from the prince—and then (cum privilegio Cæſareo) he pleads his privilege, and we hear no further of the firſt rendering which ſo well became him.

> The Devil and the King divide the prize,
> And ſad Sir Ba aam, &c. &c.

The power of a licencer thus aſſumed, was too convenient to certain perſons, not to become a mode. It paſſed as the gag did from Germany (the German word is gaghel) to every region round about! And in various ſhapes of charters, bulls, and proclamations, till at length it ended in the Star Chamber of one country, and the Inquiſition of another! Not only graciouſly condeſcending to prohibit what books ſhould not be printed—but prohibiting, alſo, books that were printed, from being read.—The

firſt

firſt ſtatute with ſuch policy, as venerable as it is gracious, yet was in a period not ſo bad as its neighbours, viz. that of Edward VI.

So much for the Typographers of Mentz.

<blockquote>
With wiſdom's voice to print the page ſublime,
And mark in adamant, the ſteps of time.
</blockquote>

OF THE

EARLY PRINTING,

THE FOLLOWING SPECIMENS ARE IN THE PUBLIC LIBRARY AT CAMBRIDGE:

Catholicon J. de Janua. Fol. Mogunt. 1460.
Cicero de Officis. J. Fuft, Mogunt. 1466.
And two copies of Durand (Rationale Divinorum Officiorum) but without place, date, or printer's name.
The Cambridge library has not either of the Meintz Bibles. The moft ancient copies there are, Bib. Latina per Matt. Moravum. Fol. Neap. 1476.
Ib. per Nic. Jenfon. Fol. Venat. 1476.
Both of which are very rare—though that of Venice is the leaft—for it never fold for more than feven or eight pounds.—After the Mentz Bible, and before thefe, were three copies, all of the fame year, 1475—at Venice, Piacenza, and Nuremberg—and one without a date—the firft Paris Bible, which is extremely fcarce, was 1476—the Englifh Bible by Miles Coverdale, 1535, is at Cambridge.

Dr. Farmer has a folio Vulgate, with a falfe date—viz. 1463 inftead of 1476.

He has alfo Fauft's Tully's Offices, 1466—4 Feb.

And Schoyffer's Valerius Maximus, 1471.

The library at Emanuel College, Cambridge, has Fuft's firft Tully, 1465.

And a Catholicon, 1460.

The Durand is not at Cambridge—Dr. Afkew had a copy (1459) and it fold for 61l. to Mr. Willet.

Conftitutions Clementis V.—No copy of this is, I believe, at Cambridge, Lord Spencer lately got a copy through

Mr. Nicol (the beſt aid on ſuch occaſions) or Mr. Edwards.

The libraries of the Royal and Antiquarian Societies are without them. The Muſeum has not, I believe, any copy of theſe books, the firſt printed at Meintz. In Sir Hans Sloane's collection, it ſeemed not unlikely to have expected Schoyffer's Herbarium, 1484—but neither that nor the Hortus Sanitatis, 1491, are, that I ſaw, there. Linnæus had no copy.—his two moſt ancient botanical books were —1540 and 1541—Dortſtinus Botanicon. Francfort—and Ortus Sanitatis, in ſix diviſions, and a Medicinal Table. Of no value, but as a ſpecimen of mere antiquity, black letter, and wooden cuts—they have a running title, and initial letters are capitals—but no numbering of the pages—no catch-words.

Theſe are, with his other books, added to the library of Dr. Smith, the celebrated botaniſt and phyſician. He bought the whole collection of Linnæus; and from nature and by ſtudy he happily has what could not be bought.

In Sir Hans Sloane's collection, the books of the oldeſt date was Hutten, de Morbo Gallico. Printed at Mentz, 1531—they both are duodecimo.

In the Britiſh Muſeum, the oldeſt date of which I have any memorandum, is the Venice Livy, 1495.

At Oxford, I was informed that there are fine ſpecimens of Schœffer and Fuſt—but by my friend's accidental abſence and failure of letters, the ſpecification cannot be preciſe.

MENTZ.

MENTZ.

THE TOWN AND TERRITORY.

> Defcenderet
> Sacrâ catenatus via!
> Sed ut, fucundum vota parthorum, fua
> Urbs hæc periret dextra!

THE town and territory of Mentz ought to be a fpot moft favourable to the powers and purpofes of man—if with all the prime ingredients in hand for external eafe and confolation, he could be left at liberty to mix and compound them as he would wifh—If the wafte of folly did not bring to nought the wantonnefs of fortune—if the froward impofitions of human violence did not thwart and fruftrate the bleffings of nature! Thofe bleffings of nature are here no lefs affluent than they are kind. In the beft glories of all land, in corn and wine, in milk and honey—with concurring rivers, the Maine and the Rhine, ftreaming magnificently at the bottom—with the fruitful mountains, of the Rhinegau, are glittering to the top!—With an hereditary fpirit in the people for deeds of good renown, of labor and difcovery, of hardihood and ufe! The contemporaries of Gefner, Klobftocke and Lefling, the defcendants from Stuptiz and Luther, from Schwartz, and from Fuft!

But what, apart from all the power of ufe, are the prerogatives of nature, and the prodigalities of chance?—Wealth that cannot circulate, and vigor not to be enjoyed?—Sacrâ catenatus, chains, whether of fuperftition or defpotifm, muft maim the limbs, and leave their bulk and elafticity, for defpoilers, like Cæfar, to calculate in vain!—In vain too, the winds blow and the waters roll, while each freight and tranfit for human good, fuch multiplied impofitions as tolls and cuftom-houfes, alfo are concurring to dam!

The North American republic ftretches through a length of 1500 miles in latitude—the territory of Mentz has but about 170 fquare miles—in America the population is four millions, in Mentz there are not 320,000 people!—And yet the expence of government, over all America, is no more than the mere allowance to the Bifhop of Mentz! a yearly total amounting to 160 or 170,000l. fterling! An expenditure, which referred proportionably to the relative circumftances of each country, muft have all the differences there can be, between good and evil, between each poffible extreme, from profperity and praife, to infamy and ruin!

He who travels with fit emotions, muft be aftonifhed and fhocked at fuch an outrage upon public policy; at fuch a wreck of public good!

The revenue paid to the Prince has been ftated as equal to the whole eftablifhment, civil and military, in America! The ecclefiaftics are above five thoufand, that is more than half the number of parochial clergy in England!—And the nobles, again more numerous than in England, differ alfo from our noblemen in education and accomplifhments! It is really difficult *out* of England, to find men fhaking off the impediments to virtue from hereditary wealth—and in fpite of the deceiving meannefs, the fpoiling fubmiffions which befet them, rifing into the rank of good citizens, at all exemplary, for patriotifm; for learning; for ufeful arts; or for any other adminiftration to the public good!

In the detail too, of each order there feems much equally to be blamed! As to the nobles, a few of them, perhaps near twenty, have from twelve to five and twenty or thirty hundred pounds a year—and two or three have ten thoufand pounds. Yet the majority of them are unprovided of any thing but hope in cafual aid. Yet, though poverty-ftruck,

* By the Cenfus laft made, 3,933,412 inhabitants.

ſtruck, they are ſlothful—and though mendicants, they are proud. Though candidates for promotion, they are not ſtudious by any talents to deſerve it—and for the badges of diſtinction, as gold keys, &c. which are ſo plentifully flung about, there is, too commonly, no plea, but pedigree and an empty pocket!

The eccleſiaſtics too, are equally ill-conditioned, both as to idleneſs and ignorance. Their educaton, inſtead of preparing men—and men who may philoſophiſe upon life, and ſtir well in its uſeful energies, turns its back on all virtuous practice, and waſtes time in all the aukward vanity of antiquated ſpeculation!—Inſtead of men, there are monks and canons—fit for nothing but the vice and impertinence of their order, the impoſitions of their cloiſter, and the jargon of their ſchool!

All this were bad enough, if literally unexpenſive. But it is much worſe, when the expence of it, with enormous preſſure, bears hard and heavy upon the people. Trade languiſhes; and is at death's door—by the mere drain of duties, more and more multiplied. In the whole eſtabliſhments of 5000 eccleſiaſtics, there are but 677 pariſhes, and of courſe need have no more than 677 to 1000 prieſts—and that number, comparatis comparandis, would be as five to one above what the prieſthood is to the population of England. While, in regard to the civil eſtabliſhments of the country, common ſenſe and feeling are equally inſulted by the multiplication of appointments, no leſs ſinecure and exceſſive!—Councils of Regency, councils of diſtricts, and councils of provinces, aulic courts, courts of aids, courts of woods, and chambers of water—ſix courts of juſtice, an eccleſiaſtical court, three committees for impoſitions, thirty cuſtom-houſes—baillies, juſtices, and runners out of number—grand marechals, grand ſtewards, grand chamberlains, grand maſters of the hunt—with above ſeventy provoſts and deans, and eight hundred canons, to ſay nothing of the

aanimals

animals, ufelefs, if not verminous, in abbeys, convents, and monafteries. Since the confecration of Nebuchadnezzar's idol, there never was any thing like it.

> Undique collecti invadunt, acerrimus Ajax
> Et gemini Atridæ, Pyrrhig exercitus omnis
> Myrmidonum, Dolopumque, aut duri miles Ulyffci !
> Ilicit Obruimur Numero !

Abufes like thefe, fome of which England fhook off at the Reformation, and which no conceivable fociety fhould bear, long fince began even in Germany to be feen, and eftimated rightly. And the late Elector, who was a prince with fome fenfe, was admonifhed by the figns of the times, and ftrove, like an honeft man, to prevent convulfion by reform. " As in the body, politic or natural," faid he, " plethoric ill has its appointed check in timely evacuation ! " —or, as when a veffel is overburthened, you fave it from " finking, if you will but *lighten the lading!*"

Accordingly he ftruck at the abufes which feemed moft offenfive and injurious. He inftantly abolifhed fome of them. And the people were called upon to co-operate for the abolition of more. With the revenues thus refcued from wafte, he mitigated the ravages of rapine ; and difpelled fome drearinefs from the fchools. Two taxes (poll taxes) were given up ! and a grant of 3000l. fterling a year, was wifely applied to introduce fome ufeful learning into the univerfity.

His purpofes are acknowledged to have had the vigor and purity of what is wife and good, and without any alloy from the imperfections too rife in each of his profeffions ! Though an overpaid ecclefiaftic, he wifhed to retrieve a primitive fimplicity for the church ! and though a prince, he felt a generous fympathy for the people !—For the citizens, he was anxious that they fhould recover their fhare in the conftitution ; a fhare wrefted from them by the affumptions of the ariftocracy. And, in regard to the

church,

church, he would have restrained and abolished the prac‑
tice of pluralities; a practice which the laws of the Elec‑
torate forbid; but which, in spite of dormant laws, is so
unblushingly perpetrated, that more than one of the most
powerful men in Mentz, have contrived to grasp out of the
church, in multiplied pluralities, above 7000l. a year! A
revenue, preposterous any where for an ecclesiastic, and a
celebate; and additionally fatal in a country like this,
where a guinea, Chesterfield might have said, has a four‑
fold effect, as well as a fourfold figure, when reduced into
German crowns!

All the chief families, in the best plight, have become so
by the plunder, which, through the church, has been taken
from the people. Even the late Elector had vast wealth,
and left behind him much more than became him!—And
the families of Schoonboin, Elz, and Ostein, each of them
have inherited from their ancestors, in the receipt of
deaneries, provostships, and various commendams, above a
quarter of a million sterling!—*Sacer nepotibus cruor*; in
enormous peculation, and family aggrandizement from such
enormity, the church of Mentz follows the church of Rome
—and at the distance only which is due between the dis‑
ciple and the master!

Thus conversing upon the subject of sinecures and unne‑
cessary placemen, a gentleman of Mentz, with more fancy
than is usual in the expression of a German, said, " As for
" the caterpillar tribe, nay, the locust, I can discover some
" incidental good from them—for they have excited the
" ingenuity of such observers as Swammerdam and Mal‑
" pighi! But as to the other reptiles we were mentioning,
" I can find nothing for it, but to stand stoutly to my phi‑
" losophy and my creed; to refer to the doctrine of final
" causes, and however arduous, to be resigned!

" I strive to bear them as I would other evils—but true
" to myself and to my condition, I must strive also to cor‑
" rect

" rect and to annihilate them. It is the proud flesh of
" morbid places, which muſt be kept under by what is
" uſefully phagedenic!—It is, as it were, a wen, for which
" there can be no cure, but cutting off, and radical extir-
" pation!"

We thought he was inſpired---at leaſt as much as Saint Boniface ever was.

The military eſtabliſhment of Mentz may be cited as an example of uſe to ſome other countries, periodically pillaged by army tricks and official connivances! The muſters and returns are never falſe! There are no corps, kept purpoſely, incomplete. No fraudulent differences between each ſtated quota of men, upon paper and upon ſervice! All the men paid for by the people, are fairly producible---and what is more material ſtill, the eſtabliſhment is reduced into a compaſs not intolerable---there are but two thouſand men in all, which are five times fewer than there have been! And in the time of peace, a large portion of them preſs with a mitigated weight upon the country, by the aid of foreign pay, or home labour, in works of public welfare! Except in having half a dozen generals, there are no jobs, nor undue influence by the multiplication of officers! And the few troops there are, for the mere theatre of parade, are not always ſo farcically employed; but in reality are of ſome ſervice, by ſaving watchmen in the ſtreets, and horſe-patroles upon the high-roads—like the gens d'armouries of the French Republic.

The expence of all this is about 170,000l. ſterling—and the taxes to produce that ſum, are on the land, on water-carriage, on conſumable articles, and by capitations—which are here, as every where, objectionable, as being arbitrary, unequal, precarious, and unwiſe. They were ſo in France under the late monarchy there! they were ſo in England when the Third William viſited the country with them, from Holland.

Lotteries,

Lotteries, another evil which was caught of the Dutch, re alſo to be complained of at Mentz! And there, as in every other country infeſted with this, the worſt ſpecies of gambling, the ſame complex miſchiefs break forth among the moſt uſeful orders of the community! Through ſloth and vain hope, the government makes men poor; through poverty they become profligate—and through profligacy, deſpairing: they are driven down from depth to depth, in proſtitution and rapine—till, in the inevitable declenſion of guilt, and its ſure conſequence, woe, they do violence on themſelves—or ſuffer the laws for doing violence to others! It is an act of undeniable merit in the French that they have rid their land of this abomination—and it is an unaccountable overſight in another nation, individually as lofty and enlightened as they are, at times, collectively hood-winked and miſled, that they ſtill ſuffer ſuch deleterious quackery of a mean mind, to taint and waſte the people!

The government of Mentz is advantageous, ſo far as it is elective: and thence increaſing the probability of perſonal merit in the Prince. The right of election is with the prime chapter; where the twenty-four canons have the reciprocal powers of chuſing, and being choſen. A power, which, as far as independence implies rectitude, they have exerciſed vigorouſly and well; reſiſting with fortitude the moſt expedient, all foreign influence whatever, even of the Emperor himſelf!

In the other eccleſiaſtical ſtates, the admiſſion of ſuch undue interference, the election of foreign princes, have made the biſhoprics in virtual vaſſalage to the houſe from which they ſprang; and involved them, more or leſs, in each rude ſhock, and temporal ſtruggle of their family. Thus it was, when Liege had ſo mixed with Auſtria or Bavaria—thus, Treves at preſent, feels an agitation ſpread through the Houſe of Saxe, ſmall, comparatively, as Saxe may be—and thus Cologne, in electing to the archbifhopric, an archduke of Auftria, feels with a kind of morbid fympathy, a confent of parts, with every council that may happen to agitate Vienna.

Thence it was that Mentz determined to rid itfelf of this impofition, and with the moft zealous unanimity in the chapter, they refolved never to admit into the office of Elector any candidate a-kin to the princes of the empire. A refolution, not more wifely conceived than furely executed For to be in any manner free, nothing can be wanting to any people, but the well-formed will to be fo!

The chief magiftrate of Mentz is an office of high rank· and power, both ecclefiaftical and civil! The jurifdiction of the archbifhopric is vaft and complex. The fuffragan bifhoprics are fourteen. Of them, three or four are of great grandeur, as Augfburg, Conftance, Paderborn, Worms, and Spires. Another yet more confiderable, Strafburg, was loft to Mentz at the revolution; when the French, in the juft fpirit of the Englifh Reformation, properly renounced all jurifdiction but their own. The Archbifhop is primate of the empire.

To the Archbifhopric thefe offices attach:
The Primacy,
Arch-Chancellor of the Empire,
Dean of the College of Electors,
Confervator of the Archives.
Infpector and Director of the Supreme Imperial Tribunal in the Appellant Jurifdiction at Wetzlaer.

Thefe offices, together, give great plentitude of political power! at the elections in the empire, he is a fort of prefiding returning officer—he convenes the electors, folely by his own authority, when an Emperor is to be chofen—and by a delegation from the college, when they are to chufe a king of the Romans, he fixes the date of the convention. He opens the diet. He directs the detail of it,

fubject

subject to the month's duration fixed by the golden bulle; he collects the votes—and which, in many cafes, may be a point of preference, not only from opinion, but for ufe, the vote laft given is his own. The vote of the archbifhop of Mentz, as of Cologne and Treves, is paffive merely; he can chufe an emperor: but he cannot be chofen.

The electorate has the rights and functions of fovereignty, vefted in the archbifhop, but chiefly exercifed by the chapter. All acts and edicts iffue in his name. In legiflation, for the tribunals, the taxes, the coinage, public works, treaties, and all ftate papers and inftruments whatever—privileges, donations, difpenfations, derive in his name: military eftablifhments, arfenals, and fortifications are at his controul—his power is abfolute, as to peace and war, life and death.

With a truft of fuch vaft magnitude and extent, it might be natural to fuppofe, and not impolitic to exact, fomething a little like commenfurate qualifications. And that as the perfonage is happily elective, there fhould be proofs eftablifhed, as in other beftowals of public confidence, that the perfonage is no lefs happily eligible alfo. But, no! in Germany they do not find it neceffary to infift, like other people, upon this. Beyond the examination for orders (there not very ftrict) which the candidate canon muft have paffed when on his probation for the diaconate and the priefthood, no further fearch is made after his pretenfions, either intellectual or moral. The obvious grand requifites of experience, temper, judgment, the knowledge and the practice of life, with the capacity for governing others, implied by the previoufly proved felicity of felf-government; all thefe, and more, are afcertained, at leaft are held afcertainable by two brief fimple operations, viz. the production of a pedigree, and of the parifh regifter. If the family have been uninterruptedly noble, in both male and female line, for fixteen generations; and if a man, with their hereditary claim to wit and worth, has completed his thirty-third year, he is then found in the ecclefiaftical ftates of Germany, at one time as well as another, perfectly qualified to be a prince.

This peculiarity, though omitted by Tacitus, or not exifting in his time, is a very curious national character! For in moft other countries, age and name do not imply a moral certainty of the character and qualifications neceffary for office—though the office may be the moft menial, no more than a clerk, a fubftitute conftable, or a watchman.

The fpecific merit of a living elector it may be difficult to afcertain or to deliver! for expreffion is not always ready with proportioned fame!—and, *celata virtus*, perfection over-delicate, may fo chance to be unknown.

One excellence, however, in fpite of all, broke forth! It could not be concealed, that he had antiquity in his pedigree, even more than was bargained for!—that he had actually the barony of D'Erthal! that when elected in 1774, he had twenty years above the ftatutable age! and that ftill, notwithftanding his years, the venerable archbifhop has the fame *ardent love of natural fcience,* and followed it with the fame avidity as was fo very aftonifhing in the late Lord B——.

The fcene of thefe experimental refearches ufed to be in the palace of La Favorite. Therefore, as far as they could give collateral curiofity to the place, the deftruction of it in the war could not but be additionally lamented. In the private life of this unhappy politician, no other noticeable peculiarity occurred!

Neither for political merit, is it poffible, with truth, to compliment the councils of Mentz! There has been ever in them an affected elation—indeed, an oftentation of apathy and difdain, utterly irrelevant to each of the reciprocal interefts which are concerned. Bad for thofe who employ government; worfe for thofe who in government are

are employed. For, fay they at Mentz, "without a fit regard to popular confiderations, what is our government, its origin, or its end?"

Popularity, at once a duty and a reward of man, cannot be too ftrenuoufly enforced by every teacher upon active life. It is well worthy of that dignifying recommendation which it has from the eloquence even of apoftolic wifdom herfelf!

Here too, as elfewhere, the providence of the plan is at once apparent: and the growth of popularity, like the moft ufeful vegetables, where moft wanted, is proportionably with eafe to be fupplied.

The procefs is neither difficult nor dear. The cheapeft courtefies, of a few words and looks, an addrefs commonly cautious; confiderations decently humane—thefe, in ordinary cafes, have fufficed. And if fuperadded, there can fubfift the captivations of manners at all fuperior, if there appear any knowledge of effect, and any power of pleafing; —any thing like philofophical fkill of diving into character, and applying it with colloquial talents to life and practice, then who can calculate the product, and limit its extent? Charming in any rank, in high place, irrefiftible, the influence of fuch powers of intellect, fo ufed, is feen and felt by all—in fpite of impediments, of all others the moft difcouraging, both from public mifchief, and from private vice! Our own Charles the Second, and Henry the Fifth (not to mention Henry IV. of France) are proofs in every body's way; the one an unprincipled invader, the other no lefs unprincipled, as a fcandalous debauchè in felfifh obdurate excefs. And yet, odious or defpicable as they both effentially ought to have been, they lived and died neither one nor the other! Even their memory, to this time, embalmed, even beyond the power of Egypt, by the fame of their manners, by the popularity of their fway.

When, therefore, as too commonly occurs, the reverfe of
this

this is seen and deplored, when a chief magistrate can suffer himself to lapse into hard opinions and disrepute; there must be something much more wrong than the mere error of chance! And when further degraded, as now and then, alas! has happened, and presented as an object of penal law, what then must be the popular opinion upon character and desert?

Certainly Charles the First, and Louis the Sixteenth, were the least offensive of their race. As certainly it is not needed, nor is it truly possible, to accuse them with the provocations, so well urging to capital resentment, the people of Rome against Nero. Yet, undeniably, with so much to deplore, there must have been not a little to condemn. Their powers and purposes must have been no less froward than their fate. If not at once heady and heartless; without fibres in the one to feel, without faculties in the other to understand, that they were amenable to the laws of conscience and sympathy, what was there in the world to hinder them from any conceivable ascendancy of fame and of merit? With any thing thing like common manhood, good faith, and the charities of nature, they might have soared far from the doom which they endured, conspicuously dear, through generations succeeding even beyond their own, in the rapturous energies of unsuborned regard—in fact, realising some of the best charms which poetry has imagined for the lavish decorations of a wished-for demigod!

Reflections such as these, more or less apt to rise on the contemplation of any great power in popular disregard, are inseparable from the present state of Mentz. The popular sentiments ran very lofty and vigorous; and there is, lamentably, nothing we could hear of about the public council to keep pace with them. The enemies of the government talked, openly, of its abolition; and even by friends, we heard the word abdication as an advice.

In

In the mean while we could not find any perfonal fet-off! at leaft not any popular fentiment at all propitious, like the lucky circumftances of the elector's lot. If his wealth has been at all enhanced by focial excellence, the people are to learn in the fenfe of obligation; the voice of gratitude is filent. If he has patronized good works, admiration alfo is no lefs reprehenfibly mute. And even the genius of government, loquacious every where as he is apt to be, abfolutely fails in his allegiance, if the elector's councils have at all laboured to leave the ftate better than he found it—lefs burthened, and lefs fhackled—more enlightened, and more free!

With fome of the hereditary princes of Germany there might be, for all this, fome hereditary excufe. But where the prince is elective, the claims on him muft be ftronger, for knowledge and practice lefs defective: in the fame proportion, as his opportunities have been more, from a birth more favourable to the ufeful energies of human nature, from a difcipline towards good upon one fide, and from folicitations to evil lefs feducing on the other fide—a difcipline more cogent, from wider experience, and from practice more matured.

The refiftance of the tempeft may prove the ftrong hold of the root. The unpopularity of the councils in Mentz yet prevails, in fpite of the late ftruggles; ftruggles not more hideous to them from their enemies, than their friends. The people feem decided for a fyftem the moft democratic. And, whether right or wrong, fuch is their wifh for change, that they feem bent upon it, undeterred by any ills, fo probable, in the changing. He muft be fick indeed, before the mind can be forced up, to fuffer a grave operation—though that operation be not painful in itfelf—but full of hazard only from accident or violence—from the ignorance of the aids, and from the barbarity of the by-ftanders.

Again,

Again, there should be considered too, each honest inference from fact. The government, comparing what it is, with what it was, has some benefit of comparison. The administration, particularly of criminal laws, has been of late, within these seven years, essentially reformed. Each process is quickened. Each expence is diminished. The accused are admitted to bail. And each accusation must be tried within seven or eight days.

The infliction of the law is, in many points, commendable; and may exemplify, to more shewy regions, on the complex objects of the law; and that it does but half its duty, if it does not try to rectify error in its source, to reclaim no less than to punish.

Such, to their credit be it said, is the disposition of their punishments! Death, a disgrace to the sagacity and temper of each system where it is frequent, is at Mentz almost unknown. At the prisons their right object, correction, is in view. They pursue it, by the tract which alone can be successful, by solitude, by discipline and labour. And that the traveller, too heedless and unprofiting to enter the house of mourning, may still be admonished by its outside; there is over the gate of the prison a device, which may catch the eye of vagrant curiosity, and well indicate the humane and wholesome purposes which are within; where the controul and education of necessity, and its reforming power over the unruly passions of men, are fairly presumeable, from the dominion obtainable over beasts, and beasts the least docile, from stubborn mischief, from levity, and from strength. Thus stags, boars, and lions are represented drawing a draft carriage. Ideally tenable, at least, from what all must know, the undisputed wonders of the yoke!

The prisons of Mentz are further to be commended for their humanity. That man is not fit for his office, either as a gaoler or judge, who, untouched by the consciousness of his own imperfections, can audit, unsympathising, the

imperfections

imperfections of others. It cannot be hoped that every one shall be like Boerhaave and Sir Thomas More—because, in the lottery of human diſtributions, there are not many ſuch prizes, as the wit and temper to emulate ſages and ſaints. But what they do at Mentz, can be done every where.— There can be a reſpect which man owes to man; the reſpect of pity, for the moral depreſſion of men! There can be the fullneſs of accommodation—that outward preſſure may not conſpire to exacerbate, needleſsly, agonies of the mind. That any ſuperſerviceable peril to the body may be warded off by the miniſters of health, by cleanlineſs and air. That there may be no ſqualid defedations. No dungeons. No chains. That there may be all reaſonable mitigations of climate. And no ſuch connivance at abuſe as the gaolers ſelling lenity and liquor, to reimburſe them for the money their places, purchaſed from corrupt power, may happen to have coſt.—Money, neither more nor leſs, than a premium for corruption! which none but a magiſtrate quite abandoned would propoſe—and which no country, but what is dark and mercileſs, can permit!

The priſons are viſited unceaſingly! once a week, by one of the upper miniſters of ſtate; and once in a fortnight by the ſuperior council. The magiſtracy of the police in the meanwhile muſt be unremitting; and to them every gaoler muſt exhibit a ſtatement of what has been done, and of courſe ſuffered every day.

Thus, conſequently, the ſuffering of the priſoners is as little as can be—and the magiſtrates have the utmoſt poſſible joy in the cheering conſciouſneſs of ſoftening a deſtiny, otherwiſe more ſevere.

The allowance to the priſoners is, daily, two pounds of bread, a pint of ſoup, and, except on faſt days, eight to twelve ounces of meat. The allowance from creditors to their debtors is, daily, two pounds of bread, and about fourpence Engliſh—a ſum equivalent to a ſhilling in England!—

and yet better ſtill, is what we further found, which was the health and paucity of the priſoners. It is rare to have any debtors immured—and rarer ſtill for any, who are immured, to die.

Even in another direction, and where from the too common virulence of political retaliation, it was leaſt to be expected, lenity towards priſoners, we rejoiced, to find had continued the rational glory of Mentz!—Even the Club-iſts, (the active agents for the *Revolution*) who had been ſeized and were impriſoned, eſcaped without ſuffering much from unmanly rigor. Intercourſe and the power of writing was, indeed, for a ſhort time denied them. But they were ſoon and finally liberated, and without any diſgrace upon the country, by any violent puniſhment!—No death! No confiſcation! No inſult upon the ſpirit by puniſhments held ignominious—but, which when unſullied by moral baſeneſs in queſtions of ſpeculative opinions like theſe, can be ſcandaliſing only, on the pretended humanity, which dare inflict them!

The contemplation of active, arduous virtue, is a ſpeculation ennobling any where. But, in high place, and ſpreading in popular application, through a wide range of beneficence, its charms are enhanced, and become much more edifying and dear, from the fine eminence of its poſition, from the finer extenſion of its uſe.

Such are the ideas and emotions with which we cloſed our political ſpeculations upon Mentz.

EXCURSION ON THE RHINE.

FROM Meintz, if the traveller be on his route towards England, he should go to Coblentz by the river, that is supposing him to be not insensible to the solicitations from ease, frugality, novelty, and delight of landscape charms!

If the traveller be not going in the direction above-mentioned, yet if Meintz be not in the route upon his return, he positively should, si fors non objecerit, indulge in an excursion like this. For in the regions which are usually the haunts of Englishmen, there is no river scenery to compare with it. For the Rhine is better than any river in Italy, in France, in Germany, or in England; and in the track now stated, from Meintz to Coblentz, is that precise position of the whole Rhine, which is, for scenery, the best.

Our passage was in the winter, in the dreariness and darkness of a German Mid-November—amidst sleet and snow, with nothing but a tilt of double dowlas, and a few chips smouldering in a little smoaking stove, to shield and sooth us under the visitations of such a sky!—And yet, even so, we found the passage, not otherwise than supremely interesting, instructive, and gay! For nature is in fine attitudes; and art, in very imposing forms! Castles and convents are in ruins. While agriculture, particularly the vineyards, flourish proportionably to these harmonising indications, how tyranny and superstition fade! The river meanwhile varies ever in its aspect and character; spreading where it is with most advantage seen, and sounding where it can be most perfectly heard.

The lands too have the power of pleasing, so potent from variety, in their shapes and surfaces. Hills and mountains are in far greater plenty than the plains. The precipice is at times abrupt, over the margin of the river. And sometimes the rock, heaving up an appendicular layer acrofs the ftream, gives an irregularity or a fall—but not more than can move the mind or the play-thing of a child. Large woods do not abound. But there are fome timber trees, and many orchards; and thefe, with brufhwood on the hills where there are no vines, fill it up for mere leafage and fcenery well enough, with no very confiderable vacuities in the eye.

The foil alfo is a fource of intereft and inftruction, for the traveller at all accuftomed to fpeculations in mineralogy, and to thofe phenomena prevailing in a country which has been volcanic. Phenomena, which feem in fome fort, like the enigmas of nature, but which refolve like other problems through the plan of providence, into new teftimonies of the attributes moft acceptable to men, a defign of mercy, and not a chaftifement of chance!

The hills which finifh on the Rhine, are the weftern extremity of the chain which arifes with the mountains of Heffe, Franconia, and Bohemia. Not improbably, too, formed at the fame time, for there are the fame marks of age and character manifeft within and without. The fame ftretched fummits and fteep defcents—the fame vertical fiffures, exhibiting in fections, fimilar variety of ftrata beneath, yellow, blue, grey, and greenifh red, the fand ftone rock, the argillaceous flate, the ferruginious loam, with calcareous ftrata, ambitioufly afcending, till fome other layer, perhaps a new comer quite, the rubbifh thrown off from fome neighbouring height, turns it from the height that crowned their wifhes, and hides them in ruin. While petrefactions, though of dirt and of decay, fhew amidft the wonders of toughnefs and cohefion, what may be done even by an error loci, by an extraneous body, if favoured by the effervefcence of a place!

The black vitreous rocks, with the prifmatic bafaltes,

which

which run along the whole of this track, are decidedly volcanic altogether, and fill the mind with a curiosity which is still awful, though the eruption is extinct! A complex emotion as much excited here, as at the Giants Causeway, at Monte Bolca, or at Viterbo—though it may be inferior to what is felt at Baia and Puzzuoli, where a flaming volcano is in sight.—To calculate on all the powers of human strength, a man must be seen in some dire extremity; some spasm of fortune, or some convulsion of his frame. To imagine all the possibilities of time and chance upon elementary matter; countries which are volcanic, must be seen.

Some of the productions, which are volcanic merely, are used, in each region near them, for the purposes of domestic life. Thus, like the lava and puzzuolana of Italy, are the tarras and the basaltes upon the Rhine.—They are the best building materials; their posts, their fences, their pavements, and their roads.

The basaltes which are in columnar prismatic forms, and susceptible of a good polish. With this they often come unwrought from the mountains, by the mere action of water! by water standing till it mines the rock at the bottom; and running to polish imperceptibly each surface at the top! Fine emblem as to the power of contrast and doctrine of vicissitudes—nay, referring, in philosophical poetry, to the prescribed action of importunity and perseverance sensible upon matter, prevailing over mind itself—

Prece molle vincuntur pectora dura.

In this country, unimpoverished by taxes and not drained by the exhausting abominations of war, building materials are still not dear. Bricks, larger than ours, are 16 and 18 livres a thousand—and the basaltes come yet cheaper still. The chief use of the basaltes is for the frames of doors and windows, for chimney pieces, and for paved floors.

The

The tarras, which forms the moſt impenetrable and petrifying cement which is known. This cement (in Italy called the puzzuolana), uſed in much larger proportions than ſtone, formed thoſe buildings, ſtill the wonders of the world, and for their duration, as well as beauty, originality of genius and force, the Coleſes, the Hadrian Villa, and the Baths of Titus and Diocletian. Leſs captivating in ſhow, but ſcarcely leſs ſtupendous in conſequences, it is now the baſis of that compoſition with which the Dutch make their dikes and ramparts againſt the ſea, and thus, upon a level in ſome places literally below it, a local habitation is formed an earthly power, which for arts and induſtry, has ever had no ſmall fame and merit in Europe.

"Scoops out an empire, and uſurps the main."

In application of the tarras to form a cement for building, the proportions are three of tarras to one of lime. Both ſubſtance, before mixing, to be reduced to powder. Fine ſand, as in other ſtucco, and in ſimilar proportions, has been uſed at times, by the builders, both of Germany and Italy. The price of the tarras, at Amſterdam, is now nineteen or twenty rix-dollars for a quantity meaſuring one hundred cube feet. Of this ſum one-fifth only is paid upon the Rhine for the raw material—the reſt of the expence is for carriage. In London, it ſells for three to four ſhillings the buſhel.

In point of ſcenery and its effects, the chief drawback perhaps is from monotony. That uniformity, by long continuance, becoming tedious in nature no leſs than in art. And both might have, with advantage, more variety here. The country in its agriculture and plantations—the towns, in the ſhape and colour of their buildings. The mixture of plaſter and ſtone, the baſaltes for the frames of doors and windows, and above all, bad unadvancing taſte, unaltered for ages, ſeems to be the ſame in all. But in all, too,

there

there is an air of ſtability, which implies comfort, and ſuch a quantity in each building, as expreſſes pecuniary ſubſtance. The villages ſwell into towns; and, in many a ſpot, there are ſo many out-buildings about a farm or two, as to make them look like a village.

For the effect of landſcape impreſſion, the widening of the river ſoon after leaving Mentz, the Rhinegauan views, and the ſcenery at Bingen and Bacharack are the beſt!

In ſeveral places, where the hills and rocks cloſing-in upon the river, favour the reverberation of ſounds, the traveller is admoniſhed by the boatmen; we accordingly fired our piſtols, and with the uſual ſurpriſes of incidence and reflection; the repercuſſions not multiplied ſo many times as at Milan, but with diſtances much more ſtriking. This led us inſenſibly to Italian and Greek architecture, and from thence the tranſition was eaſy to Ripley and Wren, to the whiſpering gallery at Glouceſter and St. Paul's, and finally to the Parliament Houſe. For Mr. Ripley's patron, Sir Robert Walpole, certainly underſtood the *management of ſounds*, in a manner not inferior to Vitravius himſelf!—And had he been able to perfect his plan, it would have produced effects far beyond any found even in the Greek theatre!

And the efficient *cauſes* would have been the *ſame*, viz.

By *brazen veſſels*, and other metallic ſubſtances on *the ſeats*.

By a given quantity of *hollow bodies*.

By a preciſe arrangement as to the *curve* of the ellipſis.

By a complex ſection with a plane, a little parabolic, as *cutting one ſide* more than the other—but by no means parallel to the baſe—and by ſome new means, happily left behind him, as to the point of *contact* and the *tangent*.

All agree it is wonderful, what by mathematics, in the ſcience *of numbers* may be done. With each dependant theory, thence finally derivable of Phonics and Acouſtics!

The exquisite, the charitable apparatus for helping weak ears!—for taking in sounds, though apparently remote!—for mollifying what is acute—and fixing what is flexible! the microphonicon, the poliphonicon, the stentorophonicon, or the speaking trumpet, refraction, reflection, and the *artificial echoes*. The more sublime mathematics are a magnificent occupation for the pure abstract mind. While the mixed mathematics, thus, with a due relation to matter, are admirably fitted for that part of the *people who trade*. Hence, and with such signal thriving, are they so well cultivated by certain gentlemen in the northern part of our islands! Hence some of the successes so surprising in life, even atchieved by the meanest of mankind! Hence, often, one man gets over another, and, sometimes, in other countries, through the corruption of foreign politics, one man is over all!

The frugality of the conveyance is another recommendation of it! For a traveller and his servant, with all their baggage, may be carried to Coblentz for two or three half crowns, in small public boats, which are passing almost every day.

These, though less likely than stage coaches to be disagreeable, are, like them, a sort of lottery, where every thing may be convertible, and good come from it as well as evil. Thus a prize, like Dean Swift, was sometimes to be met with between London and West Chester. One of the most lively and elegant men still about town, says thus he often travelled with Sterne; and another friend of mine, a very excellent clergyman in Ireland, thus once was a third to Litchfield, when the two other passengers in the same coach were Dr. Johnson and Angelica Kauffman—a lady whose sensibility and taste, which is the result of it, pervades and animates her conversation, no less than her art!

A prize of the same sort, fell to my lot, in a common boat from Mentz. It was my fortune, and I hope ever to
think

think it good fortune to meet a young gentleman, who probably will be, like his father, an ornament to our country. His education had been advantageous, both as to learning and knowledge. Useful science he had the happiness to have cultivated at Edinburgh. He had improved himself among the most instructive men of the time at Manchester and Birmingham; he had attended Lavoisier, Fourcroi, and the other great men at Paris, and the men, I know not who, who are, or at least ought to be, great in the university of Gottinghen. Added to this, he had that discipline of temper which experience only can give; and above all, he was a fine full-hearted young men, for ever restless and aspiring after rectitude, however hopeless, and who would make all around him happy, if events and objects could be found as pure and plastic as his mind!

I do not see any reason to prevent my specifying him: he was the younger Mr. W. of Birmingham. His professional position, fortunately, fills no small space in national regard, and, this may be a testimony, needed only where no other instance may be known, to show how well that position is filled.

With Mr. W. was a merchant of Naples, M. M. a gentleman of large experience, and no less honour and benignity, who had seen a great deal, and was ready in communicating what he had seen. He spoke French with as much fluency as his native language, Italian; and he spoke English too with no want of words.

In the boat there was an agreeable young German from Stutgard, and a gentleman, who, though he afterwards turned out to be an Englishman, was imagined by all present, during the day and a half we were together, to be a Frenchman, a Girondist, one of the Mountagne, and I know not what. His appearance was singular, and each singularity altogether foreign: from top to toe wrapped up in fur, and wrapped in silence too, evidently offended at Mr. W. his friends, having kept the boat past the time; but, by degrees however, he relaxed each oddity in his pellice, and what might seem more rugged in his looks, wore away, with the power that habit has over things in themselves indifferent; and he began to converse, rapidly and strong, and far from unamusingly or ill; but not a word in any other language than French.—He was asked, if he did not understand English? " Oui Monsieur," said he, balancing, " Oui Monsieur, comme ca,—un peu des mots,—a force d'y songer—ici et la en pourfuivant vos journaux, et les autres *Grands* politiques dans votre assembleè nationale. Mais, pour parler, je ne suis pas un amateur de ca!—Vraiment c'eft une etude! Et, de plus, Monsieur, c'est effectivement Moitiè Allemagne; Et Ainsi, Franchement, semi-barbare!—with a corresponding look, and tone most hypercritically full of opinion, as upon some combination *new* struck out on an object meriting neglect, if not scorn.

I have heard Mr. W. recount this little adventure so whimsically, that, if but half as well told, it might not be quite out of place here: yet much of the effect of what passed, may be incommunicable, as it arose on the incongruity of the gentleman who spoke English, thinking their fellow-traveller did not understand it.

There was no question of his being a foreigner; all that remained to ask was, from what country he might come? and there Mr. W. desired his companion to find it out; adding, " I am not quite settled in thinking him a French-
" man: and though he is not English, yet, take care, he
" may understand us!"

" He is not an Italian," said the Neapolitan.

" He is not a Frenchman," said another, " for that part
" of his face," naming it, " is rather like what we see on
" the Adriatic. He comes from Bosnia, or Dalmatia, I am
" positive!—No, sir, he has just escaped from France," said
the

the Neapolitan. " He is an emigrè—faid the boatman!"
" I fpeak from my certain knowlege"
" Then afk him," replied Mr. W. " afk him how he voted!" The German gentleman named the occafions as the apotheofis of Mirabeau, the Civil Lift, &c. &c.

Mr. W. had a little Amfterdam Horace in his hand. And the Neapolitan advifed Mr. W. to examine him in that.—Horace then luckily filled the following hour or two; and there were feveral good new readings ftruck out by emphafis and punctuation: when coming to the line in the ode Pomp. Varo.

———Sanius
Bacchabor Edonis,

The coinage of the verb, led to another made with no lefs felicity, and applied far better than by Terence, viz. in the beautiful fragment from Simonides.

Tecum mille modis ineptiebat.

Our fingular traveller, repeated the whole of that inimitable ode, and fhort as it is, yet long before the end of it, his eyes were covered with tears! One effect of them was to diffipate any little doubt there might be remaining. The emotion was evident. The caufe of it, was fuppofed, not fympathy, but fuffering. The time and place concurring. The odds were for a foreigner who was diftreffed, that the diftrefs might be French!

That proverbial inftinct, the refpect paid to forrow, is a benevolent wonder in our make. The venerable afpect of diftrefs finds or makes a friend in every heart! Emotion, when leagued with innocence and virtue, has allegiance, willingly, from all. From that moment, the traveller feemed to have more afcendancy than ever—fome flight fet-off this, for nerves perhaps too irritable!—For his tears we have fince learnt, thus burft forth, not from any fimilarity to the

fate

fate of **Danae,** but from a fenfe of diftance merely, and fome months abfence from his family and friends!

At Bingen, where they refted for the night, with the fkill and fpeed of an old traveller, he loft not a moment, till he had fecured a good room: and it unluckily turned out to be the beft.—every body, foon after, was on the fame purfuit: and finding the beft room fo quickly pre-engaged, Mr. W. faid, " He had now no doubt of his fellow-travel-
" ler being a Frenchmen, and probably too, that he ftudied
" in the old court!"

While the table was preparing, to an obfervation of the Neapolitan in favor of French eating---the ftrange gentleman ran out into an ardent panegyric, on the magic of the French kitchen, and the wines of Burgundy, calling them all by their names.—This too, though another trifle, quite neutral and indefinite, paffed for a confirmation of the French hypothefis.—And one of the gentlemen told the other what had been faid in approbation of the dinner in France, and adding that he could fee it mount, " like incenfe,
" and fume away through all the porches of the brain!"

The fupper was rather gay.—And the whole fucceeding day, with the next evening, yet gayer ftill. *Tempus in ultimum deducte.* Every body at the Coblentz table d'Hote ftill taking him for a Frenchman,—and " fes compatriotes, fes compatriotes," refounded from every fide.

Thus, he was going on at a great rate, for popularity in table talk, when he had like to have loft it all again, by two petty mal-a-propos—by making fome confufion and undue mixture of two difhes, which were maigre and gras.—And by faying, (though as he thought not loud enough to be heard) of a fmall knot of people, who were engroffing a large bowl of roafted chefnuts—" *Qu'il y en a effez, diable!*
" *pour tous les porcs de Weftphalie!*"

The eccleſiaftic, who had been according to the prejudice of his order, a little offended with the unintended
prophanation

prophanation of mixing fome ragout with his vegetables, was a venerable looking man! and with him our traveller, with evident affiduity, tried to right himfelf at once, by addreffing him in Latin, turning the converfation upon fome points in the eftablifhment of the German church. And hearing that the Germans had the good fenfe to be abolifhing tythes, and conceding a certain allotment of land in lieu of them—he faid, in antethetical, but rather lawlefs Latin, " Et imo domine reverende, incundius multo eft, & idoneus " fanè—quam incertas decimas, certis rixis obtinendas!"

On taking up his pellice to leave the room, Mr. W. obferved on the fkin, that it was not a little to be wondered why the breed of wild beafts yet continued, in fpite of the exterminating care in civil life—alluding to the practice of Alfred's time, and other humanizing laws.

He replied—" Diable M'emporte, Monfieur, mais c'eft, " incroyable ca!—Eft que vous pouvez bien imaginer une " difette des gros betes? Soyez content, Monfieur, hors " des terres Britanniques, en chaque etat, chaque gouverne- " ment du monde, vous en trouverez affez; peut etre bien " un peu de trop, de tous les monfters, concevables!"

Among other lucky things, there was a little turn too on a local circumftance that is not very lucky in the town. On the approach to Coblentz by the Rhine, the common drain of the town, very offenfive, iffues clofe to the palace. —" Ah! quels diableries font dechainès!

" C'eft l'embonchure," faid the boatman, hefitating, " des lieux du cabinet."

" Ah!" faid the traveller with no fmall foftenuto on the note, " Ah c'eft la! le cabinet de Coblentz! le cabinet du " prince! et actuellement," turning to the boatman, " qui " eft le premier?—comment s'appelle t'il?"

The next morning we were all to have walked over Coblentz together, when this extraordinary traveller, before it

was

was light, took a free French leave, and left a letter, also French, for Mr. W. but with an English direction, and with the signature of Votre Ami Anglois.

This raised a new set of busy thoughts, which continued at work till the parties met, unexpectedly in London, at the house of a prime and excellent merchant by the Custom-house—where, with other enlightened and fine spirited men, Mr. W. made the story tell better than I have done, and this Proteus of the Rhine, this reputed Frenchman, this Girondist, and what not, turned out to be, neither more nor less, than a grave English clergyman, an absolute courtier, with no more notion of politics, than he had picked up in a kind of professional prejudice for fast sermons, and the trial of the seven bishops, to say nothing of Milton, of Sydney, or of Locke!

TO WORMS.

WHILE people are humanely excluded from the temptation of conversing with the philosophers of France, the route to Italy, either by the Tyrole or by Switzerland, must continue through Germany; instead of Vauban's fine forts in succession, through Srasbourg and Huninque to Basle, the traveller must be content with what he may find in the road to Manheim, through Worms.

The departure from Meintz was by the demolished palace of La Favorite, yet smoaking and in ruins! The village of Weisenau succeeding, with delapidations, which, to our sense, seemed, at every rude gap, to be crying to Heaven for vengeance!—For what between the Prussians posted in the woody heights on the south-west, and the French batteries towards Kostheim, and the confluence of the Maine, to counteract them, this ill-fated village of Weisenau had been, literally, between two fires, and was so rent and torn in twain, that there was scarcely a single dwelling had escaped unannoyed—without lamentation!—without blood! —We stopped to talk a little on what we saw, with an officer upon a piquet. He did not look like a subaltern to the foe of mankind: but with emotions, like the colour of his trade, he exulted, without compunction, and without sympathy, on what he shewed us? And exulting over the wide-spread havock all around, he called it " a glorious " cannonading!"

We recoiled from him at once and altogether, as Nature should do from her antipathies and enmities! And dipped till we came to the contiguous wood, in an anonymous foreign pamphlet upon the advocates for devils.

That

That contiguous wood was another *aceldama* which thofe monfters had made! Mines, abbaties, and batteries, with all the brutal abominations of their train, and their effects yet more abominable, furprifed and fhocked us at every " turn.—" Vaftum filentium!—Secreti colles!—Fumantia " procul tecta!—Nemo exploratoribus obvius!"

The condition of thefe Germans is deplorable. The wild beafts, in their woods and highlands, they have contrived to exterminate or fubdue. And yet they fuffer other animals to range and lord-it uncontrouled – to perpetuate and to fatten on calamity!—Animals, whether living or dead, abfolutely of a lower order! whofe natural gifts for mifchief are comparatively poor—who, when they are called to atone for blood, cannot even then repair any part of the wrongs they have done with one poor, pofthumous, relic, equivalent to the fkin of their precurfors—the wolves and bears!—

" Rapacious at the mother's throat they fly!
" And tear the fcreaming infant from her breaft!
" Even beauty—force divine! at whofe bright glance
" The generous lion ftands in foftened gaze
" Here bleeds a helplefs, undiftinguifhed prey!"

Till the opinions and emotions of the people fhall of themfelves learn to rally as they ought; their moralifts and politicians fhould be inftant in their endeavours to teach them. They fhould excite them, as when intereft is their duty, to defend themfelves againft the vices: they fhould ftrike the door-pofts of each dwelling with the prophylactics of experience, with the blood of the flain. There fhould be, like a Court Calendar, behind each door, an elephant fheet compendium of the dead, from the firft murder to the laft, through all diftricts and ages, treaty by treaty, and battle by battle! Whether to be fuffered or to be done, they fhould determine againft fury and fucceffes, that deftruction fhould ceafe—that wars fhould be no more!

Even

Even where havock takes a lefs hideous form, and the fteps of invaders are not marked by blood. Yet the tyranny of it, fcarcely lefs oppreffive, has been infupportable to the Germans, and fo they fhould have refifted it! When the French were ufurping in this country, and entered Worms, they did not add to the many millions which, by human violence, have been flain. But as far as exaction was poffible, they were guilty of it.—They feized fix hoftages, the beft people of the place—and at their peril demanded, in three days, the payment of above 1,200,000 livres!

The contribution for fuch a petty place was enormous! It is true, it fell chiefly on the finecure chapters and convents; a department in fociety, not a little enormous alfo, for the harm they do, and the extravagant profits they have for doing it. Yet, as men, and tolerated in civil fociety, they fhould enjoy each right of man, fo conftituted; and, till they are regularly abolifhed, fhould be regularly unmolefted and free.

The detail of the contribution, as it was called, out of which the French thought proper to plunder Worms, was thus:

The Bifhop	400,000 livres.
The Chapter	200,000
Three Convents of Capuchins, Carmelites, and Dominicans	150,000
Other Convents	400,000
Four Collegiate Chapters	30,000
The Corporation	30,000

Traverfing the wood, which at the bottom leads to the Rhine, at the top to the high road, and in all parts to reflections, fuch as thefe, the way winds on to Oppenheim cheerily enough;—not with the ftronger attractions of volcanic phenomena, and fcenery at all fublime:—for the abrupt highlands, the tuf-ftone, and bafaltes, are no more—but through a country, that, with fine features, is placid and ferene.

serene. The Rhine falling on one side of the road, and a gentle hill rising on the other. The eye revels over the bold blue hills of Suabia in the distance. And the fancy, with deepest inspirations, begins to open for the purest air of health and liberty, from the approaching mountains of the Swifs.

The country, as to mere soil, is sandy; but light and practicable. The agriculture, just on this side of Blama, is chiefly arable; and open and inanimate, without cattle or shade, for there are no inclosures, and few trees.—Yet, if not exquisite in itself, what may not be made so by accident. Quod petis in te est. Every thing is an affair of temper. And the circumstances which surround us, take their form and pressure from the emotions which we feel.

If it happen to be the birth-day of an object that you love—if a tear should start, as in the eye of a father, touched by hope and gratulation, then—if the setting sun should fall through a dun water-cloud, there will form between them a half-tint of superlative tenderness and grace. If ever there was a purple light of love, it must have been from this precise degree of density and refraction to produce it!

A bewitching hue, like this, coloured exquisitely every thing around us; from the highlands of Hesse, and the summits of Suabia, where there is a pillar, to we knew not what, over the long line of wood, (like Rousseau's coffee to Eloisa, additionally dear by being rare) to the little points and projections at Oppenheim, and the new bridge of boats over the Rhine, then forming by the Prussians.

The Prussian army had here a very large depository of forage and food, horse-corn, hay, and straw. And this bridge of boats was for the convenience of fetching those necessaries from the other side of the Rhine.

A bridge of boats, as here practised on the Rhine, is a line of vessels, like the lighters on the Thames, and of the

same

fame dimenfions, lafhed together at the bottom, and united yet more firmly by the connecting wooden platform at the top. This advantage is obvious on rivers in all mountainous countries, where the ftreams are thence apt to fwell—for the boats, and with them the whole fabric floating, the bridge rifes as the waters rife.—Befides this bridge at Oppenheim, there is another at Meintz and at Mainheim.—For the paffage of the river, two of the barges open, with a valve on each fide.—At Oppenheim, the barges were towed up from Meintz (for at Mentz there is fome fame for boat-building) about fixteen of them, as we computed, for the bridge was not quite finifhed, would complete the paffage. So that the project has cheapnefs alfo to enhance its value. Such a bridge, we underftood, could not coft fo much as 400l.

Oppenheim, apart from its vineyards, has few, if any, fubftantive perfections. It looks like a little acommodating borough in England. Yet, where but in England, if the moft expert travellers may be believed, are the *complete* accommodations, as of *boroughs*, to be found?

The wines of Oppenheim and Nearftain are thought the beft on this, the weft, fide of the river.—The years 1726 and 1748 are the vintages in moft renown. The beft wine we found on the route was, at the banker's at Mentz. He faid it was thirty-three years old. That was November 1793. Of courfe, if he was exact, the wine was of the vintage 1757. Chefterfield, in his letters, talks of wine a hundred years old, for which they afked on the fpot a guinea a bottle. And even at that price, without a *fenatus confultum*, not any could be had. The whole, however extraordinary it may feem, is very credible, for on the Rhine, and on the Rhone, I have met with wine above eighty years old. And fuch are the impofitions practifed upon travellers, half-a-guinea a bottle has been given for hermitage—and at Auxerre, and at the convent in Burgundy, then owning the vineyard of moft fame (Le Clos de Vou geot)

geot) five livres a bottle I have seen given there.—The price of the beſt new wine at Oppenheim was 55l. to 6ol. for a caſk, which would yield 45 or 46 dozen.

From Oppenheim, paſſing through Wonderſbloom, where the Comte de Leinengen has built a pretty town-gate, and planted poplars in a viſta, to adorn his ſeigneurie and fief, over ſix or ſeven miles of flat arable land, relieved by nothing but ſome few orchards, and a good reach or two upon the Rhine, the eye lights upon the churches and convents of Worms.—Churches any where, by the aſſociation of ideas, inſeparable from every diſcipline and nature, come cheeringly into a view; as they ſoothe the mind with the beſt ſenſe; connecting each dependant bleſſing of peace, of neighbourhood and order! and therefore the mere fabric for external worſhip " *being when bells have knolled to church,*" is well-urged by our moſt philoſophiſing poet, as a criterion of probable character, as a proof that civilization might be warrantably implied.

The town and government of Worms, in part merit ſuch anticipation in their favour; for the points and pinnacles which they preſent, ſeem unſullied as toleration can make them. Popery is the eſtabliſhment of the place. And of the churches which appear, four are doomed to that profeſſion: but, there are the ſame number devoted to a more rational ſyſtem, three for the followers of Luther, one for the reformed.

The well earned fame, the venerable memory of Luther was indeed, I believe, a prime motive for preferring this road, and for loitering a little in the place.

> The chamber where the good man meets a doom,
> Is privileged beyond the common walks of life!

It is not poſſible to ſhake off the ſoul's allegiance to the natural and fit ſupremacy of virtue, of utility, and of truth! That man knows nothing upon the attributes and enjoyments

ments of man, who can ponder, without exalting energies at heart, over the achievements of any virtuous life, burſting with generous ambition, over each intervening bar, from pain, from diſaſter, and from diſmay, and, altogether ſublimed, above every groveling caution, for himſelf, can devote his powers to others: to toil, and to adventure, for a remote poſterity, perhaps for unknown time!

It is not eaſy to enter the town of Worms, without glowing at the ardor which once ſo gloriouſly adorned it.

No outſet could be more inauſpicious—more diſproportioned to any ſplendor of promiſe in the cloſe. An individual, unaided and alone, ſallying forth, amidſt the thick and chilling darkneſs of the ſixteenth century, from the diſqualifying cloiſters of Auguſtine, in queſt of chimeras no leſs dire, than error leagued with uſurpation and impoſition, than Imperial Edicts, than Popiſh Bulls! To think of him under the menace of ſuch prodigies, unmoved, advancing! and, in ſpite of the fate of Huſs and Jerome of Prague, truſting to the vagrant wind, to a ſafe conduct, from the Emperor! To ſee him, thus fortified alone, approaching Worms, amidſt ſuch multitudes of hard thoughts, and hoſtile paſſions, as made his few friends hold him back— left (in language then not judged inapplicable, nor extravagant), the devils in the ſtreets ſhould be as numerous as the tiles upon every houſe-top! To mark his ſteady power as he proceeds, and that ſpirit of rectitude magnanimous inflexible and pure, that Παρρησια, as Atterbury ſo finely calls it, formed, indeed, altogether ſuch a ſcene of complex excellence, with ſuch difficulty to do, and ſuch advantages when done—ſo admirable, ſo preceptive, that it is abſolutely vain, perhaps, to think of any parallel, but in the age and inſpired accompliſhments of the apoſtles themſelves!

There is delightful admonition to be gained from recollecting too the progreſs of his opinions; and from thence to infer favourably for any future advances of truth! For, that religious consummation, of liberty and found words, which Englishmen so well, thank God, are taught to prize, that ridicule and aversion with which all Europe, as it enlightens, must dismiss the frauds and follies of Rome, that glorious reformation of this country, and that authorised hope of like reform which the translated bible gives to every other region of the book-learned earth, all these, were, when they first arose to decorate and bless the existence of men, in their pretensions misunderstood, in their consequences misstated! the cry of innovation and alarm was bandied about, like an echo upon brass, through every empty head, through every hollow heart. Luther bore the brunt of obloquy and oppression. Exile and excommunication tried to drive him, if that signified any thing, from the Romish Church, and from the Ban of the Empire! The other reformers and their profession were beset, like the sun-beam with motes, with the childish brawling of nick names! Such puny efforts as edicts and proclamations attempted to suspend all liberty of speech! The art of printing, then additionally dear from the love inseparable at a new wonder, was stopped. The bible forbid to be circulated. And all copies of it already printed, ordered to be delivered up to the magistrates and the runners of the time!

Such was the fate of Luther, even in times when men far less despicable than most of their successors were in power, Leo X. and Charles V. And yet, even then, and though he made his grave with the virtuous! amidst the praises of Erasmus and Melancthon, and embalmed in the memory of the just—yet, the malice of ignorance and imposture, pursued him still; and, as far as mere clumsy invective could annoy, their efforts were not wanting to dim the lustre, which better industry will ever form, upon the name and character of Luther.

It is not unpleasant, if nonsense and mischief under any

modi-

modifications can be fo, to note fome of the expreffions thus preferved in Junctinus and Cardan. Expreffions in which things apparently moft afunder are united, the ideas and languages of both fuperftitions, in Pagan and in Papal Rome. Aftrology fettles the demerit of his death under the malignant planet of Mars, and then fate configns this moft atrocious and prophane enemy of Chrift, to the three fabulous furies and their poetic lafhes of fire.—Chriftianæ religionis hoftem acerrimum ac prophanum—ad martes coitum religiofiffimus obiit—ejufque anima fceleratiffima ad inferos navigavit, ab Alecto Tyfiphone, et Magera flagellis igneis cruciata.—Such is the fidelity of cotemporary report! and fuch the credit due to the difparagements and condemnation of any doctrine, when that doctrine may thwart the paffions of its opponents, its accufers, and its judges. Thus has it fared with almoft every martyr to truth, moral and divine! Thus Hampden and Sydney were deemed traitors —Galileo fuffered as a heretic fciolift, and St. Paul, as well as Luther, was deemed to be a blafphemer.

Befides the memory of Luther, the town of Worms is of no mark nor likelihood. It is dependent on the Electorate of Meintz; and the bifhopric, a fuffragan on Meintz, is held in commendam by the elector. The territory is about $7\frac{1}{2}$ fquare miles. The town is very fmall. The population about 3000—of whom 400 are Lutherans—800 are Reformed. Yet the bifhopric contrives to fqueeze out of them a revenue of three or four thoufand pound a year. And the reft of the ecclefiaftics, who fare proportionably well, are almoft as numerous as the people. The churches, convents, and chapters have been mentioned. With this literature, and fome there muft be in the midft of fo many opponents for ftudy and leifure, yet learned eftablifhments, ufeful efforts, there are none. I know not any claffic book ever edited at Worms. Their laws and cuftoms are included in thofe mentioned at Meintz.

The

The contribution levied by the forces of the French Republic was incidentally fpecified before. The pretended caufe of this violence, was the archbifhop's partiality, needlefsly oftentatious to the French princes and the other fugitive French. Befides that contribution, the Republicans did no further mifchief. They ftaid there in winter quarters from October to March 1. They very fairly paid for what they had; and left no debts whatever behind them.

The fugitive French, with M. de Condè and M. Breteuil, &c. were at Worms, while M. d'Artois and Monfieur were at Coblentz. And from thence they drafted to join the Auftrians and Pruffians in Champaigne, to partake of the compound immortality of their proclamations and retreats.

George the Second returned to Worms after the battle of Dettingen. It is the fate and follies of moft battles to leave their confequences quite unatoned, without any lafting good effect whatever. This battle was not abfolutely fo —for it produced Mr. Handel's Te Deum.

MANHEIM.

TO MANHEIM.

THIS is a country diſtinguiſhed, moſt potently, by the bleſſed effects of the late diſcharged deſpotiſm in France! Nature in ,making itſl at, moiſt, loomy, and fertile, ſeems only to have laid it out as a granary for Germany: but art and man's device have laboured to make it fruitful of produce, leſs trite and humble. This is a country which is immortalized by the viſitations of the moſt Chriſtian King, the Fourteenth Louis—Louis the Grand! Here—in the proper forcing-ground of laurels—in a magma animaliſed with compoſt more precious than the tribute of the brow, even though that appointed tribute ſhould be paid in tears—here he, Louis the Grand, reared thoſe bluſhing wreaths, which ſeemed in ſome eyes, to give ſuch artificial grandeur to his ſtature!

Here an order came from the Moſt Chriſtian King, and ſigned Louvois (the miniſter) to lay the whole country in aſhes!—And, here, that order was obeyed!

Here the blood-hounds of war were let looſe, under Lorges and Turenne! They raged without controul! nay, without any diſcoverable remorſe in the very wretches who led them! with apathy that rivalled Nero, they ſported with fire and ſword. They inſultingly ſerved the inhabitants, as the phraſe is, with formal notices to quit!—Notices! with all the inſolence of office, though they might be without the jargon of law. And then havoc made his maſterpiece! The Palatinate fell—inſtantly—under the moſt devouring fire! The whole Palatinate was ravaged! every populous diſtrict, each flouriſhing town! the tombs of the dead, and the churches of the living! fifty caſtles were burnt;

burnt! And from the caftle to the cottage, fcarcely a fingle tenement could efcape! The Elector, rifing from fhort, interrupted endeavours after repofe, faw at one time from his window, two cities, and twenty-five villages in flames! and even that fight, ftupendous horror as it was, is faid to have been but as a fpark to a conflagration oompared with the succeeding fhapes of guilt and cruelty—of cruelty unprovoked, of guilt irreparable; which fo monftroufly over-topt it!

Louvois, the minifter, had been long in place; and that, fays a fubtle and animated hiftorian, muft be fome apology, for inevitable abomination. And, to bring off the King, they said he was ill-advifed. Forfooth! as if advice could offer to him, without the power of rejection! Even the contemporary Courts of Europe blufhed—exclamations came from thofe which were contiguous: from Bonne, from Munich, and from Treves. The collected princes of the empire protefted. For the air all around was rent with the bewailings of the outcaft; and Germany, at leaft the weftern fides of it, was defaced, with every sad veftige of woe. And then the amiable gentleman upon the throne, the Chriftian King did vouchfafe—what?—a modeft, courtly fummons to *to do him homage*—why?—for the lands he *had feized* in Alface!

Such is the memorial of Louis the Grand, in the Palitinate! And yet fuch are the people in the Palitinate, and fuch their fapience and refignation, that troops have been allowed to form, to forage, to fly there, whofe only purpofe could be a weak, if not impoffible, attempt to reftore the great grand-children of the gentleman thus remembered.

It is pleafant, therefore, to travel through the Palatinate. For with a new infight into the human mind, you learn to fpeculate upon its poffible pliancy. And from this proved promptitude to what is ridiculous and vain, you may learn

to

to compute the probable improvement of the human powers towards what is useful, what is wife!

Otherwife the Palatinate is not very pleafant. For the whole region is a flat. Well watered, indeed, by two fine rivers, the Necker and the Rhine. But with no decoration from wood, except viftos, chiefly poplars, at the chief towns. The foil, almoft ever, is clay and fand, when it changes, therefore, it is quoad the traveller, what Dr. Young would call a change of woe. The agriculture is in the ftile of Flanders, and with the fame excellence, and the fame defects, good where corn is grown. Bad where it is grafs. The intervening crops of potatoes, turnips, and cabbages, are in a fimilar feries and fuccefs. There is not much natural grafs. The artificial graffes are the chief forage. They ufe animal manure. But not with the fame affiduity and contrivance as in Flanders: and now in France. The roads in the neighbourhood of the chief towns are paved: but where not paved, are neglected, and therefore bad.

The approaches to Manheim, on all fides, are pleafing, as there is pleafure in the fight of cultivation and fuccefs. The viftos have not fuch magnificence from the trees, as at Caverfham or Bufhey-Park; nor fuch a grand effect from extent as at Chantilli, but they are well kept, and gay; and though poplars, they feem in fome fort to fatisfy by their plentitude and uniformity. Qualities which, perhaps, make the gratification to the eye, on the review of an army in array. Beyond the eye, this array muft be to all fenfes the fame. What Xerxes faid, when he wept over it, muft be faid and done by every fentient being, by every being who can reafon and feel.

At the entrance of Manheim, by a bridge of boats over the Rhine, and the fortifications on both fides of it; with the palace and other public buildings, in large maffes, contiguous, the effect is various, and a little interefting. It was the more fo when we were there, by the valves of they

bridge

bridge opening to give a paſſage to a large detachment of the French. They loaded two large veſſels, like our weſt country barges. And they were, according to the cartel, when the Pruſſians got poſſeſſion of Meintz, removing from thence to Straſbourg. And though they were the contents of the military hoſpitals, and few of them yet active convaleſcents, yet they were ſinging their political ſongs, ſo popular in France; and ſome of them, while the papers were examining by the town-officers, wandered gaily into the town to buy bread. It was cheering to ſee ſpirit ſturdy under calamity:—and it felt it further animating, to ſee ſome Germans juſt to the fair claims of a foe: with pity for their diſtreſs, with applauſe at their fortitude in bearing it!

Manheim is, as far as it goes, one of the moſt handſome little towns in Europe. And it is ſo from the width of the ſtreets, their regularity, and the ſections and interſections being all at right-angles. Not that this excludes the pleaſure of variety. For there is no tyranny of preſcription as to outward form; and ſo, in the variety of plans and materials, you may, if you will, ſee and feel the gradations of ſociety in the well-aſſerted variations of the conditions, nay, and humours too, which may have produced them.— Sir Joſhua Reynolds taught this, as he was accuſtomed to teach other points of art, well as a painter:—and every obſerver who will be enlightened and free, ſelf taught, will feel it as a man.

For the pleaſing effect all feel in the ſtreets of Manheim, there is another provable cauſe, viz. the ſpace which the houſes have; they are not high, but wide. This is equally favourable to the buildings, both of good and bad fortune: in wealth, for magnificence; in poverty, for eaſe.

The ſtate of ſociety in crowded towns would be deplorable, if it were not ludicrous by being voluntary. To ſee two or three hundred pounds a year paid for dwellings, which,

which, in refpect to health and fcenery, cannot phyfically differ from a prifon but in name, where the fun is never feen to fhine but upon a brick wall, and where the common air cannot be felt, but loaded with all-furrounding vile effluvia from the oppofite rooms on one fide, and from their own ftables, &c. on the other.—While the poor are much worfe off ftill. They have not elbow-room If they are lucky enough to enlarge, it muft be upwards. They cannot fpread. Their houfes are like their deftinies; whoever wifhes them well, muft wifh them well towards Heaven.

When Voltaire wrote comparatively of the chief towns in Europe, for ftreet police, of pavements, &c. Paris appeared to him to be the beft. What Paris was then, may be manifeft from what it is now, without raifed foot-ways or underground drains. London is, at leaft, half a century before every other town in the world. And Manheim, even as to ftreets, is far preferable to Paris. The Mainheim foot-ways are like thofe in Privy-Garden and Scotland-Yard. If the trees and walk in the middle of the High-ftreet had been well encouraged, it had been one of the handfomeft ftreets any where to be found. For the trees, if planted after the laft conflagration, would have had above a hundred years growth.—As to the gravel for the walks, feldom found but in Englifh gardens, that too might have been had, if looked for, as well as wifhed. The Palatinate cannot be worfe off than Edinburghfhire. Yet, where are there better walks than at Dudingfton? When the old Lord Abercorn was queftioned as to the difficulty of getting the gravel—he faid, in his cool odd way—" There was no difficulty at all, " he had it from Kenfington Gravel-Pits."—Our moft accomplifhed ambaffador that we have abroad, told me that he had propofed the fame mode to the King of Naples, for his garden at Caferte. And it would be, manifeftly, very eafy.

For

For the gravel might go as ballaſt in our ſhips, which are ſo numerous, or at leaſt will be, to the fair at Salerno.

At Manheim life is not low. It is not without intellectual recommendations. There is a library; ſome experimental ſcience: and beſides that apparatus, there are collections in natural hiſtory, with occaſional lectures, not very ample in all. The multiplication of petty princes produces, with much evil, undeniably ſome incidental good. For what palace, even on a plan of oſtentation, can be complete without muſeums and book-rooms? And again, what are books, and the arts, without able men who can make the moſt of them? Learning is one ladder of ambition. And there are not a few who have mounted only by ſelfiſh patronage, and the politic affectation of it.

Hence, if not from better motives, in all the ſubdiviſions of Germany there are univerſities or academies. Even Heidelberg, the ſecond town in the palatinate, has an univerſity, with a large appointment of profeſſors, chymiſtry, botany, anatomy, natural hiſtory, experimental philoſophy, with learned ſocieties for the cultivation of political economy and practical arts. Heidelberg is indeed the moſt ancient in Germany, viz. 1386.

At Manheim there are ſimlar eſtabliſhments and profeſſors, and with more parade in their appointment and apparatus—in natural hiſtory and the obſervatory. There, as almoſt every where upon the continent, the inſtruments are Engliſh; artiſts, Bird and Dolland, Arnold and Siſſon. The ſector of the one, and the time-piece of the other are their moſt modern importation. Ramſden and Herſchel's improvements are already in Italy; but are not here. In Italy, I ſhall delight to ſtate, in the ſucceeding volume, that the fame of Herſchel is equal to his modeſty and his merit. One of his inſtruments arrived, fortunately, while I was there: and when he had the praiſe of the moſt praiſe-

worthy

worthy of the profeſſors, Oriani and Fontana, we ſhared accidentally in the honours paid to Herſchel, and felt innocently elate, as coming from the ſame country, with diſcoveries ſuch as his!

Beſides each uſual courſe of philoſophy, chymiſtry, anatomy, &c. there is a ſchool of ſculpture, drawing, &c. a military ſchool, compriſing the arts acceſſary to engineering —a ſchool where every *ſage-femme* muſt ſtudy and be vouched—an academy of ſciences, with premiums, &c. and there is a ſociety (Societè Allemande) whoſe object is the *German language* — to define, to depurate, and to atteſt it. The meetings of the ſociety were finiſhed when we were there. But, as far as I could find, it was more and more the faſhion to follow the French academy, and adjuſt conteſted orthography, with reference to pronunciation and uſage, more than to analogy or derivation. Thus their primary object is philology : but the elucidation of language, if they purſue it well, will lead to ſomething higher, both in ſcience and truth. For in learning, as in virtue, one advance facilitates another. As they analyſe meaning, they may learn to rectify it too.

The lectures, which are all gratuitous, are from October to July. The library, à fine room 100 by 48 feet, is open three days in a week. The books are uſeful, rather than curious, or rare. There are about 70 000 volumes. There are ſome antiques in the palace, and five or ſix hundred pictures, which they ſhow—and many of them are worth ſeeing. Denner's two ſmall heads (twelve or fourteen inches) are the favourites of the place, to thoſe who look no further than minute fidelity and ſuper-ſerviceable detail. Yet what is the art which is ſkin deep only, however high wrought, as theſe are, and to each petty prominence and pore, to the more arduous and more uſeful energies of a painter who dives into character, and can identify in every fibre each ſenſation that ever ſtrung it ? The firſt is the

praiſe

praife of Denner's heads—the fecond of every mafterly portrait in exiftence—from Raffaelle, Pope Urban, and the head of Leonardo, by himfelf, to the well known chefs d'œuvres of Vandyke and Reynolds, the Duke of Buckingham and Mr. Fox.—Denner was paid immoderately, twelve or fourteen hundred ducats for the two, while two living artifts, for the head of Mr. Lock, of Norbury, and for a head of Mr. Kemble, the actor, a head yet more energetic ftill, received for thofe moft admirable works but twenty-five or thirty guineas a piece! Were painters only doomed to fee a difproportion between merit and reward, not only Romney, Stuart, and Lawrence, but Beechy and Weftall might repine, that the Paris Rigaud, a century paft, had a hundred louis d'ors for a head.

In the Manheim collection thefe works are the beft—the fketches by Reubens and Vandyke, a fmall Raffaelle, a Caracce and a Pouffin. Modern pictures there are none, but two landfcapes, with much luftre, by the French Claude, Vernet—and a head of the elector by Pompeio Battoni, one of his beft portraits. There is no Englifh picture, but a hare, by a Mr. Hamilton. So tardy at times, and fo local is fame.

Literature and the arts give great circumftantial recommendations to a place. And Manheim would be no bad refidence, to thofe who can be content with a level country, if they can bear German crokery, and are ague proof.— For agues, we underftood, are frequent at Manheim— from the confluence of the Necker and the Rhine, both mountainous rivers, and both therefore liable to overflow a land, naturally not above the level of the river at low water. The drinking water is vapid and foul.

In the cure of thofe agues they give emetics and the bark. But in other Fevers antimonials are not in ufe. James's powder is little known. The fee to a phyfician is a half-florin. But little medical learning from England has found

its

its way yet into the palatinate. We saw tranflations only of Cullen, Pott, and Mofely. The hofpital is ill ventilated and dirty. And the only regulation worth any praife is, that there is a fhort feries of inftruction given by a profeffor to the nurfes, with rules and explanations on their conduct, general ideas of medicine, and inftructions to prepare them for emergencies, as hæmorrhage, fainting fits, &c. There is a lying-in-hofpital with twelve beds. This is the place where each fage femme muft ftudy practice: each community fends one fo to ftudy, with an allowance of fifteen kreutzers a day. And that is found enough for her fupport.

For the fupport of the poor there is no compulfory rate; but there is a voluntary collection, to which all people of fubftance would feel it derogation not to contribute. The receivers and managers are men of rank and character, members of the chief councils, the regency and juftice. And fuller diet, &c. to convalefcents in the hofpital is one good object of this charity. This diftribution was in one year, which we faw, 3000 loaves, and 3000 pounds of meat.

There is an orphan fchool, but is very improperly in the houfe of correction. Eighty orphans are received—and either apprenticed out, or taught manufactures in the houfe. The manufactures are fpinning thread and woollens, making cloth and cards. In England fuch charities, when well regulated, fuftain themfelves by their labours.— The expence per head, in England, is about twelve or thirteen pounds a year. At Manheim they coft not half that fum; and even that their labour does not re-imburfe: a difference to be attributed to Englifh induftry, being more fkilful and artificial, above all, to the ufe of machinery.

The prifon where the fchool is, holds, and generally has, about a hundred prifoners. Their punifhment is labour; if they

they have no trade of their own, they work at the manufactures taught in the houfe. The women, befides light work at the manufactures, wafh the linen of the houfe, prifoners', &c. On their going to prifon they are ftripped, faftened in the ftocks, and fuffer ten to thirty ftripes. Their regulations refpecting cleanlinefs are the beft part of the inftitution. Each offence againft cleanlinefs, each failure in giving notice of fuch offence, is punifhed with clofe confinement with bread and water. Their food is eight ounces of meat, except on faft days, fome foup, thirty-two ounces of bread, and a quart of beer. The women have the fame, except that their allowance of bread is but twenty-four ounces. The fick in the prifon, like the hofpital convalefcents, have relief from the voluntary fund above-mentioned. Needlefs exacerbations of calamity, chains, or dungeons, there are none. There is a chapel with fervice in it every morning.

The population of Manheim, indeed of the whole palatinate, has decreafed and is decreafing. The tyranny of intolerance, and impofition of wars and taxes, have driven away one half of the people into emigration, and the other half are driving to the defperations of political alienation and refiftance. Some years fince the palatinate produced 500,000 people. They are now computed at 200,000 or 240,000 men. In Manheim the decreafe has been lefs violent, viz. from 25,000 to 22,000. Their emigrations have been to Penfylvania; where, from the influx of fuch ftrangers, every fign and fhop-board is under-written in German. Ubi folatia, ibi patria, ftrong as the heart at firft may wifh to cling about a native place, yet what hold can continue undetached when violence inceffantly fhall affail it? What peafant can love the ground to which he is bound only by a chain? Or how will he plow and fow, where, for the harveft, the tax gatherers are to reap it?— The territory of the palatinate is 150 fquare miles.

Small

Small as this territory and population are, the contributions for support of the government, they have such reason to detest, are enormous! The country is drained of nine hundred thousand florins in mere, unconcealed, taxes! and in less avowed impositions, crown lands, as we should call them, royalties, monopolies, and tolls on the rivers and roads, not less than sixteen hundred thousand florins more! The taxes are in customs and excise! The detail and total of the accounts are, in respect to the palatinate, outrageously indecent! For, compared with the lands and population of the elector's other country, Bavaria, acre for acre, and head for head, the palatinate pays more than two to one!

And all for what?

For a chief magistrate who never resides! whose residence is at Munich.

This is a statement of the public accounts:

The public debts *exceed* forty millions of florins.

 The income was - - 31,104,289
 The expenditure - - 35,987,597

The *deficit*, of course, as in France before the revolution, is prodigious.

The late elector resided at Manheim; and the palace there, is such as must be expected when a bad original is imitated, worse.

Versailles, that vice of the times, that disgrace of moral manhood, (for it was reared on peculation and the pillage of the people) was the vain model which made so many empty mimics over the continent! and every folly, absurd and culpable, in the compass of laboured quarries above ground, was perpetrated, unblushingly, without fear of ridicule or remorse—private theatres, gaming rooms, tennis courts, and what not? Even the Third William, who lived by being antagonist to that mischievous mountebank the Fourteenth Louis, yielded obeisance to his false taste; and thus made Hampton Court, among the things not memorable for wisdom.

Manheim is so too. And with the same awkward pomp, and unwieldly profusion, almost with a similar disgust at accumulated irregularities, as in the street facade at Versailles. Versailles is likely to be an university; and so, by the popular diffusion of useful learning, may make atonement to the people for the enormous plunder they infamously bore in its production. What the palace of Manheim may be, we know not. At present it is abandoned. The elector has not seen it these five years. He, and his musicians, live at Munich. The electress lives at Okersheim—the house and chapel, in a small town, between Manheim and Worms. The King of Prussia had two or three rooms in it, in his late campaign upon the Rhine— and it has been an asylum for the Duc de Deux-Ponts, his dutchess, and their son, Prince Maximilian, since they burnt their fingers and their own place, by wisely meddling in a war with the French.

The palace is not otherwise remarkable than as being ill-placed; and without any ground. There is a little walk or two between the house and the Rhine; but, little as they are, they are made less by a part of the fortification which is in them. And the centinels and the artillery, Εις το δυστυχιν, produce effects and associations supremely gratifying at the palace. The position of the palace, bad in point of accommodating ground, is however good for the town in case of hostile attack. For in case of a canonading on the north and north-west, before the town can be battered, the palace must fall.

The King of Prussia, when at Manheim, lived, in regard to houshold and attendants, with much manly simplicity. Two valets, three footmen, three secretaries, and three or four officers, were his whole train. He dined about three o'clock, o'clock, and about six o'clock was at the play; which, having nothing in it, left him all the merit of rising from his wine.

It was six days after the successes, as they were called upon the Rhine, when the French officer sold out at Meintz, when the king entered the theatre there was no vulgar flattery from the music. The fiddlers were beginning; but the king had too much good sense and high spirit to permit it. Thus if they had read the sixth book of Virgil, and knew what he got by his **Tu Marcellus cris,** from Octavia—their motive might be the same; but not the consequences. The king had wit enough not to give them any thing for it—

" I damn ye all! go! go! ye are bit!"

The play was not in the private theatre at the palace, but at the public playhouse. There were no trappings to dizen out any particular place for the King. He sat in the plain unaltered balcony (on the left side of the actors) up one pair of stairs, Prince Nassau, Gen Geyman, and two other officers with him.

The King's dress was quite simple: a blue frock, and red waistcoat. The Prince Nassau was beset with stars and strings.—The King was distinguished by an apparent courtesy, good-humour, and, indeed, as it should seem, good-sense. Shakespeare talks of a man looking April and May. The King of Prussia is fifty. And his weight, chiefly between his breast-bone and his hip, must be, probably, eighteen stone. His countenance looks as if he had never flinched from weather or from wine. And yet—such is the force of manners, and manners which are sensible, that before the first five minutes are expired, he seems engaging, and has an advocate with all who see him. The ugliest man in England used to say, " give me but a fortnight in " any house, and I will cope with an Adonis."

The

The King of Pruſſia is a proof that he would win. For the effect of manners, in things indifferent, is not to be reſiſted.

On his entrance, he had no trick of pretended conference with his people. He came in, inartificial. Simple. Alone. The people applauded. As they will always do, without being hired, if there is merit, or if there is even dexterity, merely. The King bowed. But not like a Charlotan, whoſe object is by bowing, to beg for more. He bent over to ſpeak with one adjoining box. He nodded, and kiſſed his hand to a ſecond and a third. And to a lady in another box, he reached out and ſhook hands!—The whole ſcene, in point of good fellowſhip, was very amiable!—During the performance, which was an opera, he went into the lobbies, and converſed, not in the miſerable iterations of vacuity, but in ſounds fit for ſenſe to hear, with the people who were introduced to him.—He left the theatre, and without any ridiculous ceremonial, before the Vaudeville. —The next day he went to the camp near Frankenthall: in a coach and ſix. The coach was his own, but not better than a good hackney-coach. There were two outriders; and one man behind the coach.

As to the particular detail of the Pruſſian manners in the camp, we heard a little. But there ſeemed no good reaſon for wiſhing to hear more.

Each other memorandum at Manheim is but miſcellaneous.

The troops were between ſix and ſeven thouſand. Each corps were Bavarian. Their uniform, French grey, with various facings of green, yellow, red, and blue, like Otway's variety of wretchedneſs. All wear caps, which, with metallic ornaments, are weighty, viz. 5lb.—the epaulet alſo is ſolid and maſſy.—They are cloathed every two years.—

Their great-coat, like lord lieutenants and admirals on certain ſtations, takes three years to be made new.—The troops in Bavaria and the Palatinate, amount to 60,000. And heroiſm and happineſs are ſo cheap, that, with two pound of bread and a little fleſh meat, your hero there ſerves for ſix kreutſers (not threepence Engliſh) a day—The diſcipline is rigid, but not cruel. The call is twice a day. They are the ſecond beſt troops in Germany. They look the neateſt. But the Heſſians are, too probably, the beſt.

There are a few Iriſh officers in every corps. And their reputation is, juſtly, ſo very high, that each Engliſhman muſt wiſh to ſee them in his own.

Trade at Manheim, there is little or none. A German writer imputes it to the abſence of the court. As if any body ever heard of a court trading even in patronage or promotions!—Timber, which is floated down the river Necker, and ſome Necker wine, appear to be the articles of commerce which are beſt.

TO THE SWISS AND TYROLESE ALPS.

WHEN the traveller has turned his back on Manheim, he will have additional reason to be thankful. For, whether he is going to the Swifs or the Tyrolese Alps, he will meet with nothing but fands and German poftilions to ftop him for a fingle moment.

Bruchfal is a central point, from whence the roads deverge.—Thither you may go by two ways, the longeft by a poft and a half, is through Heidelberg; the fhorteft, through Schwetzengen. If you go by Heidelberg, you may fee the books which did belong to Grævius. And thence recollect your obligations, if you are obliged, by his Hefiod, the Variorum Claffics, and the antiquities too, alfo derived from Grævius and Gronovius.—And you may fee a few more books, chiefly on commercial arts (Technology they call the department), fuggefted, if not fupplied, by the Duc de Deux Ponts—who fo far has a merit, which belongs to no other petty principality in the neighbourhood, that his town was at work on a neat and cheap edition of the claffics: we faw it was well appearanced; and they told us it was correct.—Among the decorations was, a head of Trajan; a fac-fimile of our great actor in Coriolanus. There is a new bridge over the Neckar, where you have 720 feet of mafonry, twenty-nine feet wide, and nine arches, for 85,000 florins. Every body will tell you of the Heidelberg Tom, and you may tell every body in return, that if they affect the art of cooperage, and are ameteurs therein, they need not go further than to Whitbread's or to Thrale's.

Better than all, at Heidelberg as at Manheim, the eye will

will be foothed with the cheering vifions of toleration.—
Oppofite religions, in unbroken concord, dividing the town
between them. And though the petty policy of government is elaborate to adorn the Papal forms, yet the Lutheran and the Reformed, by the prevalence of fimplicity and truth, augment their followers, without ceafing.

If Schwetzingen is your route, you may fee what has not been feen before, the ftate of ornamental gardening in Germany. It is the prime villa of the Elector when he lived in the Palatinate: at prefent it is unoccupied. The ground plan is 360 acres, with a contiguous wood, which is immeafurable, and three or four hundred thoufand fuperficial feet of water, with trees and fhrubs enough. But the land is almoft all in ftrait alleys and terraces: the water in half a dozen ponds. And bad vafes, ftatues, and temples out of number. Orangeries 700 feet long: and doric wings to the houfe, 1200 feet taken together. From a little artificial rife in the ground, fome outlying objects are feen, as Manheim, Heidelberg, and Spire, the lofty blue highlands of Alface, Suabia, and Darmftadt, on one, which is Falfberg, is a bulky granite column, left by the Romans. But little was wanting to make it a noble palace. Which from tafte, as well as moral preferences, had been far better than the idle, the cruel wafte of fo much money at Manheim.—What figure can difguft more, than extravagance pampered by extortion?—Yet, it is the offence which infults and fickens you, in almoft every court upon the Continent! It is to the reputation of our own court, that they had wit enough to avert, from the unwieldy gloom of St. James's—and that they had honour enough not to burthen the people to build for them another palace. The only fpot completely gratifying was, a piece of twenty acres, which the Elector had given from his chace to a company, who were adventuring in the cultivation of rhubarb.—And we underſtood there had been a new plant ſupplied by Condoide, phyſician to the Czarina.

From Manheim to Schwetzingen, the road is through ſandy woods, the chace of the Elector Palatine. From Schwetzingen to Bruchſal, the woods, chiefly oak, continue, the property of the Elector and the Biſhop of Spires; a gentleman, who, for dwelling in a good town-houſe at Bruchſal, and for exerciſing, with great advantage to himſelf, a petty ſovereignty over that Biſhopric, and the Provoſtſhip of Weiſſenbourg, a little diſtrict of eight and twenty miles, is lucky enough to find people who will let him have an annual revenue of eight and twenty thouſand pounds ſterling.—This Biſhop of Spires is one of the examples of violence, unworthily, ſuffered ſince the war. M. Cuſtine extorted from him a levy of near a million of livres. The military eſtabliſhment of this petty prince, is no leſs than 300 men! And that may give a ſtrong idea of the prevalence and cheapneſs of their folly in Germany.

To the Tyroleſe Alps, you may hurry through the territory of Wirtemberg, which is ranked next to the Electorate. Where a Catholic prince contrives to draw a revenue of two hundred and twenty thouſand pounds from the people: who, as in the Palatinate, are Proteſtants—where the country is not bad, and the wine is good, upon the Necker—where there are two or three clever Profeſſors at Stutgard;—and where there is ſome reſpect paid by government to popular opinions, and to public good!—For the public debt, formerly ſo oppreſſive, (above fourteen millions of guilders) is at length nearly diſcharged.

Ulm and Augſbourg then conclude for you the circle of Suabia. Ulm, a free city, which will launch a traveller down the Danube for five livres, and, in five days, to Vienna: and Augſbourg, another free town, of larger population (33,000) and which will do better for him ſtill! If

referring

referring to the Diet and the Confeffion of Augfbourg, he can profit from the Proteftant Reformers. And rifing at the ennobling perfections of Luther and Melancthon, their zeal for truth, their magnanimity and eloquence—the Tyrolefe Alps, then bold, and captivating as they are, will yield to the more noble exaltations of his mind.

To the Swifs Alps, the route is through the territory of Baden to Bafle. A fhewy, variegated, unequal country— Non arborum impatiens—non paludibus fæda, pecorum fecunda. Full of wood. Full of wine. Where the multiplying peafants eat the labour of their hands, and repofe in their appointed reft, with no caufe, from oppreffion or from extortion, to execrate the government which they have chofen. The errors of paft adminiftrations have been rectified. Wrongs, redreffed. Taxes, remitted. The Margrave has the heart of a gentleman. His fame has ever been unftained by avarice or ambition. He has no hid treafure. He has never dealt in blood. Hofpitality and public bounty are his objects: thefe occupy his revenues! and great as they are, (above 170,000l. a year) he is carelefs of his own ftate, and lives in a wooden palace at Carlfruke!

The country and the government are Lutheran. Compared with the intervening diftricts of the Emperor, and which are Papal, they have all the benefit of contraft—in every energy of collective or individual merit, candor, induftry, wealth, fecurity, peace, and every other indication of fenfe and fpirit in the people.

The road has many charms. The agriculture has an interefting air of novelty from tobacco and vineyard, as well as pafturage and corn, here and there, all along in veins. The Rhine carries health and beauty through the valley. The diftances are Alface and the Suabian hills. And after Friburg, Switzerland rifes to the longing view.

It is hiftoric ground too: and anecdote, now and then,

adds a good ingredient to the charm. The scene exults in feudal ruins! a rational triumph to every friend philosophising and free!—Here the Imperialists and the French accursed the country with the guilty infatuation of war! And here, at Rastadt, Villars and Eugene, the first instance of generals pacificating, met, authorised, after the campaign—and formed the preliminary articles to the peace of Utrecht.—" Is it peace or war ?" said Eugene—" We are not enemies," replied Villars—" Your enemies are at your court, and mine are at Paris."

It was on Sept. 7, EUGENE signed first, followed by M. M. Coes and Cellern—VILLARS followed with M. M. Contest, and Comte de Luc.

To Kehl, a petty fortress fronting Strasbourg, Baskerville's types were carried, by Beaumarchais, from Birmingham, to print his complete edition of Voltaire! For the righteous and delicate mind of the Cardinal de Rohan, the Archbishop of Strasbourg, of Madame de la Motte and the Necklace, could not tolerate such a sin as that of printing Voltaire in the town! Kehl was planned by that despot, Louis XIV. as the avenue to usurpation on the eastern side of the Rhine. Thus becoming a printing-house, it reverses that doom, and counteracts the usurpations of despotism in their source.

After Friburg, the summits with snow on them, appear! And advancing, by easy ascents, over lands flourishing with cattle, cultivation, and woods, amidst the highlands of Suabia and Alsace, united by the providential bounty of nature, dissevered only by the mischief of man! And then the view revels over the valleys and mountains of Switzerland! The sensations on the eye thrill with rapture on the heart. Each emotion rises with the surrounding wonders of the scene—and the sublimities of nature, impress morals and politics equally sublime!

Dole is the entrance into Switzerland, where the opening

ing, as at the Blenheim portal, is worthy of the whole! where the Lakes appear! and the feries of Alps, from Dauphinè to St. Gothard!

Bafle is but a wicket. With a few fhowy mountains, and the Rhine, there is a ftream of paftoral and romance.

But all other, the ideal preferences prevail, and rufh with undiminifhed blifs upon the mind! Each excellence of the people, and their inftitutions, perfonal and focial! Their eafe; profperity and peace; their power of forcing fortune—peopling the defart, and fertilifing the rock!— Maintaining, venerably, the fimplicity of nature, and the dignity of man—admired for fafe virtue, for practical knowledge, for defenfive valour!

Thus you approach Bafle.—You breathe the air of freedom. And your wifhes would fain afpire to virtue. Prejudice and perverfenefs, like the dark and foggy meteor are below you. And the fpirit brightens at the look of light and life! Memory fondly ftrains after EULER and MAUPERTUIS, BERNOUILLI and ERASMUS—and, firm and lofty in natural elation, you would foar after the objects you are privileged to attain, the COMPLEX PERFECTIONS OF THOUGHT AND ACTION, the FAME OF THE KNOWING, AND THE MERIT OF THE GOOD.

THE END

AT Augſbourg the late Lord Baltimore printed a meagre quarto of proſe and poetry, Latin French, with Vignettes and engraved title page. He inſcribed it to Linneus, with a prediction, ſoon well fulfilled, of the eſteem and admiration which awaited him.

The title is—

GAUDIA POETICA,
Latina, Anglica, et Gallica, Lingua Compoſita.
A. 1769.
Auguſtæ
Litteris Spathianis, 1770.

At Augſbourg this book is not to be found. The only copy known is in the collection of Linneus.

There are the four following letters from Linneus to Lord Baltimore. They are a curioſity, and elſewhere not to be had. The reſt of the work is not worth remembering.

FAMILIAR AND FRIENDLY LETTERS,

BETWEEN

LORD BALTIMORE

AND

C. LINNÆUS,

ON THE SUBJECT OF LORD BALTIMORE'S WORKS.

EPISTOLÆ
Urbanitatis Caufa Scriptae,
Inter F. B. & C. L.
Ad
Originem hujus operis fpectantes.

Vir longè fapientiffime,

SI omnes, ficut ego, cogitarent non folummodo capfulas aureas, fed maximos honores et emolumenta pro te darent· Felix qui te audit, et eft ter felix patria, quæ te poffedet. Res abditæ, quas non fcripfifti ex timore cæcæ malignitatis humanæ, plus valent quam thefauri fcientiarum tuarum, quos fummâ confideratione perlegam, et te inter celeberrimos philofophos in æthere locabo.

F. B.

Helmiæ, die 16 *Jan.* 1769.

To C. LINNÆUS, &c.

Most learned Sir!
WERE all men of my mind, not only golden coffers would be at your service, but every thing which honour as well as emolument can do. Happy he who hears you. Thrice happy the country which possesses you. The undivulged discoveries which you must have, and which from fear of human violence you may have suppressed, I hold in more account, than even the treasure you have made known. Over these I ponder with incessant consideration. They must raise you to the highest exaltation of philosophic fame.

F. B.

Stockholm, Jan. 16, 1769.

T. C. de B. S. P.
C. L.

UTI in te, illustrissime domine comes, præsente miratus sum, summam sapientiam posse nasci in viro opulento, ita et nunc magnanimitatem tuam: dum projicis aurea dona vilissimis homuncionibus, qualis ego sum. Mehercle cana prius gelido desit absynthia campo, quam uti immemor vivam. Incede viam tibi soli perviam, dum ego legam suave manuum tuarum opus.

Upsaliæ, Junii die 18, 1769.

To LORD BALTIMORE.

My Lord,
WHEN we were together, it seemed to me astonishing that a very rich man should ever become a very wise man. Now, am I struck at your magnificence; which can be thus

lavish

lavish to a man so humble as I am. The wormwood shall sooner cease to love the cold plain, than I can think to live with any coolness in my remembrance of you.

Go on in advances accessible only to yourself, and let me profit by what you may produce.

LINNÆUS.
Upsal, June 18, 1769.

Illustrissimo Comiti, de B. S. P. D.

C. a L.

QUOD tam cito attigisti oras Ruthenicas, illustissime comes ex animo gratulor; quod vero mei, homuncionis, non oblitus es, mihi pleno gaudio gratulor.

Pro continuatione carminum tuorum de itineris progressu grates reddo devotissimas. Video, quam tu non sis factus *sed natus poeta!* Dum Virgilius describit Μετεμψυχοσιν seu animarum transmigrationem, de se dicit: olim Achilles eramsic tu dicere possis: *olim Virgilius eram.* Audivi multa de imperatricis magnificentia; nullus tamen eam magis te vividè delineavit. Legi jam bis opus tuum de itinere orientali, idque summo cum oblectamento. Polles eâ sapientiâ, quâ potes paucis verbis magis vividè delineare argumentum, quam alii diffusissimo sermone. Sequor te votis meis, teque tanquam coram me sisto, quoties intueor donum tuum, pretiosissimum omnium, quod ab ullo in vita accepi sint tibi fata prospera.

Upsalia, 1769, 15 *Aug.*

To LORD BALTIMORE.

My Lord,

I congratulate you very heartily, that you are soon arrived in Russia: and, it adds to my congratulation, joy, that you can, in spite of distance, be mindful of me.

You have my sincereft thanks for the continuation of your poetical tour [*]. It is manifeft that poetical compofition in you is not an artificial knack: but, that you are a poet born!

If Virgil, defcribing the metempfychofis, could fay of his own tranfmigration, that in a pre-exiftence he had been Achilles. To you it may be equally fuppofeable that you have pre-exifted as Virgil!

I have heard much of the Czarina's magnificence. The moft vivid delineation is from you.

Twice have I read the oriental part of your tour; and with undiminifhed pleafure. You can, fuch is your fkill, fay more in a few words, than others can exprefs in an elaborate declamation.

I follow you with my beft good wifhes. And, indeed, we are not afunder, as I think of your bounty to me. Bounty [†] the moft magnificent, I ever found in my life. May fate, fir, ever favour you.

C. L.

Upfal, Aug. 15, 1769.

Viro Immortali de B. S. P. D.

C. L.

ACCEPI aureos tuos Verficulos, Illuftr. D. Comes, quibus iter tuum Drefdam ufque defcripfifti; nec pulchrius legi unquam. Selecta enim verba ita exprimunt puriffimos fenfus, ac fi oleo inuncta affent. Lector horam tamquam per paffus Te fequor toto itinere, ita vivis coloribus depingis peragratas regiones. Faxit Deus, at feliciter ab-

---

[*] In hexameter Latin verfe. No lines of which appeared tolerably worth repeating.

[†] It does not appear what the prefent was which Lord Baltimore had fent to Linnæus.

folvas,

folvas, quæ reftant itineris, dum me participem reddere non dedigneris fatorum tuorum, fcias neminem te puriore et majore effectu profecuturum, neminem puriore gratitudine te culturum, neminem e tuis litteris majorem voluptatem unquam obtenturam. In te enim *prifca virtus* radiat. Tu in fumma felicitate non fucô, non aurô externè fplendes, fed fummâ fapientia internâ fulges. Te fapintiorem certe vidi neminem. Aurea tua carmina legi et relegi millies ; quod me his exhilarare voluifti, grates reddo, et reddam dum vixero, fummas. Mihi fumma gloria erit, numerari inter tuos cultores vel infimum. Deus te fervet incolumem.

Upfaliæ, 1769. *November* 13.

To LORD BALTIMORE.

My Lord,

I HAVE received your excellent verfes, which defcribe your journey to Drefden. I never read any thing more beatuiful: either for purity of idea, or for felection of phrafe. Labour never was more fuccefsful. The Reader can go with you all along: and difcriminate throughout the whole form of each veftige—the very colour of every view.

May God grant that you may end as well as you have began: and let me not be difdained, to fhare in whatever may befal you. None can follow you with more grateful emotion. The pleafure I have from your letters, is as great as can be.

For, in thee beams forth the antique virtue. Your diftinctions are not external only, from mere hue, and feparable circumftances; but from internal qualities and inalienable fkill! More fkill, I never faw. Your admirable lines I have read again and again. And as you wifh to

pleafe

pleafe and cheer me, again and again you have my thanks; as long as thanks fhall be mine to give.—It is a prime wifh in my heart to be among thofe who refpect and love you. —May God blefs you, Sir, &c. &c.

LINNÆUS.

Upfal, 13 *Nov.* 1769.

Illuftriffimo Generofiffimoque Comiti.

B. S. P. D. C. a L.

ACCEPI tuas, vir fapientiffime, d. 6. Januarii Augfburgh datas, cum inclufis divinis iis carminibus. Nefcio, utrum in his idearum puritas an etiam verborum pictura præponderet, ubi ambæ facratiffimô connubio ita junctæ fint, ut fimile non viderim. Quod autem mihi infcribere velis immortale opus, non cupio; vereor magis, ne meo rudi nomine nitidiffima tua carmina tanquam levi figurâ oblinas. Novit nemo me melius deblitatem ingenii propriam et Παροραματα mea heu nimis multa: nifi eô velis umbram addere picturæ, ut purior exfurgat tanquam pulcherrima Venus fuliginofo Vulcano nupta* etiamnum formofior evadit; vel etiam cum fata tibi foli et conceffere fatis opum, et fimul fapientiam fummam, ut *non opus habeas flectere genua regibus*; eos imitaris, qui, cum non habeant panes, beneficia fua conjiciunt in infimos homunciones. Nunc vero, dum *video placuiffe tibi*, mihi infcribere immortale opus, id effecifti, ut anxia femper mente colam fapientiam in te fummam.

Dabam Upfaliæ, 1770. 6 *Feb.*

To

To LORD BALTIMORE.

Moſt learned Sir,

I HAVE your letter of January 6 from Augſbourg: with the very ſuperior verſes which were incloſed. Again, I know not, which to prefer, your imagination, or expreſſion; both are united; and with unexampled force.

That you ſhould incline to inſcribe the *immortal* work to me, cannot be my deſire. I rather fear it. Leſt there may be ſome ſhade from my rude name to dim the ſplendor of your verſe.—Though, perhaps, knowing myſelf, my few powers, and many overſights, you may, perhaps, purpoſely take them for the effect of contraſt, as ſhadow to your picture. For beauty herſelf, in contiquity with Vulcan, ſeems, as from a foil, more captivating and fair.

Or it may be, as fortune favors you no leſs than knowledge, ſo that you have no need to fully your knee in courts, you may aſpire after that ſyſtem which we adore—which, far above all, is laviſh of bounty to the leaſt!

In your determination of inſcribing your immortal work to me, you do it, I ſuppoſe, that my anxious mind may be ever obſequious to your worth.

LINNÆUS.

Upſal, Feb. 6, 1770.

Illuſtriſſimo Comiti de B. S P. D.

C. L.

HODIE iterum habui honorem ſapientiſſimi comitis, d 25 Januarii ſcriptas accipere; ad mores devotiſſimum meum reſponſum dedi ante aliquot dies. Quotidie lego et religo tua *divina* carmina, et quotidie magis magiſque intelligo

pro-

profundiffimam tuam fapientiam. Te non non tangat malitia humana: novifti *homines* effe *natura malos,* folâ culturâ et fapientiâ evadere bonos. Letare, quod habeas invidiam, et rideas *mifer natus eft, qui caret invidia.* Quo major felicitas, eo major invidia. Tu longe fupra invidiam pofitus es; te non attingat. Profecto, fi effem in tua felicitate, ut tu, viverem. Quæ major felicitas quam paffe vivere, ubicumque placeat, videre orbem et gentes, habere, ut nihil deficiat, omnia? Pro honore, quo me velles cunmulare, grates reddo devotiffimas, novum hoc effet documenfitum favoris tui in me: fed dudum receptus fui non tantum in Societate Regia Londinenfi, fed et in Anglicana occonomica quæ curat, et Edinburgenfis etiam; fum enim *membrum* Societatis Londinenfis, Anglicanæ, Edinburgenfis, Parifinæ, Monfpelienfis, Tolofanæ Florentinæ, Bernenfis, Cellenfis, Berolenenfis Petropolitanæ, Holmienfis, Upfalienfis, Naturæ curioforum vifi de bonenfis, adeo plurium, quam quibus poffum fatisfacere.

Tu ne cede malis, te noverit ultimus ifter, te Boreas gelidus. Te feliciorem novi neminem, modo ipfe fcias Quid levius homine verba metuente Luna properat fuum curfum, nec tetratus canum curat. Tibi plura Dii conceffere. O! ter quaterque felix! bona fi tua noris.

Dabam Upfaliæ, 1770, *d* 16 *Februarii.*

To LORD BALTIMORE.

My learned Lord,

TO day I had the honour of receiving your letter of January 25; and, according to my cuftomary zeal towards you, I anfwer it without delay. Your excellent verfes, which I have read and read, more and more convince me of your mind. Human perverfenefs has no part in thee. Men naturally evil, are by education and accomplifhments difciplined to good. As to the envy you may have raifed;

at that you may rejoice. Miserable must he be, who is not somewhere enviable.

As to envy, you are thus far blest:—by the provocation of your happiness, by the immunity of your rank. How can envy ever reach you?

Truly, were I as you are, so happily like you would I live. For what can be more pleasant, than to do as you please —to go every where—to see every thing—and to have every thing you want in what you see?

I am much obliged to you for your intended honour; but I am a member of all possible academies and societies, London, Edinburgh, Paris, Montpeliere, Tholouse, Florence, Stockholm, Bern, Berlin, Petersburg, Upsal, Vienna —enough to satisfy me, and more than I can satisfy.

As for yourself you may defy accident. You have tried it in latitudes that are remote. You are happy beyond example: if you would but know it. And are you to tremble at a few words? while even the moon may teach you how to treat each animal that may bark below. To know yourself and your condition—to be conscious of what you are— and to exult in your appointed round.

LINNÆUS.

Upsal, Feb. 16, 1770.

SPALLANZANI's TOUR

TO

VESUVIUS, ÆTNA, GROTTE DEL CANE,

&c. &c. &c.

APPENDIX.

SPALLANZANI has written three fmall octavo volumes of Obfervations on the Regions in Italy, where volcanos are either ardent or extinct—viz. in the Ecclefiaftical State about Naples, in Sicily.

The work of a man with fuch decided excellence in the department which he profeffes, feems likely to be current. As far as it is didactic on thofe parts of the creation which refer to volcanic phænomena, it certainly muft raife curiofity, and probably not raife it in vain.

But, as that object may be of very limited enquiry, as many of the perfons who let it occupy any part of their time might wifh rather to read it in Italian, and as, in either language, the readers are, from the peculiar circumftances of Europe, lefs difpofed than ufual, to a ftudy, like this,

com-

comparatively minute—it did not feem an expedient rifk of leifure, to tranflate the whole work, till fome experiment might afcertain, a little, the eventual likelihood to the bookfeller.

As that experiment (the firft chapter of Spallanzani) is now tranflated. If names enough are fent, the tranflation will be forth-coming in two or three months.

SPALLANZANI's TOUR

TO

VESUVIUS, ÆTNA, GROTTE DEL CANE,

&c. &c. &c.

ON the 4th of November, 1788, Sig. Spallanzani, accompanied by his friend, Dr. Comi, commenced their visit to Mount Vesuvius. Sig. Spallanzani, the Professor of Pavia, is well known to every man of science in Europe. His companion Comi, is a young physician of Abruzzo; already distinguished in natural philosophy, and for medical fame.

July was at first the time appointed for their attempt. But they changed the time, from these considerations: because they were assured by some friends, already practised in the same pursuit, that there would be obvious and sure profit by this delay, since in the month of July they had not failed to find the eruption from the volcano was but scanty and faint. While in the other month, they might expect it to be forcible and full.

The expectation of November giving a more striking attitude of things, of more movement within the mountain, and of more flow of lava without it, was not disappointed. For at the time abovementiond, on his route from Sicily, even at the distance of Capre, before the rising of the sun, he he had the furprife (to him not ungratifying) of feeing a current of lava, ftreaming through a new aperture on that part of the volcano which he calls the Flank.

At Rometaggio de Salvatore, but two miles from Vefuvius, Spallanzani and his friend Comi paffed the night. The night was, happily, favorable. The fky was wont to reft.

The obfervations were thefe:

That each heaving of the lava was very vifible—that comparing one throw with another, the explofions were not equable—that in form and colour they were like red flame, fenfibly fpreading as it rofe, enduring for a few feconds, and then feen no more.—But refumed and feen again after fhort intervals; the intervals were fo fhort, as never to exceed five feconds.

As the volcano was thus labouring, the philofophers alfo, it may be thought, could not long be at reft. They rofe before the fun. At four o'clock they were on foot, and began to mount in their much-expected way!

As they drew nearer to the volcano, their obfervations on it were alfo nearer to the truth. They afcertained points not perceivable at a diftance—viz. that in each burft of the lava, the detonation heard was precifely proportioned to the quantity of flux which was feen.—And that when diftant but half a mile, that the difcharge of the lava was feen before the report or explofion was heard, only one fingle moment, and no more. That the fhowers of ftony matter, which they compared to hail, were literally particles of lava, as it were foldered in the external air—confolidated—rounded.

This difcharge prevented, in one direction, their further advance.

On the eaft fide of the volcano, there was no fuch fall of ftones. And there they obferved, not without furprife, the lava burfting, as before, by fnatches, or with interrupted
throws

throws—but not, as before, each burst followed by a detonation!—This absence of all sound, they note, accurately, to have happened eighteen times together! The nineteenth burst they record to have been with detonation, as before—and therefore the detonation, they rationally conjecture, to have been anomalous, or accidental!—A conjecture, afterwards well fortified at Naples by the Abbe Fortis, who observing on the same object, had made an inference which is the same!

In the usual progress of curiosity, he was led from contemplation of this phenomenon, to the tracing of its cause. And thus, very ingeniously, he tried to trace it.— The caprice in the phenomenon, if it can be called so—that is, its irregularity, its intermissions, the reader should be reminded, has not been noted by any preceding observers on the volcano.

The theory of Spallanzani is this:

The fire is, of itself, not sufficient to form explosions. There must be with it an elastic fluid, which disengages itself from the liquid lava, forces up on high a portion of it as it flows.

Thus, it may seem, that it must ever be. But, continues Spallanzani, but I do not think I err if I say it can be only in certain limits.

Every time that the elastic fluid disengages itself acting against the lava, then with a force, single, abrupt, and violent, the explosion or report of such action must be proportionably loud.—But, on the contrary, the report shall be little or none, when the force (of the elastic fluid disengaging from the lava) shall be in a series of actions uninterrupted, uniform, equably sustained! And this difference of explosion may surely happen, though the matter exploded may be the same.

This perspicuous idea is well and beautifully expanded by

the familar inftance of the pop-gun*—let that well known toy, the aperture at each end well clofed, as ufual, on the atmofpherical air, fills the tube within, if the pellet be additionally driven out with fudden force, the found of it will be fmart—if the force be flow, the found will be little or nothing!—for it is the prerogative of fplendid parts to brighten wherever it touches—to aggrandife what to common eye feems little, and fometimes faint image of creation, to draw light out of darknefs, and form fomething out of nothing.—Thus every body may recollect, the chief fages' doctrine of light and colours, from the fchool-boy's foap bubbles as he trifled in wafhing his hands! And thus a leading fyftem of the univerfe became explained by obfervations fubtle and profound, on the fall of a common apple!

This clever train of new thought on the volcanic hail will end as well as it was began; for he fays, that though there was no perceivable detonation, it is by no means conclufive that there was none:—on the contrary, probably there might be fome, though from cafual circumftances of diftance, &c. the obferver could not hear it.

On the lava then, thus falling on the flank of the mountain, the obfervations of Spallanzani were thefe—that between the fouth and the eaft—that the diftance from the crater was about half a mile—that the vent-holes, or chimneys, (his word is *fumajoli*) on the declivity, were more than fixty—that the opening in one of them was about nine feet diameter—that the cavernous part of it had but little depth—that the foil on the fpot from which thefe vent-holes rofe was of a yellow tint, as formed by murratico-ammoniac falt—that the heat of the ground was fuch, the foot could not bear it, though at fome diftance, even for a few feconds.—As for this local heat, he traces it to the fingle fource of contigruity and communication with the fire within.

* The wind-gun.

On the south side, at fifty yards distance from the spot, where three months before the lava had flowed, the lava was now as hard as a stone. He saw it flow, first in a trough; it then issued at two miles distance from the summit of Vesuvius, forming a current, quite uncovered, to the open air!

Curious to inspect the trough—these were the appearances he has preserved:

The figure of the trough was an oval, twenty-three feet diameter—the sides, almost vertical, were four feet and a half high—the lava was old, which filled the bottom—and had a movement from north to south.—A thick smoke rose, and reverberated by, and on the burning lava produced a red light, which hurt the eye, at a great distance during the night.

This smoke was loaded with acid-sulphurious exhalations. These hid the liquid lava. And it was only when the wind favoured the view, and by getting to windward, that the observer could speculate at his ease.

Then leaning over the trough, and his lower limbs but five feet distance from the lava, the heat was such, as, from time to time, forced him to retire!—The lava flowed from north to south—and hid itself in the fissures of the lava which had become hard.—Its surface was red—like burning coal; but without the least show of flame. He compared it to bronze fusing in the furnace! covered with a whitish foam; at times, bubbling; the bubbles soon bursting, not without noise, and a little throw.—After which the lava smoothed and flattened a-new.

Spallanzani then let fall into it some fragments of the old lava—the only hard substance which presented itself—and on dropping, the sound was such as when a stone falls upon soft earth. Of these fragments, about one-third of their volume was steeped in the lava, and thus were carried by it as it flowed.

The velocity of the lava's current became cognizable by this experiment! for the speed of the stream was defined by the motion of the stone—which in half a minute had over-ran a space but of ten feet and a half!—A tardiness of motion to be explained only by the little slope in the ground.

It was obvious why the fragments of old lava, when flung in, were steeped only one-third of their volume—for they were of a spongy texture, and of specific gravity, less than the body on which they fell—in the same manner as a globula of glass cast upon glass in a state of fluidity, is observed not to sink, but to swim.

As for the degree of heat in the lava, as it flowed, unfortunately he could not ascertain it!

He could have done it easily and surely, with the thermometer of Wedgwood. But that thermometer he had not with him.

With that thermometer, he could have attempted to decide, not only the superficial and external heat, but that which was deep seated and within!

Failing of that instrument, he would have used the following expedient. He would have had one of the cylinders closed in a sphere of thick iron, suspended by the iron chain, as the iron fluxes not in a common furnace, there would have seemed a probability that the metal might have resisted also the lava as it flowed—but, if it had not, the metal had melted. Thus melting so far, it would have become a kind of thermometer in itself.

Though this experiment may not ascertain the heat of every lava—yet, in this instance, as far as it went, it was decisive. And not being able to return to Vesuvius, he could decide no more.

To those who would repeat this experiment, there is no denying that there was some danger in it. But they, who have

have too quick a sense in finding danger, must be content, without searching into the awful wonders of volcanos!

Having departed from the trough, and passing over a mile of ancient lava, they make record of these discoveries. That, in the ancient lava, there was still such intense heat as to burn their shoes!—and that under the solid lava, they were as sensible of a fluid; they heard and they felt it, as indisputably as in passing a frozen river; there is often a sure sense of floating water under the upper surface of ice!

Thus, luckily, illustrating the elements and qualities of nature, by their contraries the most opposite, fire with water, and burning lava with ice, Spallanzani reviews his sensations under each extreme—and, as might be expected, he adjudges the impressions to be less from mountains of snow, than from streams of fire! And no wonder, when against Alpine horrors there are the obvious mitigations of diet and clothing—these simplify the suffering—there may be hardship, but without hazard. It is fatigue only, but it is not fear!

Following then the lava, it descends over an inclined plain, forming with the horizon an angle of about 45 degrees—the run of the lava was then eighteen feet in a minute.

There, in spite of the heat, intolerable when the wind blew towards them, Spallanzani and his friend, approached the lava within ten feet! They threw into the burning stream some more fragments of the hardened lava—and the sound was the same as of one stone upon another! A statement this, agreeing with the observations of Sir William Hamilton: he also flung a larger fragment of the hardened mass into the fluid lava as it flowed with such singular rapidity in the year 1766, and the impression was very trifling, though he flung with all his force.

Of this lava, the light, the liquidity, the speed, all were in different degrees proportioned to the diſtance from the ſource, and the contact with cold air diminiſhing its heat. After two miles the current ſtopped, forming a kind of ſolid lake, ſolid at leaſt ſuperficially—and it loſt all the colour, red, at 200 ſteps before it finiſhed its career! in contracambia.

Here it is that Spallanzani, ſuperbiâ quæſita meritis, ad‑dreſſes M. de Luc, and invites him to the Univerſity of Pavia, to ſee in the unrivalled muſeum there, a cylinder of lava 18 Italian inches long by 5¼ thick!

The cylinder is curved. The curve it received from the hands of the perſon who had curved it, when in a ſtate which was ſemi-liquid.

The Monſ. de Luc above-mentioned, is a ſtudious gen‑tleman of Geneva, who, ſo far back as 1758, had ſhewn, in his cabinet, with ſome ſmall elation, a ſpecimen of lava, marked alſo when it was ſoft and plaſtic, with the ferrula of a walking cane.

Theſe obſervations are then compared with thoſe of the Doctor Serrao, of Father la Torre, of Monſ. de Luc, and of our accompliſhed countryman Sir William Hamilton—and with theſe opinions, Spallanzani on the chief points for the moſt part agrees.

But he differs utterly from others who have erroneouſly aſſerted on Veſuvius, that the lava was not liquid, but only ſoft—that it falls in a ſtream-like form only by the effect of its proper weight. Aſſertions which he diſproves from his better views of the lava, not only in the open air, but where a judgment on it muſt be moſt ſure, and where and before him unattempted in its paſſage through the trough.

Analytically examining the lava, he found the baſe of it the roche cornea roccia de corno—the colour a blackiſh grey—the ſubſtance moderately hard—dry to the touch—
when

when broken, fhewing earthy particles mixed with colour-
lefs granites, and with fhorles—it moved the magnetic nee-
dle at three lines and a half diftance—it ftruck fire—the
fhorls exifting in the fluid lava were not altered by the fire
—while on the contrary thofe burfting from the crater in
globular forms have endured incipient fufion.

In the furnace of a glafshoufe, and by the word furnace
he means that of a glafshoufe always, the lava changes into
an enamel (bollicofo) coloured like fhining pitch, fticking
to the fides of the crucible—the fhorls were fufed—but
the granites become whitifh without lofing their luftre.

After infpecting this recent lava, he was eager to examine that which fell in November 1785, and his obfervations on it, he very allowably thinks may be the more interefting, the fubject for what he knows not having been
touched by any body before.

Of the lava in November 1785, the extent was great.
The greateft quantity was in a valley under Maffa, and on
the fide of Salvatori, formed in beds feveral feet deep, but
the continuity broken by many a cleft. The furface was
irregular and often rendered rugged by a vaft number of
cylindrical bodies twifted like ropes, and probably formed
by the lava when it ceafed to flow. As this lava, in its
precipitation from a high rock muft fall as a fort of cata-
ract, its appearance in the darknefs of night muft have
formed a fpectacle very rare!

Although in this fall the obvious action of the air muft
have much mitigated the actual heat, yet notwithftanding
the fluidity, one evidence of remaining heat continued very
far—and on the fide of Maffa, meeting a plantation of oaks
in its track, fome of the trees where the current came, inftantly dried up and withered! while in fome on the fide
oppofite to the current, vegetation and verdure were ftill
kept!

There

There were other difaftrous phenomena in its track! The church of La Madonna della Veteranna, now quite deferted, was the firft fpoiled? The lava flowed againft the door. The door was burnt! The walls next were eafily demolifhed, for they were of foft tuffo, and the lava then fpread throughout the church. In the church-yard fome lime trees were blafted and black!

For fifteen months the lava flowed! and in the twentieth month, after it had ceafed to roll, there ftill was heat, and it fmoked lightly here and there!

About a mile from Vefuvius, below Salvatori, is the ample hollow, called Foffa Grande. It was formed by the rain. This was the way by which Spallanzani returned to Naples, and thefe are the confiderations which made him glad that he did pafs that way.

For thus he has been able to illuftrate, with new light, a part of mineralogy hitherto obfcure.

On the formation of thofe curious fubftances which are called fhorls and feldfpates (there is, the tranflator thinks, no trivial name) naturalifts are divided. Some think them to have been formed while the lava was ardent and fluid, others when the lava begun to cool and to indurate—and many, perhaps more, judge them to have been primitive exiftences, original in the rock, prior to any produ&ions from a volcanic change. Even Bergman, who opened on the queftion, has not clofed it conclufively. And Spallanzani himfelf was not able to decide till he faw the abovementioned appearances in the Foffa Grande. His decifion, as might be expe&ed, is, for the laft opinion, that the fhorls and feldfpates are exiftences not derivative but primitive in the rock.

The nature of the rock in one part is mergaceas, with lime-ftone (carbonat de calci) however prevailing in it, no calcined, but as we fee in ftones not volcanic.

It

It is proveable that they have not suffered from fire—for on breaking them numerous feldspats are seen cryftallifed and externally the fame as thofe in other currents of the lava from Vefuvius. There are to be feen many feldfpats, and yet more fhorls, untouched, that I could, and I would, augment the clafs of undamaged ftones.

But, as for the prefence of the feldfpats and the fhorls, and their different cryftallizations in the lava, there is now no difficulty to afcertain and underftand them. There is no need of recurring for their origin to any circumftance of the lava, whether hot or cold, or fluid, or fixed, fince as they are found in the lava, we can alfo find them in the ftony fubftances from which they derive their being.

Such were the obfervations, fuch are the opinions of Spallanzani on the volcano of Vefuvius. Our learned readers have of courfe perceived that he has done much, perhaps as much as could have been rationally expected of him —he has been fedulous, acute, inventive, original, and juft! He has feen appearances which had efcaped preceding feers! He has thought with novelty and with force, where fo many qualified perfons had been thinking before!

WHILE the publication was by an accident delayed, the affiduous kindnefs of two or three friends fupplied further information relative to the books firft printed at Mentz, &c. The following are the copies of them, in other libraries at Oxford and Cambridge.

IN THE BODELIAN.

Biblia Latina—2 vol. fol. *circa* 1450 *(fed abfque nota loci five anni)*—Editio Primæ Vetuftatis. Typis Mogunt. Joh. FUST Evulgata, Cujus Parifiis Adfervatur Exemplar in Bibliotheca Mazarinea. (The Mazarine Bible fuppofed to be unique).

⁎ Such is the opinion now given to me, and it is to be received with the attention due to learning and judgement, both of great account. Yet there are grounds for doubt— and till minute collation fhall decide the abfence of all variation between the copies, the probability, from paft trials of the fame fort, muft be in favour of the prevalent idea, that the Mazarine copy is unque.

Of the copy which was fold in M. de Gaignat's fale, 1769, there was for a time a fimilar opinion; but, on comparifon with

with the Mazarine Bible, the opinion was found not tenable. The two or three bibles lately brought into England are, it may be conjectured, the same as that fold at M. de Gaignat's.

Continuation of the Bodelian Books.

The Durand, 1459, is there.

The Bible, by Fuft and Schœffer, 1462, (tom. 1mus. in membr.)—This is what is commonly called the Mentz Bible.

Idem Liber, 4 tom. 1462.

Tully's Offices, by Fuft, 1465.

T. Aguinas, by Schœffer, 1467.

St. Hieronymi Tractatus et Epiftole, by Schœffer, 1470.

Valerius Maximus, Schœffer, 1471.

St. Auguftine, 1473.

Pauli de Sancta Marie Scrutinium Scripturarum. Pet. Schœffer. 1478.

Barth. de Channis Interrogatorium. P. Schœffer. 1478.—Thefe are all the Bodleian Library has by Fuft and Schœffer. —There is the Livy of the fecond Schœffer, 1518—but neither the Catholicon nor the Conftitutiones Clementis V.

The oldeft Pfalter in the Bodleian is 1476—printed at Naples, by Hen. Alding and Perigren. Bermentelli—8vo.— A fcarce book this; though not fo fcarce as the Venice Pfalms in 1486—nor the third edition of the Mentz Pfalms in 1502.—The firft and fecond have been mentioned in the chapter upon Meintz.

AT CAMBRIDGE.

Added to what was alfo ftated in the chapter upon Meintz, there is nothing by Fuft or Schœffer in the libraries of Trinity or St. John's.

At St. John's—the firft Pfalter is by Aldus, at Venice, 1495.

Their firft Bible, by Coburger, at Nuremberg, in the year

year 1500.—This is remarked, by Thomas Baker, to be the laſt book printed by Coburger.—This book, he might have added, I believe, is of no great value. Leſs, indeed, than the firſt copy by Coburger, 1477. And that never ſold in any of the great ſales of M. de Soubiſe, Duc de la Valiere, &c. for four pounds.

Their firſt Tully (de Officiis Lugd.) is 1556.

The firſt Valerius—Milan, 1508.

At Trinity College—Alſo, there are not any ſpecimens of the earlieſt printing.

The firſt Pſalter there is, the Paris Quincuplex, 1508—the Bible—that by Aldus, Venice, 1518—the Ximenes Bible is at Trinity.

INDEX.

INDEX.

	Page		Page
Mr. Pott, Fourcroi, Lavoisier, &c.	2	East India Commerce	9
Edinburgh, and London	2	Pragmatic Sanction	10
Pavia and Padua	3	The American Crusade	10
Fabricius and Harvey	3	Cork	11
Bologna	3	Government and Law	11
Florence and Fontana	3	Scotland	11
The Pope's State	3	Sheerness	12
Francis I.	3	Emigrants	12
County of Kent	4	Sir C. Grey	12
Sir R. Taylor, Lord Eardly	4	American Republic	13
Sir R. Boyd	4	Inscription	15
Sir Gregory Page	5	Flanders	16
Falstaffe, Mr. Henderson	5	Travelling in Flanders	16
Westminster Bridge	5	Stivinus	16
Becket and Erasmus	5	Nieuport, Dunkirk, St. Omer, Lille	16
Taylor and Hooker	5		
Stukeley	6	Canals	16
Dover and Cinque Ports	6	Duke of Bridgewater	17
Itinerary f Autoninus	6	Brindley and Smeaton	17
Sir H. Oxenden	7	Cost and Profits of the Bridgewater Navigation	18
Foote	7		
Churchill	7	Virgil	18
Mr. Wilkes and Humphrey Coates	7	Roman want of Canals	18
Passage from Dover	8	Flemish Canals	18
Samer and Montreuil	8	Agriculture in Flanders	19
Ostend	9	Implements of Husbandry	19
Trade	9	Ploughing	19
		Manures	

INDEX.

	Page		Page
Manures	20	Public Offices	35
Scavengers in London and Paris	20	Feudal Impositions	35
Practice at Bruxelles	20	Harry VII.	36
L'Ecole Veterinaire	20	Joseph II.	36
M. Chubert and M. Flandrin, and Duc de Charrot	20	Ecclesiastical Corporations and Endowments	36
Buffon	21	Useful Part of Government cheap	37
Boerhave and Linnæus	21	Appellant Jurisdiction	37
Fens, Flemish and Romney Marsh	22	Admiralty Court	37
Jurisprudence for Cattle	22	Justices in Eyre	37
Victualling Trade	22	Philip's Wars	37
Thrale and Whitbread	23	Ecclesiastical Courts Checked	37
Lace and Hat Manufactory	23	Reubens	39
Flemish School of Painting	23	Crayer and Van Hout Horst	39
English Academy	23	Road through Aloft	41
Tradesmen of Flanders	23	Hanover and America	42
Charles V.	24	State of Tenants and Labour	42
Education in Flanders	24	The late French Court	43
The Printing of the Plantin Family	25	Sketches of Reubens	44
		Martin and Erasmus	44
Exports and Imports	25	Hospitals and Goals	45
Theatres	26	Nero and Tiberius	45
College of Medicine and Pharmacopœia	26	Louvois	46
		Crequi	46
Grotius and Father Paul	27	Bruxelles	47
Queen Elizabeth	27	The Park, Bois de Soigne, &c.	47
Pacification of Ghent	27	Dean Swift	48
Reubens and Vandyke	27	Pestilence and Wars	48
Dumourier	28	The Roman Roads	49
Churchmen	28	The French	49
French Bishops	28	Population	49
Flemish Bishops	29	Military	49
Revenues of Clergy	30	Gobelin and Sabloniere	50
Age for Orders	30	Flanders Lace	50
Card. de Granville	30	Buildings	51
Bruges and Ghent	30	Duke of York, Col. Gardiner, &c.	51
The Government of Flanders	33	The Archduke's Villa	52
Union with Lorraine	33	Venice Glass	52
Treaty of Aix-la-Chapelle	33	De Lance, Le Roi, Montoyer	53
Barrier Treaty	33	Grounds, Welbeck, Clumber	53
The Constitution	34	Chantilli and Versailles	54
Abject Nobles and Clergy	35	Wentworth, Oatlands, Richmond	54
		M. Walker's	

INDEX.

	Page		Page
M. Walkeer's Villa	54	Interest of Money	73
The Derbyshire Ilam	ib.	Minors	ib.
Guimard	55	The Chancellor	ib.
Nanci, in Lorraine	ib.	Van-de-Velde	ib.
Handsomest Coffee Rooms	ib.	Duc d'Aremberg	74
The Theatre	56	M. Walkeers	ib.
Statues, Roubiliac and Banks	57	The Carnival	ib.
Lord Aylesbury	ib.	Vandernoot and Vonk	ib.
His Inscription	58	Spiegeleus and Vesalius, Breighel	
The Government of Brabant	59	and Van Meulen	ib.
Marechal Koueyfegg and M. de		Boileau and Racine	75
Meternich	60	" One Arnold" and Gen. Burgoyne	ib.
Routine of Law	61		
Qualifications of Nobles	ib.	Le Grand Arnaud	76
English Nobility	63	Duke Albert	ib.
Tiers Etat	ib.	French Fugitives—Condé, Monsieur, &c.	ib.
Session of the States	64		
Charles V. and VI.	65	Louis XIV. and James II.	ib.
Privy Council	66	Justus Lipsius	ib.
Conceil des Finances	67	Van Vein	77
Law Proceedings	ib.	Laws, &c. administered by the	
Roman Law, and Commercial		people	ib.
and Criminal	68	Marriages, Baptisms, Burials	ib.
Lisle	ib.	Pluralities, Orders and Rural	
Bruges and Bruxelles	ib.	Deans	78
Liege, Juliers, Cologne	ib.	St. Gudule—the Revenues	ib.
Turnhout	ib.	Hospitals, Madhouses, &c.	ib.
Qualifications for a Lawyer	69	Lyons, York, Milan	79
Thonlieu	ib.	Length of Life	ib.
Mayor's Court	ib.	Population, England, Naples,	
Imprimatur	70	Holland	80
Judges and Town Officers	ib.	Diseases and Meteorological Observations	ib
Alexander Farnese and Charles of Lorraine	71	Georgical and Manufactures, Printing, &c.	81
Revenue and Interest of Money	ib.		
The Chief Prison	ib.	Roads and Streets	ib.
Lotteries, a little atoned by their application	72	Wine and Water	82
		Academy (des Belles Lettres)	ib.
Italian Lotteries	ib.	System of Life	ib.
Mont de Pieté	ib.	Freight, Labour, Travelling, and Provisions—their price	83
Pawnbrokers	ib.		
Coeberghcr	73	Taxes	84

INDEX.

	Page		Page
Bills of Exchange, Germany, Switzerland, England, France, Italy, Dantzig	84	Game Laws	111
		Game Laws in France and Italy	112
		Chantilli	113
Defeat and Slaughter of the Germans and French	86	Lists of Game and Persons	114
		Dogs and Horses	115
Scenery on the Road from Bruxelles	87	Stables—Buxton, Petworth, Woburn-Abbey, D. of Queensbury, D. of Orleans, &c.	116
Louvaine	88		
The University	89	Dog-houses—Goodwood	117
Boerhave, Blackstone, and Lipsius	ib.	St. Trond	ib.
Octennial Bill	91	Bracton	118
Popular Decline	ib.	Liege	ib.
Brewery	92	Abbe St. Farre	119
Warburton	ib.	P. of Cobourg's Levy	120
Graduation and Patronage	ib.	Loss of Liege and subsequent operations	ib.
Apostolic Months	ib.		
Empress Queen	ib.	Yhler's Retreat	121
Lectures, Session, and Vacations	93	Depopulation of Liege	ib.
Greek Manuscripts, and Bible of Bessarion	ib.	French Iron Works, Birmingham and Brosely	122
Schools of Divinity, Law, Medicine, &c. Text Books and Classics	94	Fabius the Bourg-Master	ib.
		Fame of the Liege Prince-Bishops	123
Printing, Elzever and Plantin	96	Number of Ecclesiastics	124
Emigrants, Nonjurors, &c.	ib.	Tythes and Church Lands	125
The Reformation	97	Queen Ann's Augmentation	126
Thomas Stapleton	ib.	Proofs of Nobility	ib.
Sir Thomas More and Garetus	99	Card. de Granville and Wazon	ib.
Garetus	ib.	Patronage	127
Justus Lipsius; his Epitaph	100	English taking the Vail	ib.
Inscription on Alardus, by Erasmus	101	Government of Liege	129
		Law Proceedings and Lawyers	131
Inscription on Professor Lupus	102	Punishments	132
Rickius	103	Debtors	ib.
Goldsmith	ib.	Prisons	134
Reform at Louvaine	ib.	Florence and Vienna	ib.
Horrid actions about St. Tron, Neerwinden and Landel	108	Mr. Cruickshank	ib.
		Liege Pharmacopœia, Physicians, &c.	135
Marechal Luxembourg	ib.		
Tirlemont and Hulans	109	Trade and Manufactures of Liege	136
Duc d'Aremberg and Sir W. G.	110	English Commissary	ib.
Blindness	111	Charleville and St. Etienne	ib.
Mr. Stanley, Lord D. &c.	ib.	Nail Trade, Watch-making, &c.	137

Geneva,

INDEX.

	Page		Page
Geneva, Lord Stanhope, Gold Alloy	137	Magistrates, Senate, Town-Wards, &c.	175
Hat Trade	138	Penal Laws, Debtors, Appeals, &c.	176
Pit Coal	ib.	Police; Suspended Animation	177
Foreign Trade	140	Fire Insurances, Bankers, &c.	ib.
Landed Property, Rents, Leases, Soils, Agriculture	ib.	Encouragers of America	ib.
		Protestants	178
The Money Trade	141	Trade and Manufactures	ib.
Registered Counties	ib.	Capt. Cooke	179
Mont de Picté—Fire Insurances	142	The Rhine, Speed, Freight, &c.	ib.
Dumourier	143	Price of Provisions, Taxes, &c.	180
Sir John Mandeville's Inscription	ib.	Soldiery	181
English at Liege	145	Reubens	ib.
Scenery upon the Meuse	147	Viscount B——	182
New Road to Aix-la-Chapelle	149	Univer. of Cologne, Professors,	
Popular Spirit at Aix	150	Lectures, Text Books, &c. 184 &c.	
Gambling	152	Hospitals, Foundlings, &c.	189
Inscription on the Czar Peter	ib.	Inscription	190
Spa Water	153	Students, Fees, &c.	191
English Scenery	154	Doctorates	ib.
Emigrants	156	Early Printing, Caxton, &c.	192
Lake of Geneva	158	Paschal and Rochefoucault	ib.
Remarkable Vicissitude	159	Adam Schall, Vondell, and Maria Schurman	193
Trade at Aix	162		
Regulation at Divine Service	ib.	Inscriptions	194
St. Barnard	164	Mylius, Strahan, and Allen	195
Inscription—Charlemagne	ib.	Course of Exchange, Money, Coins, &c.	ib.
Aldenhoven	165		
The River Roer	166	Scenery on the Rhine	197
Juliers	167	The First Vines—Painshill	ib.
Treaty of Munster	ib.	Italian Vineyards	198
Bavaria and Prussia	ib.	Agriculture	ib.
The Sacrament	168	Soil, Price of Land, Taxes, Leases	199
Scenery	169	The People	200
Cologne	171	Bonne	201
The People	ib.	Versailles and Manheim	ib.
Their Representatives	172	The Praise of the Prince	202
The Clergy	173	The College—Anatomy, Botany, Library	ib.
The Aristocracy	ib.		
The Archbishop	174	Theatre	ib.
The Elector	ib.	Professors in the University	204
Rousseau and Hume	ib.	Mr. Kedgell	ib.

Mr

INDEX.

	Page		Page
Mr. W. and Lord	204	Reforms by the Chief Magistrate	240
Human Calculus	206	Augsbourg	242
Proscriptions against Cologne	207	Territory and Revenues of the Electorate of Treves	ib.
Jews	208	Real Representatives of the People	ib.
Pedigrees	ib.	Ecclesiastical Jurisdiction of Treves	243
Clergy	ib.		
The Elector—his amusements and pursuits	209	The Military	244
Mineral Water	212	Position for English Tradesmen	ib.
Mr. Repton, Lord Bacon and Browne	213	Taxes	245
		Life at Coblentz	ib.
The Palace, Pictures, Natural History, Library, Baskerville, and Boydell	214	The Palace	ib.
		Lawrence, Biechey, Raffaille, and Leonardo	246
The States and Taxes	215	Fontenelle and Euripides	247
Distribution of Landed Property	216	Road to Frankfort	248
Officers of Ordnance	218	Ehrinbreillein	ib.
Clubs	ib.	Woods and Farming	249
St. Martin—Helen, Julian, Drusus	219	Francfort and Tradesmen	250
		Code of Carolina	251
River Scenes	220	Treaty of Westphalia	ib.
M. de Calonne	221	Exemplary Chapels	252
Inscription	223	Mich. Angelo, Bramana, Palladio, and Wyatt	ib.
A Parsonage—in Germany and England	224	Pantheon, &c.	253
Zinzendorff and Warburton	ib.	The Fairs—Regulations on Bills of Exchange	255
Hammerstein Rocks — Seven Mountains—Dutch Dykes	225	Taxes, Elections, &c.	ib.
Andernach, Drusus, Cæsar, &c.	ib.	Laws, Debtors, Criminals	256
Neuwred	227	The Guillotine, Bochius, Caracci	ib.
A becoming Prince	ib.	Arts and Amusements	257
Coblentz	231	Mr. Maty	ib.
The French Princes there	ib.	No Annoyance of Soldiery	ib.
Their Court there	232	Custine	ib.
The Elector's Court	233	Scaliger	258
Embassadors and Councils	234	Old Printing	ib.
Mr. Fox, Mr. Sheridan, and Mr. Burke	235	The River Maine to Mayence	259
		Surrender of Mentz	ib.
Condorcet and Montesquieu	236	Prussian Hospital	260
The Moselle	238	Neckar, Lord C. the Marino, and Voltaire	261
The Simois and the Tyber	ib.		
Wine	239	The Scenery upon the Maine	ib.

Modern

INDEX.

	Page		Page
Modern Piety and Glory	261	Dr. Farmer, Mr. Willet, Dr.	
Hockheim, Weisenau, La Favorite, Cassel	263	Askew, Lord Spencer	290
		Royal and Antiquarian Societies	
Mayence after the Siege	264	British Museum, Sloane, &c.	ib.
Capt. Cooke and Sir R. Curtis	265	Linnæus and Dr. Smith	ib.
The Architect Manzin	ib.	Oxford, the Bodlæian—Fust,	
The Palace	266	Schæffer, &c. &c.	ib.
Havoc of Human Nature	ib.	Mentz—Life, Local and Popular Characteristics	
A Jubilee to the Fish	267		291
Sufferings, price of Provisions in the Siege	ib.	Expence of Governments	292
		German Clergy	ib.
Stores taken	268	English Noblemen	ib.
Debts of the French	269	German Titles and Sinecure Places	
Bill Money and Paper Currency	270		293
King of Prussia's Money, and new Money of the French Republic	271	Constitutional Reforms	294
		Taxes	295
		William III.	ib.
New Works at Cassel	273	Lotteries	297
Printing at Mentz	275	Elective Chief Magistrate	ib.
Lawrence Coster	ib.	Undue Influences and Bad Alliances	
Guttenberg and Fust	277		298
Peter Schæffer	ib.	Qualifications and Examinations	300
First Idea of Types—Harvey and Newton	278	Popularity, Charles II. Henry V.	301
		Charles I. Louis XVI. Nero	302
The Psalter—Vienna, Paris, Lord Spencer, &c.	279	Revolutionary Spirit	303
		Laws and Punishments	304
Duke of Marlborough and Buckingham-house	280	Prisons &c.	ib.
		River Scenery from Mayence to Coblentz	
Mr. Cracherode's Library	281		307
Fust and Schæffer's Works	ib.	Mineralogy	308
First German Bible	282	Monte Bolca, Viterbo, Baia and Puzzuoli	
Bodoni and Bulmer	283		309
Valerius Maximus and Cicero	ib.	Tarras and Puzzuolana	310
First Classics in Italy and at Paris	284	Roman Antiquities and Dutch Dykes	
State of Printing in England—Caxton, Pinson, and De Worde	ib.		ib.
		Echo, Ripley, Wren, Sir R. Walpole, Milan, The Rhine	311
Erasmus, the Greek Physicians, Linacre	285	Angelica Kauffman	312
		Mr. W. of Birmingham	313
Press first groan'd under a Licence	286	Germans abolishing Tythes	317
Star Chamber and Inquisition	287	La Favorite	318
Libraries at Cambridge	289	Condition of Germans	320

Scenery

INDEX.

	Page
Scenery and Soil	321
Oppenheim	322
Bridge of Boats	ib.
Wines	323
Burgundy, Clos de Vougeot	ib.
Worms	324
Luther	ib.
False Alarm, Bible Forbid	326
Leo X. Charles V. Erasmus, Melancthon	ib.
Junctinus and Cardan	327
Crimina's, Traitors and Blasphemers, Hampden, Sydney Galileo, St. Paul	ib.
French at Worms	328
George II. Dettingen, Handel	ib.
Manheim	329
Discharged Despotism	ib.
Louvois Lorges and Turenne	ib.
Louis XIV Bonne, Munich, Treves	330
The Palainate, Soil, Scenery, Agriculture	331
French Prisoners	332
Buildings of Manheim	ib.
Sir Joshua Reynolds	ib.
Voltaire, Paris, Lord Abercorn, Caserte, Kensington	333
Use of Petty Princes	334
Heidelburg	ib.
Herschel	ib.
Oriani and Fontana	335
Mathematical Instruments of England	ib.
Lectures, Books, &c.	335
Romney and Stuart	336
The Pictures at Manheim	ib.
The Ague, other Diseases and Remedies	336
Cullen, Pott, Mosely	337
Hospitals, Poor, Orphans, Prisons, decreasing Population and Emigrations to America	338

	Page
Enormous Taxes, Crown Lands &c.	339
The Palace, Hampton Court	340
King of Prussia at Manheim	341
Troops, Pay, Cloathing	342
Trade	343
Roads to the Alps	344
Bruchsal	ib.
Heidelberg, Grævius, Gronovius, Whitbread, and Deux Ponts Classics	345
Toleration	346
Ornamental Gardening, Schwetzingen	ib.
Roman Column, Cultivation of Rhubarb	ib.
Bishop of Spires and Custine	ib.
Wertemberg, Prince, Diminution of Debts and Taxes	ib.
Ulm aud Augsbourg, Luther and Melancthon	347
Baden	ib.
Vines, Tobacco	ib.
Rastadt, Villars and Eugene	348
Kehl, Baskerville, Voltaire, the Cardinal Rohan, and the Necklace	ib.
Switzerland, Dole and Basle, Euler and Maupertuis, Bernouilli and Erasmus	349
Gaudia Poetica	350
Lord Baltimore and Linnæus	ib.
Letters between them	351
Virgil and Achilles	355
The Czarina	356
Dresden	357
Augsbourg	359
Spallanzani	361
Academies and Societies	363
His Tour to Vesuvius, Ætna, Grotto del Cane	364
Comi of Abruzzo	365

Sicily

INDEX.

	Page		Page
Sicily, Capre	365	Fluid under Solid Lava	373
Rommetaggio de Salvatore	368	Sir W. Hamilton	ib.
Bursts of Lava	ib.	M. De Luc	374
Detonation	369	Sir W. Hamilton	ib.
Abbe Fortis	ib.	Pavia	ib.
Theory of Spallanzani	ib.	Lava of November 1785	375
Volcanic Hail	370	Massa and Salvatore	ib.
Trough of Lava	371	Feldspates and Shorles	376
Heat	ib.	Bergman	ib.
Thermometer of Wedgwood	372		

FINIS.

Books printed for J. DEBRETT, oppofite Burlington-Houfe, Piccadilly.

PARLIAMENTARY REPORTS, 1794.

This Day is publifhed,

Numbers XXVII. and XXVIII.

Revifed and collated, with the Notes of feveral Members, and which completes the Debates of laft Seffions, with copious Indexes, in Three large Volumes, Price 1l. 11s. half-bound and lettered.

INCLUDING,

Befides a faithful Report of all the Important Debates in both Houfes—Supplies—Ways and Means for 1794—Appropriation Paper, fhewing how the Money given for the Service of the Year 1793, has been difpofed of; Eftimate of Services performed by the Office of Ordnance; and Eftimate of Charges of the Office of Ordnance for 1794.—An Account of Monies iffued out of the Civil Lift Revenue between the 14th of February and 5th April, 1793—An Account of the Surplus of the Confolidated Fund—Total of Army Eftimates—Salaries granted to Lords Hertford and Malmfbury, and Sir Gilbert Elliot—Pay and Half Pay to the feveral Commiffaries at Home and Abroad—State of Nova Scotia and New Brunfwick, including the Correfpondence of Governor Wentworth with Mr. Secretary Dundas—Reports of the Secret Committee on certain Seditious Societies, &c. &c.

THE Parliamentary Regifter; or, The Hiftory of the Proceedings and Debates of both Lords and Commons; containing an Account of the moft interefting Speeches and Motions authentic Copies of all important Letters and Papers laid before either Houfe during the laft Seffion.

Of whom may be had,

The Parliamentary Regifter of the Third Seffion of the prefent Parliament—Containing, befides a faithful Report of the Debates and Proceedings in both Houfes of Parliament, revifed and collated with the Notes of feveral Gentlemen—Authentic Copies of the Treaties with Sardinia, Ruffia, and Heffe Caffel—Report on Commercial Credit—Refolutions for the Government of India—Lord Auckland's Correfpondence prefented by Lord Grenville—Lords Proteft on the Bath Peerage, and on the Scots Election—Correfpondence between Lord Grenville and M. Chauvelin, complete; an Account of the Charges and Income upon the Confolidated Fund to the 5th of January 1793—Total Produce of the Duties on Cuftoms, Excife, Stamps, and Incidents, to October 10, 1792. Total Net produce of Cuftoms and Excife in England and Scotland, &c. &c. in Three large Volumes, Price 1l. 8s. half bound and lettered.

www.ingramcontent.com/pod-product-compliance
Lightning Source LLC
Chambersburg PA
CBHW032009220426
43664CB00006B/182